LETTERS FROM PRISON

LETTERS FROM PRISON
James P. Cannon

PATHFINDER

New York London Montreal Sydney

Edited by George Lavan Weissman

Copyright © 1968, 1973 by Pathfinder Press
All rights reserved

ISBN 978-0-87348-307-0
Library of Congress Catalog Card Number 73-79781
Manufactured in Canada

First edition, 1968
Second edition, 1973
Fourth printing, 2009

Cover design: Toni Gorton
Cover photo: Top, GIs demand to be sent home, 1945. Bottom right, auto workers on strike at General Motors, 1945. Bottom left, striking coal miners, 1943. (Wide World)

Pathfinder
www.pathfinderpress.com
E-mail: pathfinder@pathfinderpress.com

Acknowledgments

These letters, written twenty-four years ago, are finally published as a result of a unique combination of circumstances and the participation and collaboration of three other people, whose part in the project is here gratefully acknowledged.

In the first place, Rose Karsner had to be in New York on the receiving end of the correspondence so that I could continue, in effect, the conversations which went on in our house all the time. I could write with confidence that everything I had to say would be listened to and understood, and that her information, criticisms, and suggestions would prompt further discussion.

In the second place, on my return to New York in January 1945, Sylvia Caldwell, secretary extraordinary, gathered all the handwritten letters, typed them, and filed them away neatly for possible future reference.

They slept in the files for twenty-three years and would be there yet if Beatrice Hansen hadn't showed up, read them, and decided that they should be published. She then proceeded to retype them and ship them off to Merit Publishers.

These three collaborators are part of the book, and I am proud to call myself one of the four.

James P. Cannon
LOS ANGELES
JANUARY 10, 1968

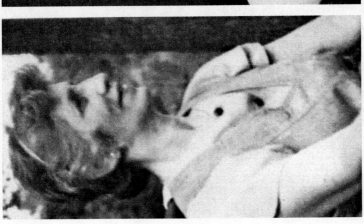

Rose Karsner in 1940's

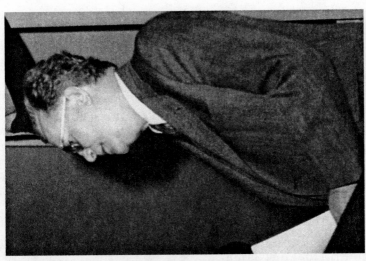
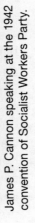

James P. Cannon speaking at the 1942 convention of Socialist Workers Party.

Contents

ABCs must be learned again • Sympathy must not obscure political judgment • The bridge for the petty bourgeois union policy • Programmatic firmness and political objectivity • Boyhood memories • A pedagogical trick • The 'trade-union analogy' and the Soviet state • The dialectic of factional struggles • John L. Lewis and Stalin • Trotsky on the *Socialist Appeal* • News from Italy • Constructive start of the discussion

of library • The worst fault of the thinkers' faction •
The convention was a great triumph

A five-year publishing plan • Three departments of
publishing activity • A petty-bourgeois prejudice
• The Servant of Man • Pioneer Publishers' great
tradition • *The Militant's* function • Human solidarity
at Sandstone • Against conciliationism in international
field • Revision of previous ideas about the press •
Courtesy and compassion in prison • The price of *The
Militant* • The principle of paying, not the amount
paid • *The Militant* as a combination tool • Man does
not live by argument alone

The Achilles' heel of the *Appeal to Reason* • A
tentative program for the literary secretariat •
Materials needed • Books proposed • The national
training school • Dangers of centralization and of
amateurism • Democracy or snobocracy • Genius
and men of common clay • All prisons are the same •
Leadership and the leader cult • The old movement had
many techniques • Appeal to the young • The thought
of a better future • Dewey's philosophy • Objectivity
and subjectivity in politics • Insensitivity toward
criticism • The recent party discussion • The 'Three
Theses' • The source of 'leftism' • Why attitudes to
other organizations changed • Lessons are lost • More
books proposed • A party organizer is a joiner of
people • The Sandstone assignment is finished

Introduction

This collection of letters is in reality a prison journal recording the daily thoughts and impulses of a rebel behind bars. In these letters James P. Cannon addresses himself specifically to the problems of organization and politics faced by the Socialist Workers Party in the United States of 1944. But the book's central interest and importance is not as a history of that period of the revolutionary movement. The most striking thing about these letters, written a quarter of a century ago, is that they deal with the most important problems of party-building that confront young revolutionaries today.

In the last few years, growing numbers of young people have begun to reject the evils of capitalist America—war, racism, poverty, its sick culture. More and more of them want to replace capitalism with a better system. But how is this to be done? What kind of organization must be built to lead this struggle? What kind of men and women will the job require? These are the very questions discussed in *Letters From Prison*. Thus it is a basic handbook for the organizers, propagandists, and educators of the present generation who are beginning to face up to these questions.

On January 1, 1944, James P. Cannon began serving a sixteen-month sentence in the federal prison at Sandstone, Minnesota, for opposing Roosevelt's imperialist war policies. He and seventeen of his comrades, leaders of the Socialist Workers Party and of Minneapolis Truck Drivers Local 544-CIO, were the first victims of the Smith Act.

As National Secretary of the Socialist Workers Party, Cannon was the chief defense witness; his entire testimony has been published in book form under the title *Socialism on Trial*. In it he outlined his party's view that the goal of America's rulers in World War II was to dominate and exploit the postwar world and that, far from fighting for democracy, the American ruling class was the enemy of democracy here and abroad. He predicted that this would be clearly demonstrated during and after the war.

To Roosevelt's expansionist war, Cannon counterposed revolutionary socialist opposition to capitalism and fascism. He also forecast the economic, social, and political squeeze on the working people that would inevitably take place as American imperialism waged war—and the resistance from the workers this would eventually evoke. The sentencing of the eighteen took place December 8, 1941, at the same hour that Congress was formally declaring war.

At that time the American Trotskyists were almost alone in their antiwar stand in the radical and labor movement. Unlike the first world war, when thousands of American radicals headed by Eugene V. Debs were jailed for their antiwar views, World War II saw the Communist Party and Socialist Party, along with the AFL and CIO officialdoms, quickly line up behind Roosevelt's imperialist war policy. The Communist Party and a section of the labor bureaucracy even praised his crackdown on domestic dissent and the jailing of the eighteen.

The Civil Rights Defense Committee, with James T. Farrell as chairman and George Novack as secretary-treasurer, was formed to mobilize support for the Trotskyists indicted under the Smith Act. By the time legal appeals were exhausted and the eighteen were put behind bars, the CRDC had gathered thousands of supporters in the labor movement who saw the imprisonment of the Trotskyists as a blow against their own right to dissent or struggle for better conditions during the war. This list of supporters was to grow during the period of imprisonment. The miners' strikes and the 1943 explosion in Harlem were the first expressions of mass opposition to the sacrifices demanded by the warmakers and foreshadowed the postwar strike wave and the bring-the-troops-home movement that began less than a year after the eighteen had served their sentences.

When he entered the federal penitentiary at Sandstone, Cannon had already spent thirty-seven of his fifty-three years as a revolutionary socialist. He had been an organizer and strike leader in the Industrial Workers of the World and a member of the left wing of the Socialist Party. In 1919, under the inspiration of the Russian Revolution, he became one of the founders and leaders of the American Communist movement. Expelled from the Communist Party in 1928, he was the initiator and principal leader of American Trotskyism and a founder, in 1938, of the Socialist Workers Party.

Federal prison regulations strictly limited the length and frequency of letters between prisoners and the outside world. Rose Karsner, Cannon's wife and companion, was "approved" as a correspondent by the authorities. Like Cannon, she was a veteran of the Socialist and Communist parties and a founding member of the Socialist Workers Party. All of the letters in this volume, save two, were written to her. Thus Cannon's handwritten letters—restricted under the rules to one sheet of paper—to Rose Karsner in New York City, at first two, then three, and finally four a week, and her letters to him—also restricted in length and frequency—were his channel of political communication with the Socialist Workers Party.

Cannon's letters often expressed ideas and proposals that had been crystallized in discussions with his fellow leaders of the Socialist Workers Party at Sandstone. Rose's letters contained not only information, suggestions, and ideas of her own, but the replies and opinions of the functioning national leadership of the party. Both incoming and outgoing mail was completely censored, so people's names were often disguised in order to protect them from possible victimization.

Because of the prison censorship, Cannon could not express some of his innermost feelings. Nevertheless, in the glimpses of Cannon as a human being that come through, the reader gets a fuller understanding of his character and personality. One of the pleasures and values of the book, especially for young revolutionists personally unacquainted with Cannon, is that this element of the letters was not edited out.

It is important to place Cannon's communications in the context of the concrete conditions that faced the Trotskyist movement internationally as well as nationally at the time they were written.

Leon Trotsky had been assassinated by an agent of Stalin only four years earlier, and the responsibility for forging a genuine international leadership of the Trotskyist movement weighed heavily on the prisoners at Sandstone. This task was made all the more difficult because of the conditions that Trotskyists faced during World War II. They were hounded and persecuted not only by the fascist governments and the Kremlin but also by the "democratic" powers. Trotskyist leaders found themselves in detention camps in England and in prison in the United States. Throughout the world they had to work in underground conditions.

Trotsky's death had come soon after a deep-going factional struggle within the Socialist Workers Party. A section of the membership, headed by James Burnham and Max Shachtman, under the pressures generated by the outbreak of World War II, had led an assault on the basic theories of Marxism and the political program and organizational principles of the Socialist Workers Party. The Shachtmanites, who composed 40 per cent of the party membership, challenged the Trotskyist concept that the Soviet Union was a workers' state, bureaucratically degenerated though it was, which had to be defended against imperialist attack, just as a bureaucratized trade union had to be defended against attack by the bosses and their government. The grouping likewise challenged the whole concept of the party as a disciplined, centralized organization rooted in the political life of the working class.

The education received by the party ranks in the intensive discussion that defeated the Burnham-Shachtman tendency, an education in those very concepts against which the Burnham-Shachtman faction centered its attacks, steeled the Socialist Workers Party for the future. Consequently it was capable both of withstanding the wartime repression and responding to the opportunities that the effects of the war were to create in the labor movement. This last political struggle in which Trotsky participated is documented in his book *In Defense of Marxism* and in Cannon's *The Struggle for a Proletarian Party*.

Shachtman's concepts, followed to the end, logically led to the liquidation of the revolutionary workers' party. This was confirmed by the subsequent evolution of his split-off group which eventually disintegrated, dissolving into the Socialist Party.

While the struggle against such concepts centered in the Socialist Workers Party, it had its repercussions and echoes in almost all the sections of the Fourth International, the World Party of the Socialist Revolution founded under Trotsky's leadership in 1938. The difficulties of worldwide communication during the war years, however, left uncertain the extent to which the international movement as a whole had absorbed the lessons of the Shachtman fight. These lessons were important, as Cannon repeatedly pointed out, because the end of the war would see massive upsurges of the workers and peasants, in revulsion against the horrors they had endured. A revolutionary leadership on a world scale was essential if these upsurges were to result in victory for the workers. A defeat of the workers and the restabilization of capitalism, especially in Europe, would place World War III on the agenda.

As more and more of the crimes of the Stalinist bureaucracy came to light, and as American and British imperialism clearly seemed headed for victory over their German and Japanese competitors, the pressures increased to abandon revolutionary politics in deference to bourgeois democratic public opinion. In response to these pressures a small group of party members, under the leadership of two of the eighteen prisoners, Albert Goldman and Felix Morrow, began to echo some of the petty-bourgeois concepts embraced by Shachtman. Much of the dispute with the Goldman-Morrow faction revolved around its disagreement with the Socialist Workers Party that uprisings of the European workers and revolutionary upsurges of the colonial workers and peasants were sure to occur. This made Cannon even more determined that the Socialist Workers Party should do everything it could to help educate and prepare the Trotskyist nuclei in Europe and the colonial lands for the opportunities and responsibilities that the postwar crisis would soon present.

Cannon's persistent inquiries about the English Trotskyists, his questions concerning Natalia Trotsky in Mexico, his eagerness for reports from the American Trotskyist merchant seamen who at that time were the only real communication links with the foreign sections of the world Trotskyist movement, his eagerness for every piece of information about the emerging European workers' movement, and even his urging that American Trotskyists learn foreign languages, all reflect the importance he attached to doing what he could, even in prison, to be part of a leadership team of international collaborators. In one of his letters to Rose Karsner, he wrote: "Without international collaboration—that is what the word 'internationalism' means—it is not possible for a political group to survive and develop as a revolutionary party in this epoch."

Nationally, the seeming hypnosis that the outbreak of the war had imposed on the American working class was already wearing off as the eighteen Trotskyists entered prison. Afro-American dissatisfaction, which had shown itself at the beginning of the war in the response to the projected March on Washington, burst out in the explosion in Harlem in 1943. Discontent was becoming more and more evident in the organized labor movement. This was to explode in 1945–1946 in the biggest strike wave in American history. Even American workers in uniform would display a new kind of combativity in the bring-the-troops-home movement in both Europe and the Pacific after Japan's surrender.

It was to this growing militancy of the American working class that Cannon wanted the Socialist Workers Party to orient all of its activities. The results of the early 1944 subscription drive to the party's weekly paper, *The Militant*, showed that a growing number of increasingly dissatisfied American workers were open to the ideas of revolutionary Marxism. The necessity of settling accounts with the Goldman-Morrow faction assumed its real importance in relation to this new wave of working-class militancy in the United States.

Was the party to prepare itself on all fronts—from the character and size of its newspaper to its projected educational and publishing programs—for the rapid expansion that would be possible as the American workers threw off their extreme subservience to the Roosevelt administration? Or was it to dabble in prolonged and futile literary discussions with circles like Shachtman's Workers Party, destined to be bypassed in the postwar upsurge of the American workers?

In other words, was the party to be a workers' combat party, seriously preparing for coming events in the arena of the class struggle? Or was it at that very juncture to dilute its disciplined and proletarian character?

It was to answer these questions that Cannon's proposals for developing and expanding the various departments of the party were written. At the same time they rebutted the shortsighted and dilettantish perspective put forward by the Goldman-Morrow grouping.

More than anything else these letters reflect the importance Cannon attached to all the problems of the organization, education, and development of the revolutionary party. Today, just as in 1944, the building of a revolutionary party is the central requirement of our epoch. And its urgency is nowhere greater than in the United States, where the richest, most powerful, and most highly organized ruling class in history must be defeated.

The rulers of American capitalism are today fighting a bloody war to dominate Southeast Asia. They will fight even more fiercely against any challenge to their rule at home. Only a revolutionary party of the workers that is totally conscious of everything involved in disarming and defeating American imperialism on its home ground can hope to succeed. Without an adequate leadership the resistance and upsurges of exploited Americans will come to nothing— with consequences that can doom the human race. This is why it is so important to understand how best to organize, educate, and inspire those critical-minded and dedicated men and women who compose and will compose the American revolutionary party.

The concepts touched on in these letters extend from the scope of the revolutionary party's education to its field organizing, from the necessity for it to have a professional leadership and staff to the purpose of its democracy, from the character of its newspaper to the inspiration of its youth. It is the elaboration of these concepts, outlining the organization of a Leninist party in the United States, that constitutes Cannon's major contribution to Marxism.

The accomplishments of Cannon and the Socialist Workers Party in this field received their major test to date in 1944. With much of the central leadership in prison, a second-line leadership stepped in and, in the midst of World War II, led the party through the year of its greatest growth. The performance of the unjailed leaders, the capacity of relatively young and inexperienced organizers to meet the challenge of new opportunities, and the response of the women in the party, who shouldered a greater part of the duties at the party center, were measures of the accomplishments of the previous period. Cannon watched this process unfold with keenest interest.

A great weakness of many young radicals today is their tendency to dismiss the importance of continuity in the development of revolutionary leadership. This in large part is a reaction against the systematic betrayals by the Communist Party, which dominated American radical politics for so many years, the reactionary policies of the AFL-CIO bureaucracy, and the quiescence of the American labor movement. But radicals who have no accurate appreciation of past experiences can have no serious perspective for the future. They are ill armed compared with the rulers who learn from both past successes and failures and thus stand upon the shoulders of their predecessors. Those revolutionists who fail to do the same condemn themselves to failure.

Giants and geniuses in the short history of the modern revolutionary movement are rare, but the march of history does not require each of us to be one, nor to wait for one to come along. *Letters From Prison* does not challenge each of us to be a Marx, a Lenin, or a Trotsky. We are simply challenged to be ourselves, to study what went on before, and to apply the discoveries of our predecessors to the problems of our time. By standing on the shoulders of the earlier working-class fighters, American Marxists, as a *team* of revolutionists, can accomplish the tasks before them.

New insights into revolutionary theory and better understanding of revolutionary practice will doubtless come from the new generation of American radicals. But they will come from those who are consciously part of the continuity of the international movement to change the world that began in 1848 with the *Communist Manifesto*. Those who, in the name of the quest for the "new," reject the use of the tested insights, understandings, and accomplishments of the last century or more, will merely repeat "old" mistakes.

The current struggles in Latin America, Vietnam, and America's black communities testify to the contradictions and continuing decline of imperialism. These struggles bear witness anew to the combativity and courage of the working masses. The central question remains the same as it was when Cannon was viewing the United States and the world from prison in 1944: How are revolutionists to build a party equal to the task of leading the working masses to the conquest of power?

Building such a political instrument can no more be an avocation than maintaining capitalist exploitation is an avocation of the leadership of the ruling class. One thread that runs through *Letters From Prison* is that a revolutionist does not play at politics. Revolutionary socialist politics is his chosen vocation, the center of his life, not a pastime or incidental interest. Everything, from the nature of one's education to the mode and conduct of one's life, is determined by the conscious decision to be a revolutionist.

In one letter Cannon says approvingly, "The young relate the word to the deed. They are moved and inspired by *example.* That is why they demand *heroes;* nobody can talk them out of it."

The two principal heroes of many young radicals in the world today—Malcolm X and Che Guevara—embodied the qualities of a revolutionist about which Cannon wrote in Sandstone Penitentiary a quarter century ago. They appealed to the best in men by challenging them to commit themselves to the great goal of liberating the oppressed that transcends the petty interests and concerns of everyday life. They sought to acquire and impart to others a knowledge of history and a confidence in the inevitability of their eventual triumph. They imbued their comrades with a faith in mankind's future that would follow the eradication of capitalism and racism. Their studies, their personal modes of life, and their integrity reflected the goals they had set for themselves. And each, after long experience and struggle, became preoccupied with the search and struggle to construct the type of organization that could lead the oppressed to victory over the American imperialist rulers and their international allies.

A prime obligation of a revolutionary leader is to explain the reasons for what he proposes and does, thus enabling the entire movement to participate in his thinking. In doing this he offers the younger generation what he knows. *Letters From Prison* is an important contribution from James P. Cannon toward fulfilling this obligation.

Jack Barnes
SEPTEMBER 1967

Letters from prison

This is the twenty-seventh anniversary of the day the Russian Bolsheviks took hold of the world and changed it, and in doing so, changed and reshaped our lives too. I am grateful today to the Russian Bolsheviks, and I am convinced to the bottom of my soul that it is better to be here with them, to feel that here I am one with them, than to be anywhere else under any conditions and be against them.

—From Letter to Rose Karsner,
NOVEMBER 7, 1944

Fifteen of the eighteen Smith Act victims surrender themselves to U.S. marshals (far right), December 1943, to begin serving their sentences. **Left to right**: Jake Cooper, Ed Palmquist, Clarence Hamel (face hidden), Emil Hansen, Harry DeBoer, Max Geldman, Carlos Hudson, Grace Carlson, Felix Morrow, Farrell Dobbs, Albert Goldman, Carl Skoglund, Oscar Coover, Sr., James P. Cannon, V. R. Dunne.

Above: George Novack speaking at a February 1945 meeting of the Civil Rights Defense Committee on the release of the eighteen: **Left to right**: Oscar Schoenfeld, Karl Kuehn, Farrell Dobbs, James T. Farrell, Osmund K. Fraenkel, Albert Goldman. **Below, Left to right**: James P. Cannon, Felix Morrow, and Albert Goldman.

January, 1944

LETTER 1

SANDSTONE JANUARY 3, 1944

Dearest Darling,

This is the first opportunity I have had to write you and let you know that I am OK. We have to go through thirty days of quarantine. After that I will be able to write oftener. I listed Walta as a regular correspondent but am not sure I gave the right street number. Please send it to me and tell Walta she can write to me. I feel lonesome for the baby. Did you have a good New Year's? I suppose it wasn't so gay for any of you under the circumstances, but I hope you didn't let that prevent you from celebrating. I was thinking of you all the time and hoping you were having some fun.

I am sorry I missed Carl. Tell him he doesn't need to worry about me. I am a soldier too, and can take things as they come. I suppose Joe told you that we finished our work on the book. I hope it will not be delayed now. I gave Joe my watch to take back to you. You will also receive my clothes. They will need pressing and cleaning. Did you have eggnog for New Year's?

Love ever,
Jim

LETTER 2

SANDSTONE, JANUARY 6, 1944

I am waiting anxiously to hear from you and to learn how you are getting along. Concern for you and lonesomeness for you are my two main problems. I am taking everything else as it comes. I hope that by this time you have received my first letter and that you know where I am and how to write to me.

I am writing this at 6 P.M., just about the time the paper should be going to bed. This will be the second issue prepared without us and without our seeing it. Nevertheless, I am sure it will be OK.

I was at the library today. James T. Farrell will be pleased to learn that five of his books are in the library. Only one was available, however. The rest are "out"—in the hands of other readers in our community.

I am anxious to hear how the fifteenth anniversary fund is coming along. You should be careful not to crowd the branches too hard on this matter. It was a mistake to send out that letter asking them to shorten the time for the fulfillment of their quotas. I heard that it caused some resentment.

I saw by the Minneapolis paper yesterday that the Supreme Court refused for the third time to review our appeal. That seems to make it final. We will have to reconcile ourselves to sixteen months' separation. But the time will pass and we will be together again. Meantime we can live on memories of the past and hopes for the future. The memory of last summer in the country is especially sweet and dear. I must thank you for that, as for everything.

Was the baby disappointed because she couldn't go with me? I think of her fondly. I couldn't keep the pictures I brought along, but you can mail me some others if they are not too large.

I am resting, reading, smoking and marking time. That is all there is to do for the thirty days of our quarantine. I have had a physical examination and am apparently OK in that respect.

I am sorry I did not have time to correct the stenogram of my plenum speech. Tell Sylvia to save it for me or give it to you. I will get around to it some day. Too much of my blood is in that speech to let it be lost and forgotten as so many others were.

Write, darling, especially about yourself. Every detail of your life is of vital interest to me. Be sure, above all, to tell me if you are taking care of yourself and not depriving yourself of any opportunity to make your life pleasant during my absence.

LETTER 3

SANDSTONE, JANUARY 10, 1944

I forgot to tell you in my last letter to send my ration book to me here. The regulations require it.

Did you write to Father and Agnes? If not, I wish you would do so and tell them when I left and that I am all right. I do not intend to write to them from here. I hope Father received the humidor so that he can keep his cigars in good shape. I got smoking tobacco and a corncob pipe from the commissary here, also oranges and candy—thanks to the money the CRDC gave me. I have enough to last me during January and February—I am only allowed to spend a maximum of ten dollars per month, so there is no need to send more.

I am doing quite a bit of desultory reading—the first for a long time without feeling that I was neglecting something else. This is one of the positive sides of my present situation. It is rather pleasant to feel free to read uninterrupt-edly for hours—and days—and to know there is nothing else to do.

I just finished reading Balabanoff's memoirs. There is some useful information in this book, but on the whole it is a pathetic reflection of the centrist mind. Lillian Symes and Clement helped her prepare the book, and it reads like it.

The library here is small, but there are enough books in it to keep me occupied for a while. I am not permitted to have books sent in to me from the outside unless I order and pay for them myself out of the ten dollar maximum we are allowed to spend each month. You can be sure I will have to *want* a book to order it under such circumstances. Tobacco, oranges and candy come first! However, if you will send me the correct titles, publishers' names and addresses and the prices, I think I will order the Clausewitz book on war and Aristotle on logic. War and philosophy are about the only two subjects that can tempt me to spend money these days.

I am waiting anxiously for the pictures—of you and the baby, and if possible the picture of me and the baby—if it came out right. I hope, if the holiday mails have not been unduly delayed, to have a letter from you tomorrow.

LETTER 4

SANDSTONE, JANUARY 12, 1944

I got your first letter last night. It was a bright occasion for me. I was confident it would come and looked forward to it. In the future you should sign your full name and address at the bottom of your letters, according to the regulations. Walta can write to me, as I have listed her as one of my correspondents. These must be confined to relatives under the regulations.

I wish you would send Father a copy of the paper marked to call his attention to my speech. He can compare it with Robert Emmet's. By the way, I know this speech very well; I was raised on it, so to speak.

I note your concern about my health. So far I am all right. Perhaps you will be interested in my daily routine. I rise at seven-thirty, wash and make up my cot, and breakfast at eight. From then to one, I read and smoke mostly. The big meal of the day is at one and so far I have always eaten my share. After dinner I shave and take a shower, then smoke and read some more until suppertime at five. After that there are five solid hours to read, smoke and play checkers until lights go out and we retire at half-past ten.

That is the day's routine, with the following interruptions: After breakfast I clean my quarters; really clean them—sweep, dust and mop until there is not a trace of dust on anything or in any corner. The monotony has also been broken by trips to the library and commissary, to the "school" for intelligence quizzes, to the doctor and dentist for examinations and—last but not least—to the doctor *twice* for typhus inoculations and smallpox vaccination. I had these two together yesterday, and feel just a little droopy tonight. Otherwise I have felt good, and after the first few nights, have slept well.

My reading up till now has mostly been in biography. I finished two books about William Allen White. He represents an interesting, if now out-of-date, phenomenon in American politics. Now I am reading alternately the *Life of Jesus* by Renan and—by a mere coincidence—a book about Walter Winchell who is not quite the same type.

I must spend my first month in quarantine. That means that the daily routine I have described above will scarcely vary during this period.

LETTER 5

SANDSTONE, JANUARY 17, 1944

I have a partial report on my physical examination. The doctor says my heart, lungs and blood pressure are normal. I have had no stomach disturbances since coming here, and since that is the only point I definitely knew to be wrong in the past, I assume that I am all right on the physical side. I also had a "psychiatric test," which is part of the routine here, but I won't bother to ask a report on that.

I wish you would send Father a picture of my bust. I also promised to send one to Mona. You can tell her where I am to explain why I don't write to her.

I am wondering if the manuscript of my history book has been put in shape and given to the printers. There is one small point I wish you would call to the attention of Joe and Usick. In the chapter on the Minneapolis strike I use the expression (regarding Shachtman's cowboy hat): "Why in God's name he wore it," etc. Leave that in, but eliminate any other mention of the deity that may occur in other chapters.

I wish you would thank Usick for the going-away present he gave me (through Joe). I enjoyed it immensely and remember it fondly. Tell Usick I would rather have the memory of his sixteen-year-old bourbon than a drink of ordinary stuff right now. Having said that, you might drop the gentle suggestion that he begin now to canvass the situation and see if he can't arrange to duplicate the gift when I come out. That would be something to look forward to—for a man with a well-preserved thirst and a taste for the best.

I am anxious to get some detailed news of what my friends are doing. Is the magazine out yet? What is the status of the second edition of my trial pamphlet? Has the six-page *Militant* been established as a regular procedure? What is the situation with regard to the anniversary fund? Is E.R. Frank still on hand?

Did they go ahead with Thomas' suggestion to invite Frank Graves to come to New York? I am in favor of this project and meant to write to him, but the last hours were too crowded.

Since I wrote you last I have finished reading two more books. One is *As Long as the Grass Shall Grow*—a book about the American Indians. This subject has always interested me, but I never seemed to get time to study it outside. The other book is *Louisiana Hayride*—a book about Huey Long and the regime which rode high, wide and handsome for a few years after his death until its disgraceful collapse. I found it an interesting facet of rural politics.

LETTER 6

SANDSTONE, JANUARY 20, 1944

Today I am recuperating from the last of three shots of anti-typhoid serum. None of them made me really sick, as is frequently the case with others, but I felt a little droopy yesterday. As far as I know, I have now gone through all the necessary health measures and will be out of quarantine a week from Friday. That will be four weeks since my arrival here. I am feeling well and except for slight symptoms of indigestion after each of the three typhoid injections have felt well ever since I came here.

I am out of the dormitory where I was first quartered and am now in a cell block. I like it better as I have a single cell to which I can retire whenever I want to be alone. It is quieter and I sleep better too. I am taking rigorous care of my health, and barring unforeseen difficulties, confidently expect to come out of here in shape for some serious work. The diet here is supposed to be balanced, but I am balancing it a little more on the side of the vitamin vegetables as against the starches. I also take care not to eat too much as I aim to reduce about ten or twelve more pounds at the rate of one pound per month. The vegetables I mentioned are mainly carrots and rutabagas— this is the heart of the rutabaga country—so when I tell you that I eat them prodigiously, you, remembering how I spurned such fare in the past, can realize that I am really disciplining myself to eat for health, not for pleasure.

My pleasure is more in the thought that I am pleasing you and preparing for the future. Another pleasure which I permit myself is the anticipation of meals I am going to eat with you when we are together again. You know I have never been much interested in food, but the subject has taken on a fascinating importance since I saw you last.

I have worked out a plan to inform you of special dishes which make the most imperious appeal to my appetite from time to time, and to ask you to record each of them on a sepa-rate page of a little memorandum book with the best recipe for its preparation. Then, when we have the opportunity, we can turn the pages, one by one each day, and know what to cook for dinner. Put porterhouse steak, french-fried potatoes and a salad on the first page. A long list will follow.

I am also anxious to hear how the membership campaign is progressing. No time should be lost on this project. And it is very important that the *pattern* of the last two campaigns be followed. Sylvia has all the circulars in her file. Moish should begin with a roundup report of the other campaigns showing the totals branch by branch, the average per month, and setting the new goal. Let me know all about this.

LETTER 7

SANDSTONE, JANUARY 24, 1944

I received two letters from you last week. The second, however, came before the first, probably because it was not signed properly. Walta's letter has not been received. The rule is to write on *only one side* of the paper and sign the *full name and address.* You and Walta are the only correspondents I have listed so far. I am allowed to write only *two* letters per week, but may receive *seven.*

The ruling against sending books as well as subscriptions to periodicals from the outside is permanent, unless there is a special ruling from Washington in our case.

I understand 5" x 7" photos may be sent. I am eagerly waiting for them. You are here with me all the time anyway, but still I would love to have a picture of the face I adore. I want one picture of you *alone.* Any one will do; it is not necessary to have a new picture made. I think I like best the old one of you walking in Washington Square. (I think Frank Lovell was on the other half of it.)

Can you quote in your next letter what Joe wrote about you in his story? I would like to read it. I am worried about Evelyn. Her cold has been hanging on too long. She should have an examination when she gets back from the country. If she is not absolutely OK she must take a long rest even if it means making some changes in the CRDC.

Since writing to you last I have read *No Hiding Place,* a biography by William Seabrook, the selfish, egocentric nut who wrote *Asylum.* Also *King News,* another autobiography by Moses Koeningsberg, one of the big figures of Hearst's journalistic menagerie. There is some useful information in such books, but I would never take time to read them in normal circumstances. That is one of the compensating luxuries of my present situation—that one has time for such indulgences. I am now reading *The Doctors Mayo.* This is a solid, well-written book about two men and their father who really achieved something worth writing about. I am enjoying this book immensely.

I am again playing with the idea of making up some outline notes for my memoirs. For this—in order to do it properly—I need some factual material about Father's early life. Where he was born; at what age he went to work; his first trade; some information about *his* father, his trade, his characteristics and what happened to him; at what age Father came to America; where he first went from New York; how long he stayed in Providence; when he married my mother; when and why he came to Rosedale, etc. Can you write to Agnes and ask her to send it to you?

I am more and more convinced that Pioneer Publishers do not advertise their *list* sufficiently. It should not only be advertised frequently but should also be printed on good paper in a separate circular for inclusion in all letters and in a general circularization of the mailing list of the party press. Ask Lillian about this.

LETTER 8

SANDSTONE, JANUARY 27, 1944

You have not mentioned in your first three letters whether or not you received my clothes. I wish you would let me know about this. If they have not been received I will ask to have the shipment traced. I don't want to lose my precious Hollywood suit.

I finished the monumental book about the Doctors Mayo and have now started on another book, *Indians of the United States.* This is a history on a subject which I have long wished to study, but never felt that I had the time since it is not connected with the current needs of modern politics. In the meantime I read two novels. One, *Valiant Is the Word for Carrie,* is a sentimental story which had a big sale a few years ago. It is all right if one has nothing else to do. The other book is a murder-mystery story of sophisticates in the radio racket. I felt that I needed a shower bath after I finished it; and on top of my repugnance for all the characters, the author and the milieu he deals with, I blamed myself for indulging, even in jail, in the most stupid of all pastimes—the reading of "mystery" stories.

I have received my "time" report which shows, "good time" being allowed for, that my release date is January 23, 1945. Put a ring around this date on your calendar so you can remind me of it in case I forget. I can already think of so many things I want to do when I get out that I wonder how and when I will ever get time enough for them all. But before I start on any task I want to eat a few meals of special dishes I can think of and see a few shows. Perhaps you and I will be entitled to a little vacation, commencing January 23, before settling down to new tasks. What do you think?

There are two small corrections I wish Joe or Usick to make in my *History* manuscript. In the chapter dealing with the negotiations with the AWP I speak of Salutsky as hating us "as the devil hates holy water." This should be eliminated for fear of misunderstanding. In the same chapter, or thereabouts, I speak of lukewarm people and follow the reference with a biblical quotation. It is not precisely accurate. After my own words: "Woe to the lukewarm!" follow with the quotation as follows: "Because thou art lukewarm, and neither cold nor hot, I will spue thee out of my mouth." Tell Joe this is from Revelations 3:16. I looked it up in a Cruden's *Bible Concordance* in the prison library. I had to come to this place to make the acquaintance of this most valuable book. I wish Sylvia would get one for my library. It is a well-known book and should be found in some secondhand store.

I also want a rocking chair to rock Mickey in, when I tell her stories and sing her songs at bedtime. Also, tell Walta to practice up on crepes suzette and teach you how to make them. I will want plenty.

LETTER 9

SANDSTONE, JANUARY 31, 1944

I received your letters of January 19 and 25, making five letters in all. The New York winters don't seem to be good for you. You should have gone to Florida. It is cheaper than pneumonia. After my long years of hammering on the subject, nearly all of the comrades acknowledge—"in principle"—the necessity of having a professional staff of party workers, but very few, and even you are not among them, really understand that you can't have it unless you pay for it.

The party has a big investment in every qualified party worker. He represents an accumulated capital of experience, tradition, facility in the performance of tasks which are not easy to learn, habituation to disciplined work, loyalty, etc. To say a vacation in a warmer climate is "too expensive," when the health of a party worker is involved, is like "saving money" on repairs and maintenance of a costly building until it falls down in ruins, or like a farmer haggling over a veterinarian's fees when his expensive horse gets lame. The analogy is far from perfect because the sensible property owner keeps his buildings in repair as a matter of course; and the first rule of the good farmer is to take care of his livestock.

I note from Walta's letter that you are thinking of accepting the invitation of good Bess Gogol to spend a week with her in Florida. But I think it is absurd for you to limit yourself to a week's vacation there. Even if Bess's accommodations are not available for a longer period, there is no reason why you shouldn't rent a room or go to a hotel so that you can stay in the Florida sunshine until the backbone of the winter in New York is broken. No reason, that is, except expense; and that is the party's problem, not yours, since you are an experienced and proven party worker.

The news in your letter of January 19 is very agreeable. There is no reason you cannot send this detailed information regularly. I am limited to *two* letters per week and may only use one sheet of paper, but I am entitled to receive *seven* letters and they are not limited as to length. I wish you would check all my letters to see if every question has been answered in detail. Otherwise I may repeat them, as I keep no copies.

I was highly pleased to hear of dear Evelyn's plan to spend forty of her fifty dollars contest prize on a party for us when we come out, but I still think the best thing she ever gave us is herself. Meantime, both you and she must bear in mind our agreement to say nothing to anyone about the contest until we return. This is important.

Tell Evelyn I received the pardon application and will send it on in a few days.

Thank Walta for her three-page letter of January 26 with the welcome *detailed* report of the activities and developments of my precious Sweetums. I will keep all her letters and acknowledge them in my letters to you.

Practice up roasting prime ribs of beef to a *pink* turn with Yorkshire pudding.

February, 1944

I have finished my period of quarantine and am now quartered in a dormitory. It is not so lonesome as the cell block; there are fifty-one others here with me. I am one of two "orderlies" (janitors) whose daily task it is to keep the dormitory clean. I try to do this job, like every other, in good, workmanlike fashion as a matter of principle. Besides that, I have another incentive: I think my co-residents, as well as myself, are at least entitled to a clean place to live.

If Freda comes to live with you, as you say may ensue if Frank leaves, the project ought to work out to your mutual satisfaction. Freda is good company as well as a good cook. You also have some points in your favor.

Joe pointed out several mixed metaphors in my history manuscript and made me sensitive on the subject. Now I recall another one. It is in Chapter 3, I think, toward the end, in which reference is made to the CP faction leaders. "I think some of them were bad eggs from birth" is the sentence, as I recall it. I thought the figure of speech was pretty good, and appropriate to the subject, at the time. But it occurs to me now that eggs are not born. So the metaphor must be changed. Let Usick figure out a better one and blame Joe, not me, for any difficulty he may have. Maybe "from birth" can be changed to "to start with." Anyway, the *mixed* metaphor must be unmixed.

Walta's letter was a delight. She made my little Sweetums live on the page. I miss her poignantly, and am impatiently waiting for the picture.

I will return the pardon petition to Evelyn with a brief one-sentence reason motivating the petition. I hope she understands this petition *only* as a formality and that her campaign is not *in any way* to be based upon the petition, but upon the merits of the case as CRDC has already explained them. *Our press must not even mention the petition.* It has absolutely nothing to do with the issue. Our press has its own line and needs no ACLU angles.

No mail since last Thursday. Are you ill again?

LETTER 11

SANDSTONE, FEBRUARY 7, 1944

I received your letters No. 6 and No. 7, and you can be sure I felt thankful to medical science and its miracle sulfa drug for your speedy recovery. Your illness harassed me all the more because I was so far away and unable to cook for you and bring things to you. I keep reading slipper ads in the newspapers, remembering that I bought a pair for you when you were sick last winter. It is best for you to stay in the house anyway until the time comes for you to go to Florida.

Your report about the functioning of the party staff does not surprise me, although I was glad to hear it and to have the reassurance. Between ourselves, it was planned and selected that way—not without time, experiment, struggle and effort. My conception of the staff is different from other conceptions; more often there are lack of definite conceptions on this all-important subject. I am firmly convinced—and nobody can unlearn me—that team-workers are superior to self-centered "stars" who usually are made of tinsel anyway.

Walta's idea of keeping a written record of the baby's development in the form of letters to me is a very good one. I will save the letters. Then, when I come home, we can have them bound in leather with a gold-lettered title: "Lorna's Third Year (Letters to Bam)." Won't that be a nice "personal history" for Sweetums to read some day?

I got the pictures and will have them framed on a piece of cardboard to stand on my little iron table. Remind Evelyn that our ten-dollar monthly allowance should begin on March 1 and be sent on the first of each month thereafter. That is all we will need—we cannot spend more—until next Christmas when, in accordance with our old ILD custom, we should receive a combination "Christmas—Going Out" present. I heard indirectly of the wonderful work CRDC is doing, but should get more detailed information from you.

I wish you would quote what Joe said about the baby in his article. You don't need to write double-space. Single-space serves very well and enables you to write longer letters for less postage.

In addition to a printed list, Lillian should also get out a printed folder—a modest adaptation of International Publishers catalogue—describing the items briefly. She has enough books on her list to warrant such a step, and it will also give her present customers, as well as prospective ones, a better impression of her rather imposing business.

The news of Larry's illness struck me very hard. I am anxiously awaiting further word. It is time for the club [party] to make a definite decision that all employees be provided with adequate medical and dental care as part of their compensation and that it begin with provisions for immediate, and thereafter periodical, examinations in order to detect incipient weakness in either department in time to treat them properly.

Next Friday I would like above all to have chicken stew with dumplings for my birthday dinner. Perhaps the family can have it and let Mickey have an extra portion as my proxy. Add this to your menu list.

LETTER 12

SANDSTONE, FEBRUARY 10, 1944

If Evelyn is to make the rib roast, remind her that Yorkshire pudding must go with it. She had better begin to practice up; otherwise we will have to send for Demila.

Your scheme to buy a country place for $180 and build a house on it sounds utterly fantastic. I don't want to become a property owner and have to worry about taxes.

Pay no attention to the parole blanks sent to you. I have not applied for parole and have no intention of doing so; we are applying for a pardon (which we won't get).

Apropos the six-pager. It is, it appears to me, solely a question of an adequate staff.

The appointment of Freda to full-time work is an important step forward. Every timely and well-considered addition to the professional staff yields a double value: it strengthens the party cadre and also widens the knowledge and improves the training of the individual. Freda begins with good assets. She has demonstrated the qualities of endurance and loyalty and she *lives* in the party. She has ability enough too, I think.

If she does the new task properly, that is, thoroughly, there is little reason to doubt that her appointment will give all-around satisfaction and, perhaps, establish her permanently as a functionary. In that case, perhaps Evelyn can gradually shift more of the responsibility and more of the details to Freda while we mull over the idea of another field of work for Evelyn, possibly on the press.

I intend to write Walta more than one letter before I finish my sojourn here. However, I still have many things to crowd into the limited space of my two letters a week to you and it will be some time before I catch up with the notes I have already made.

I was delighted to learn that Dot cooked and took care of you during your illness, and that Grant took his evening meals there. Is it not possible that the combination of good cooking and good company helped the sulfa drug to bring about your speedy recovery? I have been wondering how Grant is getting along on his job and wish you would let me know.

How many new members up to February 1? I am anxious to know the *percentage* of the full quota reached each month. I think this should also be a feature of Moish's monthly bulletins to the branches.

I would like to get some *concrete* news about the progress of my history book at the printer's. When the publication date is approximately in sight Lillian should send out a bulletin, and the pre-publication notices and ads should be readied for the press.

If part of this publicity work is done in the month before publication, the selling campaign can be carried through all the sooner, and the decks cleared for the next book. I think Moish should check the introduction which I hope is fairly brief and informative, and raises no controversial questions which might divert attention from the book itself.

Put a hot pastrami sandwich on your list.

LETTER 13

SANDSTONE, FEBRUARY 14, 1944

I received your February 7 letter on the 9th. I get your letters as promptly as you get mine, but can't answer them right away as I write only on Wednesday and Sunday nights and date them the next day, when they are mailed. Your letter was delivered to me at 10 P.M. Wednesday—the regular mail delivery time—but my letter for that day had already been written.

Now that the fifteenth anniversary fund has been successfully completed I want to hear something about the no less important membership campaign. What was the total of the old campaign up to January 31? Are the branches being lined up to concentrate on the new campaign? This is the most important question now.

My job is all right. It is more manual labor than I have been accustomed to for many a year, but I am getting used to it. Perhaps the exercise is good for me, and I still have plenty of time for reading and study. I don't think I need any vitamin pills. I feel OK. As far as the duodenal ulcer is concerned, I know, as I have known for a long time, that it is there, but as long as it doesn't bother me I don't see why I should bother it, or talk about it, or hear about it. I watch my diet far more carefully here than I have done for several years. My method, which is very simple, seems to work well so far. If I think anything is not good for me, such as all seasoned and spiced foods—hamburger, meat loaf, sauce, etc.—I just pass it up and take a couple of extra scoops of carrots or rutabagas and call it a meal.

I finished a history of the American Indians by Wissler and now have a rough knowledge of all the various tribes who inhabited the U.S. when the white man first came; their background, traditions and customs; their wars against the white man's encroachments; their present locations on the various reservations; and the results, up to date, of the white man's attempt to "civilize" them. It is a fascinating subject. The author gives a great deal of essential information in compact form but his prose lacks wings. I had to walk the whole length of the way with him.

I also read a splendid book entitled *Zapata, the Unconquerable* by Pinchon. This is a biography of the greatest leader of the Mexican Revolution. It makes one feel it was well worth while to come to prison to make the acquaintance of this beautiful, heroic personality and to live a few all too brief days with him, oblivious to all external surroundings.

I hear much indirectly in commendation of Joe's piece about our departure. I get a double sense of satisfaction from this: 1) It is good for the cause—all parties and all people must continuously be inspired and reinspired. Those who don't understand this can never lead a *movement*. 2) Joe's selection for this task was also one of those things I picked out of the air. Can you send me an outline of the main points of his article with a few salient quotations?

LETTER 14

SANDSTONE, FEBRUARY 16, 1944

I have received the following pictures from you up to date: one of you, one of Walta, one of Ruth and two of the baby. The other pictures you have mentioned have not been received.

＊

In the first bound volume of the old *Labor Defender* there is an article of mine entitled: "The Cause that Passes through a Prison." I am not sure whether all or part of this old article would be suitable for republication, with an appropriate explanatory note, but you might check it and see.

I have been thinking about Leon Sedov, and how shamefully our press has neglected to keep his memory alive by observing his memorial day. We also barely mentioned the Old Man last August. I suppose the main reason for this is that everybody forgets the day until it is just around the corner, and then there is a hurried, usually too late rush to get or find an article somehow or other.

We have often talked of getting up a *calendar* of our movement. Nothing ever came of it; perhaps because it was visualized as a big and elaborate undertaking. What is needed right now—something that can be worked out in a single staff meeting and promptly executed by a single designated person—is a typewritten *calendar of dates* for the guidance of the editorial and administrative offices. With this on the wall or under glass on the desk, important events and memorial occasions would be noted long enough in advance to allow for early preparation of special articles, whole pages and even special editions.

LETTER 15

SANDSTONE, FEBRUARY 21, 1944

I received your letter of February 14 last Wednesday. You indicated that you had a setback and said you would write again at greater length the same night. I have heard nothing from you since. I can only hope that this does not signify a turn for the worse which prevented you from writing. If you do go to Florida be sure to notify the authorities here of the change of address and the reason for it. Do this promptly, and notify me at the same time, as permission must be secured to write to you or receive letters from you at a different address.

I wish you would send me the final scoreboard on the fund—quotas, contributions and percentages. I am more and more uneasy about the failure to get any information about the membership campaign. Does this mean that it is not succeeding, or that someone has the stupid idea that I should be told only good news? I, like any other adult, would be obliged to get the truth—and get it straight—about everything. The membership campaign is the most important thing now, in my opinion, and it must be organized as a *campaign*.

I wish you would send me the list of books Evelyn sent to Washington for approval. Otherwise it is quite pointless for me to make any suggestions—it might only duplicate the list. I ordered the works of Aristotle. If approved, it will cost me five dollars—that is half a month's supply of my commissary goods.

My action in ordering the book under such circumstances is the most convincing way I can think of at present of demonstrating to Usick that I am taking his guidance in the study of philosophy seriously. I hope he was consulted on the makeup of the list sent to Washington, so that the appropriate works to follow up on Aristotle will become available for the Sandstone undergraduates.

I am anxiously waiting for more detailed information about George's accident and his present condition. Also about Larry's progress and the affair of Frank's little finger. It is especially important that information on such matters, which are most vitally important to us, be supplied to us promptly and fully one way or another.

The report of the big snowstorm in New York—and the sub-zero weather here—reminded me painfully of the heating situation at the headquarters. I have felt very sorry that I only talked about providing supplementary heating before I left, instead of making sure it would be done by doing it myself. I feel in my bones that the staff is still at the mercy of the erratic janitor, shivering on cold days and endangering their health.

This is entirely unnecessary. I have read several ads in the Minneapolis papers about electrical heaters which are just about what is needed. They are rather expensive, but what better purpose can we put our money to than providing the necessary conditions to facilitate the work and safeguard the health of our staff?

I read Oscar Ameringer's autobiography.

I am now reading a life of General Grant as an antidote. This resolute campaigner is more to my taste. Much more. In fact, next to John Brown I like him best, I guess.

LETTER 16

SANDSTONE, FEBRUARY 24, 1944

Your letter of February 17 came Monday night and the contents—as well as the fact of receiving the letter—greatly relieved the anxiety which had weighed upon me over the weekend. We ought to reconcile ourselves to the delays and uncertainties of the mails these days, but it is hard to be rational sometimes in a place like this. I suppose I am more fortunate in this respect than others, but uncertainties and apprehensions about your health upset me sometimes.

I am calmly objective and patient enough about other things. No philosophy, however, has ever yet taught me reason and logic where you are concerned. I don't think Aristotle, whom I am going to get acquainted with next, will be able to help matters in this regard. (The commissary clerk told me that the book should come from the publishers any day now. I am eagerly awaiting it.)

I am overjoyed to hear about the certain prospect of your trip to Florida. I want you to go as soon as possible and wait there until the New York winter is finished. I am less inclined to approve your proposal to come here for a visit. It will be a long and wearisome trip and I don't think it will do you any good. Better wait and come to meet me when I am released—eleven months from today—January 23.

I am sorry I cannot see or hear from Carl. You should

not encourage his fatalistic moods. Many good things can happen to a man after he is thirty and he should look forward to them. His problem is to find out for sure what he wants to be and do—not what somebody else wants him to be and do, but what *he* wants—and then do it in spite of everything. This is the beginning of all personal wisdom and philosophy.

I am delighted to learn that Larry is coming along all right, but George's burns were felt here in Sandstone, I can tell you. Third-degree burns—those are very serious aren't they? Please send me promptly every scrap of new information you get about his condition.

Isn't it quite a striking coincidence that I wrote you about Sedov just when Usick's article was going to press? I had completely lost track of the date—had a hazy impression it was in the fall—and that is what started my train of thought about the calendar.

I am very glad Joe got little Mickus down on record in his article for the magazine. I wouldn't have had that left out for anything. I am thinking about her every day and living future times with her in anticipation. Tell her to have my slippers ready.

What became of the plan to make a pamphlet out of the farewell speeches, Joe's report, etc.? In my opinion this is absolutely necessary to complete the record of the case. You say my messages have been conveyed but you don't say what has been done about them. That is the main point of my concern. Perhaps just because nothing ever happens here I expect things to happen quickly every time I send a suggestion.

You might remind our friends that while I can't do anything here, there is nothing to prevent me thinking—possibly all the more clearly because there is no pressure of immediate action upon me—and expecting action from others.

LETTER 17

SANDSTONE, FEBRUARY 28, 1944

I received your letter of February 18. I didn't say that I was making notes for my memoirs but only that I was mulling over the idea. Meantime I am reading other biographies and autobiographies, partly to observe the patterns others have used for projects of this kind. At present I am reading Jim Farley's story of his life and work. His pattern would never do for me. He disposes of his entire boyhood and youth in a single chapter. Such a "biography" is something like a tree without roots.

I read some reviews of Sean O'Casey's autobiography—I think it was his—in which his boyhood and adolescence each were allotted their rightful place, namely, approximately one-third of the whole, in the form of separate, self-sufficient books. I am interested in O'Casey anyway, and I would like the CRDC to include his books in the list they plan to donate to the library here. Farley's account of his political activity and experience is interesting, in its way, to a born "politiker" like myself, but it never occurred to him that his game is a penny-ante one. *Our* politics is bigger, so much so that it has the difference of quality.

I have definitely decided now that I want to study Greek history while I am here. I want to know the milieu in which Aristotle wrote. Ask Usick to give the CRDC a small list of the most necessary books on this subject. These, in addition to the books on philosophy to follow my reading—rather, my study, line by line—of Aristotle are all the books I will need, for my part, for the balance of my sojourn here.

How strange it is to have the opportunity thrust upon me at this late day to satisfy in some measure the most poignant desire of my youth for study and contemplation, free from the pressure of immediate responsibilities and the clamor of the day.

If you have not already done so, don't you think it would be timely to send Natalia a roundup report of all that has happened, including our affairs here, our health, our activities, etc.? You can tell her truthfully that we all think of her fondly and speak of her often.

The favorable news of Wil [Workers International League] and the others [in Britain] is most welcome. Indeed, this question worried me so much I was afraid to inquire about it. They constitute the most important link in the international chain at the present moment, and if they fail to rise up to the level of their responsibilities it will take a long time, when time is so pressing, to repair the damage. There is no other way for them than the one we have already pointed out more than once.

The outline of Joe's article which you sent me only raises once more the question: Why have the farewell speeches not been printed in a pamphlet with Joe's article as an introduction? I am absolutely unable to understand this incredible lapse. The historical record must be completed. If it is a question of money we will agree to provide it, if necessary by authorizing Evelyn to "check off" 50 percent of our "wages" until the bill is taken care of. This is a true expression of our sentiment on the matter. Tell Joe I am especially glad that he put in the section about Dewey and the trials. How the Old Man would have loved that!

March, 1944

SANDSTONE, MARCH 2, 1944

I got your letter of February 24. I don't get mail on any set days. The mail is delivered here every night, except Sunday, just before bedtime.

I wish you would send me the chapter titles on my book. I want one more chance to consider changes in them before the page proofs are made up. Also: Ask Usick to delete the parenthetical remark in my farewell speech when it goes into the pamphlet. In speaking about the gold watch I mentioned that I wouldn't be able to take it with me and added, between dashes—"they figure, etc." Leave out the part between the dashes. Perhaps it detracts a little bit from the dignity of the context.

As I remember, the *Labor Defender* article had a fine center-of-page illustration. Perhaps it can be used if the article is reprinted—even if it has to be rephotographed or redrawn.

The contributions from "friends" to our anniversary fund are very interesting. Can you tell me more about them, how they were given, amounts, etc.?

It is too late to cancel my order for *Aristotle*, although I haven't received it yet. I want it for my own anyway. The Modern Library edition of Plato is in the library here, as also is the Modern Library edition of Keats and Shelley in one volume, so these two books can be omitted. Ask Usick to substitute volumes of other ancient Greeks. I intend to live with these chaps as much as possible while I am here.

*

Too much fuss should not be made about Philadelphia's delinquency. The branch has suffered disintegration, and scolding will not help them. They need a blood transfusion. As far as I can see, that can be accomplished only by colonization. Some reinforcements along the lines we sent to Frisco and Akron should be undertaken if possible. After all, Philadelphia is one of the founding units, and besides that is strategically very important. It should not be allowed to disappear.

During your absence I do not want to rely on Walta for the prompt and full information I need about everything going on in our circles. Better have Sylvia write you all the news two or three times a week, and you can relay it to me. Also, you can send Sylvia my suggestions, which are not intended as general observations but as concrete proposals for action to which I would appreciate concrete and prompt replies. Walta is obviously overloaded now with her double task of housekeeping and Mick-raising.

Our California girl wrote me a very sweet letter, just before I left New York, about the *Struggle* book. I didn't get a chance to answer her in the crowded hours before leaving. Will you drop her a note at San Diego and thank her for her letter? It is in my desk somewhere. Her letter pleased me very much.

LETTER 19

SANDSTONE, MARCH 6, 1944

I received your letter of March 2 on March 4. My trouble about writing letters is the opposite of yours. I never can find space enough, and the notes I make of things I want to say keep piling up. If you adopt the system of making notes, and remember that I have no other contact with our world except through your letters and that I want to know about everything, you will not lack material to write about.

I am losing weight, steadily and systematically, according to plan and disciplined procedure in regard to diet. The only thing I am worried about is my Hollywood suit. I don't want to lose it. Do you think we could get it altered? Otherwise I am afraid I will have to give up my slimming program.

You must decide for yourself about Florida. If you wear yourself out with transportation difficulties and get bored in isolation among strangers, the trip might do you more harm than good. You ought to know best what you need most. The main thing you need, in my opinion, is heat and sunshine. Perhaps, if you stay in New York you had better get your sun-ray lamp fixed, or if that is impossible, get another one. A sun-bath or two every day may carry you over till you can go to the beach.

I am very much interested in your plan to get a beach place for a long period. I am also very anxious for the baby to have an uninterrupted summer in the sun. I hope something can be worked out for the maximum benefit for all, without putting too much work and responsibility on you.

I hear the Minneapolis branch made a big success of a rummage sale, to top New York's success with the musicale. Wouldn't it be a good idea for Moish to get a report from the Twin City organization and then send out a bulletin to give the other branches a hint on a way to raise money?

I will send more suggestions for books in another letter for the next shipment. I would like to be clear about Frank's draft status. Does "limited service" mean deferment, and if so, for how long? If he is deferred he should study French to make his international work more fruitful.

I heard indirectly of some criticisms of Joe's article and

have the impression they are somewhat of an echo of the plenum discussion and the sad affair about the introduction to my *Struggle* book. If the article is published in the pamphlet and thus becomes more "official," it would be well to remember that these "criticisms," like those raised around Usick's introduction, are not in reality directed against Joe's artistry—that is only a pretext, common in shyster politics— but against another object.

It is usually best to ward off these "sneak attacks" by small concessions, even at the cost of literary perfection or full self-expression. For example, the decision to start the "march" at 2:30 from the Minneapolis headquarters should not be ascribed to me personally, etc.

I must again express my satisfaction at the inclusion of the section on Dewey. Can you send me this quotation?

Have our friends noted the Paris Commune date on their "calendar"?

LETTER 20

SANDSTONE, MARCH 9, 1944

I found the following books about Greece in our library here: *The Life of Greece* by Durant and *The History of Greece* by J.B. Bury; *The Works of Homer; The Works of Plato; The Works of Thucydides.* I will read the first two first in order to get a general panoramic view of the whole subject and then go on to the Greek authors themselves. My *Aristotle* has arrived from the publishers but has not been delivered to me yet.

Tell Usick to include, in the next list made up, the essential Greek authors missing from our library. I also suggest that he include the three volumes of *Capital.*

I hope our staff is not working under too much pressure.

That is necessary in emergencies, but our friends have a long pull ahead of them. For that they need a steady pace and a regular daily stint—no more. We don't want to come back and find them worn out from overstrain just when it is time to start some big projects germinating in our minds.

I would like to suggest that Moish take a census of the party membership in order to get an exact picture of the composition with regard to: 1) sex; 2) average age; 3) length of membership; 4) previous political affiliation; 5) occupation; 6) union membership.

I think the census will show a surprising percentage of new members since the split with no previous political affiliation or experience. This leads me to the thought that our press has to undertake a systematic work of education for their benefit on the hundred-year history of our movement. Historic dates, indicated on our calendar, should not be treated perfunctorily or neglected altogether, as was too often the case in the past, but made the occasions for thoroughgoing treatment of the subjects: what happened and why, and the lessons to be derived.

The Paris Commune, for example, should be treated this year from the point of view that perhaps hundreds of our members and thousands of our readers have only a hazy impression, if any at all, of this great historic event. There should be one simple explanatory article giving the essential facts for the benefit of beginners; a political review and analysis; and perhaps, if space permits, a reprinting of some of the classic comments on the Commune. I suggest this as a sort of pattern for all the important dates on our calendar. The extra two inside pages of the six-pager are made to order for such projects.

Moreover, the *public* observance of important dates— meetings, lectures, etc.—is an especially good medium for propaganda in these days when discussion of contemporary events is restricted in certain respects. When I finally get a chance to read the bound volume for 1944 I hope to find a number of special editions and special inside pages far superior to our handling of the great anniversaries in the past because they represent a work of planning and preparation in advance.

LETTER 21

SANDSTONE, MARCH 13, 1944

Wednesday was a red-letter day. I received your two letters of March 5 and March 6 plus one from Walta, and the pictures of me and Sweetums together, and of her alone. It was a feast. Isolation is the all-pervading fact of prison. Letters are the sole means of contact with the world one has known, and the prisoner's day is pointed toward mail time.

I am somewhat disturbed about the "intransigence" of some of our friends regarding the criticisms of Joe's article which is now to be included in the pamphlet. It is not profitable to fight over trifles. Also, in politics—as distinguished from art—it is not sufficient for a statement to be "the truth" in a literal sense nor for an action to be "correct"; statements and actions—in politics—must serve ends also. Otherwise they are better left unsaid or undone. *In no case* can the pamphlet appear with my picture on the cover. The cover must express what the pamphlet is concerned with: the issue and the speeches *of the eighteen.* Far better a pamphlet with no illustration on the cover; this might be better in any event. I had to learn these simple lessons through blows over the head. I hope our friends can learn them the "easier" way, as Farrell recommended at the plenum.

You do not say whether you got the sunlamp fixed. Since you have decided to stay in New York for the balance of the winter, I think this is most necessary. I remember the lamp did you a lot of good when you had it in operation at our place on East Tenth Street.

I was very pleased to hear that Edith wrote to you a sweet letter which, as you quoted it, impressed me as a reflection of her personality. The next time she writes I would like her to indicate her and especially Mike's impressions of my *Struggle* book and the *History* book. They were written, in part, for their benefit. In these two books I tried, for the first time, to give a thorough-going and all-sided exposition of the troublesome "organization question." Edith and Mike should be good judges of how well I succeeded or wherein I failed. The "organization question," properly understood, is nothing less than, it is only another name for, the central question of our whole epoch—the question of the party.

I guess we can let the chapter headings stand as they are.

Je suis enchanté with the report of the place you have rented on Long Island. This assures me that your summer is provided for and that mine will be made easier as a consequence. I love to think of little Mickus living the whole summer long in the sun until she is "brown as a berry" and "sound as an apple." I think she should be taught to swim this summer already. I have seen newsreels of kids her age swimming and diving. What others can do she can do.

Is there open territory near the house where Wong and I could take long walks without running into too many neighbors and their dogs? Is the furnace fitted for coal, gas or oil?

LETTER 22

SANDSTONE, MARCH 16, 1944

The news about *The Militant* is just right. Now is the time to start the sub campaign which was derailed by the trouble with the mailing rights. I offer the following concrete proposals:

1) A special rate of twenty-five cents for six months.

2) The goal should be 3,000 (yes, three thousand) new subs.

3) There should be a definite *time limit* for the reduced rate campaign—sixty or ninety days, no more. (Otherwise you will endanger the financial structure of the paper by getting people out of the habit of paying the regular rate.)

4) It should be an all-out, high-pressure party campaign. (This is timely, and the morale in the ranks can sustain it.)

5) The financial transactions and technical details of the campaign should be handled through the regular business manager's routine, but the *party* must be mobilized and driven into action from the National Office and all party attention and activity centered on the attainment of the quota goal.

6) Quotas should be assigned to the branches, taking as a minimum basis and obligation *four subs from each member.*

7) The subs should be printed on *prepaid postal cards* so as to eliminate all unnecessary bookkeeping and addressing of envelopes. (This method was one of the secrets of the great success of the old *Appeal to Reason.*)

8) The campaign should be strongly publicized in the paper, and not announced until every technical detail is worked out and ready.

9) Don't fail to use a *thermometer* to illustrate the progress of the campaign in the paper, and this time make it a good one.

✳

I keep thinking of the new house on Long Island as a place to camp in when I write my next book. I hope the furnace has an automatic oil burner so that precious time need not be wasted shoveling coal.

I am not inclined to take the *World-Telegram* story about the CP too seriously. There may be something going on there but it is most likely a dispute as to the *interpretation* of Stalin's wishes. That is as far as Foster's courage could take him.

We should be very careful in our interpretation of the events in the ILGWU, etc. These are anti-CP but by no means pro-revolutionary manifestations. I really mourn for the poor, deceived and doubly betrayed Jewish workers in the needle trades. They are like a lost tribe. Most of them are too old, too disillusioned to find their old faith again without a genuine and general revival of the revolutionary movement on a world scale.

Your reference to the CP's new "Jefferson School" reminds me of some elaborate projects I have been thinking about for our own school—to be undertaken when we come back. But I will leave that for another letter; most likely, for several letters.

I am very glad indeed to learn that Mexico translated and published our plenum resolution.—The new list of books should be held open till April. Before then I will send you a number of additional titles needed here.

LETTER 23

SANDSTONE, MARCH 20, 1944

We learned indirectly that three books had arrived at the library here, presumably from the CRDC. They are *Dialectics of Nature, Treasury of Science* and *My Native Land.* Two of them had already been taken out. What happened to the others? And what about this?—On March 2 you wrote that the list had been approved "and will go forward this week." Does it take two weeks for the mail to bring an order of books, or was the "this week" a euphemism for "sooner or later."

And what became of the request to include a number of books on U.S. history? These questions are for the CRDC. Nothing causes more bitter resentment than negligence, indefiniteness and delay in attending to the details which may mean little in the normal run of things but mean everything to the prisoner who is *waiting!* I know very well that the comrades in the CRDC are busy with many tasks, but I also know that prisoners' requests and needs must always take first place in a defense committee's routine because explanations never do a prisoner any good.

I propose the following inflexible routine in these matters:

1) Submit a list of books to the Washington authorities on the *first of each month.*

2) Include every title requested, if it is to be had.

3) When the list is approved, ship them *the very next day.*

4) *Simultaneously* notify me of the date of shipment and the titles included.

If this is done we will know exactly what to look for and when to look for it; this will prevent needless misunderstandings, and nobody will eat his heart out with the thoughts that golden hours of study on a prescribed subject are being lost forever because details are not attended to properly and promptly.

Include the following titles in the next list submitted:

English: *Oxford Book of Greek Verse in Translation; Plutarch's Lives;* Rostovtzeff: *History of the Ancient World* and *Social and Economic History of the Roman Empire; Works* of Sophocles, Aristophanes, Aeschylus and Euripides.

French: Voltaire: *Candide, The Philosophy of History, The Ignorant Philosopher;* Dumas: *The Three Musketeers* and *The Count of Monte Cristo;* Jules Verne: *Tour of the World in Eighty Days;* Villon: *Poems;* Anatole France: *Penguin*

Island and *Crime of Sylvestre Bonnard.*

Spanish: Five or six books with their corresponding titles in *English* for use in advanced study of the language.

Ask Usick to make, if possible, one *final* correction in the *History.* In the "Dog Days" chapter—I think—I say, "we survived because we had the help of Comrade Trotsky," or words to that effect. Change it to read: "The help of Comrade Trotsky and our international organization." Then, after the reference to Comrade Trotsky's special help, add: "The intervention of the International Secretariat was a decisive help to us in the solution of our difficulties. We sought their advice and were sensible enough to heed it when it was given. Without international collaboration—that is what the word 'internationalism' means—it is not possible for a political group to survive and develop in this epoch." This *final* change is very important—it is for the Britishers.

Moish should be sure to make it a specific proviso that the twenty-five-cent, six-month subs are for *new subscribers only.* On the old *Labor Action* we broke down the regular subscription rate by overlooking this detail. Tell the CRDC to send *money orders* and tell the wives all to use money orders for our remittances. Checks take three weeks to collect.

LETTER 24

SANDSTONE, MARCH 23, 1944

Two more books have arrived: L.D.'s *History* and Clausewitz. We still don't know what others to look for. We need the whole list. Include the following in the April 1 list: Modern Library edition of *Homer* (the copy here is always out); Diogenes Laertius: *Lives and Opinions of the Eminent Philosophers; Heraclitus on the Universe.* (All the classical titles not available in Modern Library or Everyman's Library cheap editions can be gotten from The Loeb Classical Library published by the Harvard University Press, Cambridge 38, Massachusetts. Write to them for the Loeb Library catalogue.) Always get the cheaper editions if possible.

Include also: Everyman's Library editions of *Eugénie Grandet; Lost Illusions; The Quest of the Absolute; The Rise and Fall of César Birotteau.* In French: *Comédie humaine* (i.e., the Collected Works) or the above four volumes and *Le Père Goriot.* (The French can be bought at G.E. Steckert on East Tenth Street.)

*

I was especially glad to hear that all is well with "the boy" and Don and Demila. I think of him often and want to do something for his future. He should think of me as his American Uncle whom he can always rely on.

By chance I saw a copy of Dwight's new magazine. My impression of it is cogently stated, I mean concisely stated, in the title of the inaugural editorial: "Why Politics?" Why, indeed?

I got my book of Aristotle and have started to work on it. There are 1,487 pages. This is quite a bite but I will chew it up, and digest it too, before I leave here.

Are the photos of the bust a good representation? Nobody here thinks the photos are good likenesses of me. Be sure to let me know anything more you learn of Charlie's movements. Even if Wong goes to live with you in Long Island I think you should take Brownie too. Mick is entitled to have a little dog of her own. What is the matter with that arm which she keeps spraining? Maybe she should practice on a boxer's punching bag to make it strong. I think you should rent the sunlamp in any case. Don't they have a heat globe as well as the sun-rays?

The lack of level ground around the new house is a drawback but it is not as serious for me as it would have been last year. I will have less weight to carry up hills a year from now. I am thinking most of all these days of a place to study and write in. That is the most attractive feature of the place on Eleventh Street—the front room, I mean.

We get the *New York Times* here and keep track of what is going on, in a general way. We also get the Minneapolis papers. I spend very little time, however, on the newspapers. A glance at the front page of the *Times* and then the index to see if there is anything of special interest listed. I am far too much occupied with the Greeks and my other studies to waste time reading the newspaper page by page.

Your report that the *NI* is serializing Ciliga is interesting. I have some thoughts on this subject which I will write about when I get more space. "Cut-rate" Trotskyism obviously will not work. One cannot cut away "quantities" from the unified doctrine without eventually coming to a qualitatively different one.

LETTER 25

SANDSTONE, MARCH 27, 1944

The arguments for the three-month or six-month sub for twenty-five cents are both equally valid, depending on the conception of the main purpose of the special campaign. The three-month argument is OK if one is thinking of *trial subs* primarily, preparing the way for a second canvass for full-rate subs. However, I think this conception is too narrow for the present situation. The fault of my previous letter on this subject was my failure to mention a different primary motivation for the campaign.

Our main object now, as when we started the program of mass free distributions, should be to get a wider spreading of our message while our case is still alive regardless of the immediate effect on our permanent subscription list. Three thousand papers going every week for six months to the *same people*, who have not been getting the paper before, should be more effective than the same number of papers being distributed, more or less at random, as with the mass distributions.

The appeal is more concentrated and, moreover, is directed in the main to people who we have reason to believe are interested to a certain extent. Nevertheless, in our present financial situation, no one could make a reasonable objection to *giving away* three thousand more papers weekly if we had good spots to put them. The reduced-rate subs, of course, are better because they reach a more receptive audience and the extra cost is nearly, if not entirely, covered.

From my point of view the six-month sub is more than twice as good as the three-month sub because the repetition of the message for double the length of time should have more than double the cumulative effect. Of course, there is nothing fatal in the difference, however the decision is made. One method can be tried first and the other later, for that matter. But keep this in mind: Now is the time to spread out, not count pennies too closely.

*

I will write about the school when I have thought it out more completely. I already have several pages of notes for a *thesis* on the subject.

The supplementary information about the Long Island *settlement*, which is now enlarged for the benefit of the hardworking functionaries, is very welcome here. Evelyn went about this just as we would have decided if we had been asked to state our maximum preference. But doesn't she always?

*

Here is a preliminary note on another subject: New York should get *double* the reduced-rate subs, proportional to membership, as the rest of the country. We should never forget that New York is the Capital of the *world*. We must strengthen our base there at all costs in preparation for the future. With the further development of international events, the resounding crash of all traditional organizations and tendencies will create the biggest vacuum in New York.

It will be filled; it has been known since Strato of Lampsacus (280 B.C.) that "nature abhors a vacuum." Our party, and ours alone, must *be there, and be known,* when the betrayed and disillusioned youth angrily turn away from the false teachers who have lied to them, and seek a new road. New York is *far* more important than any other place. We must prepare *now* for things to come *there*.

I have finished the first reading of Aristotle's *Rhetoric* and have started on his *Ethics*.

Why can't I get any news about Sweetums and her doings?

LETTER 26

SANDSTONE, MARCH 30, 1944

Once the U.S. history books get here there will be no special hurry about the others. The important thing is that when we are told they are coming—or when we are told anything else, for that matter—we know we can rely on it. You can tell the CRDC that I was not complaining about a personal grievance. Also that I was only moderately angry—which, Aristotle said, is the mark of "the good man." It should never be forgotten, however, that the prisoner service is the most important side of CRDC work and must always get priority, never be handled casually or carelessly. No matter how long the CRDC may remain in existence it will never find a "reasonable" prisoner.

The procedure you outline seems to be OK. Notify us when the list is approved—itemizing the entire approved list—and again when invoices are received. In this way we will know what is coming and when to look for them.

Ask Usick if he can still make one final correction of the "final" correction I sent last week. Where I say "no group can survive and develop" insert the words "on a revolutionary path." I think this is important enough even to change a page makeup (some other words can be chopped out to make room).

I want the monthly remittance for Agnes to continue during the whole time I am away. Whatever she gets from Carl she can consider extra and use it to equip her house with labor-saving devices to make her housework easier. Please send the answers to my questions about Father; I will probably want to follow up on this inquiry when I see the answers.

We all think our "Senator" [Grace Carlson] got the toughest break, but there is nothing we can do about it. My decision to come here with the others, instead of going to a closer place for reasons of personal convenience—which you may remember I made so promptly and firmly—was one of those decisions that are *given* to me. I always know I am right in such cases without even thinking about the matter. Those who made a different choice so shortsightedly and light-mindedly will never know how gravely they erred.

Did you give Carl a key to our house? He could sleep in my room when he is in town overnight. Also, you could invite him to live with us if he locates in New York next time.

I think I would like to have a file of the radical press to glance through when I return: *New Leader, Call, Labor Action, NI.*

I think time will pass more easily if you undertake a definite task to accomplish in a given period. I think often of our making another visit to Natalia. Why don't you acquire the German language in the meantime in order to facilitate conversation with her? It ought to be easy for you. Ask Sylvia to investigate the "Linguaphone" method advertised in the *Times* Sunday magazine.

I finished *The Life of Greece* and have started on Thucydides' *History of the Peloponnesian War.*

It is snowing here this afternoon as I write. It makes me think of my boyhood and my first sled. I am going to get a sled for Mickey. A nice red one, with green and yellow figures on it, and sharp, shiny runners.

April, 1944

SANDSTONE, APRIL 3, 1944

I think of Wong often and miss him cruelly. He would
be good company for me here. I look forward to the time
when I will take him for a walk again and rest on a rock on
the hill to think out some problem of philosophy.

It is good to hear that Sylvia will have a place with you
in the summer house. I want her to think of herself as
partly my guest there and that when she is resting and
having a good time there she is doing me good thereby. Is
she plugging away on her stenotype practice? We are going
to put that machine to good use some of these days and I
hope she will be ready when I am. The pact we made one
day in Pennsylvania for her to perfect her shorthand by
going back to school for more speed practice yielded rich
results for our cause. With the stenotype we will do more,
much more.

Why don't you want me to "lose too much" weight? You
know I never do anything by halves.

We are not impatient about the new book list. As long
as this—and all similar matters—are handled in regular
routine fashion we will be fully satisfied. There is no need
for hurry or strain. What we can't stand is uncertainty and
indefiniteness.

What arrangements have been made to help Lillian manage her double problem of little Charley and Pioneer? In view of the big stock Pioneer is accumulating and the expansion of its business in general, shouldn't the executive board begin to consider 1) safe and adequate storage space, and 2) fire insurance?

Page 14 of the March 29 *Times* has an interesting speech by Senator Aiken. I wonder if the paper is spreading this material from the *Congressional Record*. Statistics on the losses of merchant seamen will be appropriate in connection with the speech. Is some member of the staff in special charge of the *Congressional Record* reports? Is M. Stein writing his column regularly?

The Battle of the Buffoons—Messrs. Hillman and Dubinsky in the ALP—is a fit subject for satirical treatment. Shakespeare must have been thinking of them when he cried out: "Man, mere man, / Drest in a little brief authority, / does such fantastic things before high heaven / As make the angels weep"—or words to that effect. These undersized Lilliputians actually think that their hustling and bustling, their bawling and their caterwauling have some great significance. It is good to have a quiet jail and a timeless philosopher to resort to. The Spanish language has a word for these gladiators who fight with pigs' bladders. *No importa*—"it does not matter."

You speak of "the Editor's Month in Review" in the March *FI*. I hope this reference to the editor in the *singular* is a typographical error on your part, and that the editorials appear as sponsored by "The Editors" or "The Editorial Board." I can't find anything in Aristotle's logic to warrant the party's magazine appearing as anyone's personal organ. I know the present executive editor is as eager as anyone to break this outworn pattern which does not even deserve an honorable place in the party museum.

The new door at the party headquarters is appreciated. The old one, Ray said, "looked like an old ice house."

LETTER 28

SANDSTONE, APRIL 5, 1944

Your March 31 with picture of Natalia came April 3.

＊

Under the new rules for correspondence I am allowed [to write] three letters per week. Correspondents, on the other hand, must restrict their letters to *two* pages. We are allowed to receive seven letters per week. Photos must not be larger than 4" by 6" and must be kept down to "a reasonable number."

The *New Leader*, March 18, advertises *Zapata* at the Rand Bookstore for $1.19 (original price $3.00). Are we selling this excellent book?

Your report that we have a cartoonist for the paper was joyfully received here. This is bigger news than the restoration of the second-class mailing rights. Tell her she has appreciative supporters and ardent well-wishers at Sandstone.

You are correct, as we read in the *Times*, that Dubinsky denounces the ALP as "a cover for the communists," but you are quite wrong, literally and politically, to add, "which of course it is." The new leadership of the ALP is a cover for the Stalinists, but they (the Stalinists) are not communists, and we should never acknowledge such a claim even by slips of the tongue. We make our own terminology and do not let the Stalinist traitors or disillusioned renegades impose theirs upon us. There is a very important political meaning in these distinctions of expression. I earnestly hope the present editors will tolerate no carelessness in this regard.

I am somewhat disturbed by your reference to "Tito-Brezovich," especially by your statement that we will "carry an exposé" in the paper if GPU connections are established. We must be careful not to give an inch, directly or indirectly, to the Russophobe renegades. Wright's thesis-article on Yugoslavia last year in the *FI* must guide us on this question. We are against Stalin vis-à-vis the proletarian revolution, but *for* the bureaucracy (in our own way and with our own methods) vis-à-vis Mihailovič *e tutti quanti*. I do hope that the friendly attitude some Social-Democrats are showing toward our case and toward the CRDC does not induce any of our comrades, unconsciously, to soften up toward these swine in a political sense. That would be a real disgrace.

*

Include the following books in the next list: *Flowering Earth* by Peattie; *The Mediterranean—The Life Story of a Sea* by Emil Ludwig; *I Knew Them in Prison* by Dr. Mary Harris.

I think we can make a compromise on the special sub campaign which will combine the strong points of each proposal and be better than either. Sell the cards for twenty-five cents each on a three-month basis. At the end of that time canvass the list for renewals at the regular price. Those who do not renew should be *kept on the list* for another three months and then canvassed again. I see the point of those who want to follow up on the subs at the end of three months. I hope they also see the advantage of broadening our circle of readers in this period even if it requires the most extraordinary methods.

Your reports of Don make me feel real good. I fully intend to follow up on that front and make another visit as soon as it is possible.

My self-prescribed curriculum for this semester at Sandstone University is as follows: 1) Philosophy; 2) Greek History; 3) French; 4) Spanish. I work at each subject every day.

LETTER 29

SANDSTONE, APRIL 7, 1944

Your April 3 came April 5. In your March 31 you speak of a letter to be written the "next day." Evidently it was lost in the mails. Don't forget the new rule limiting letters to *two* pages hereafter.

Grote's *History* [of Greece] arrived but has not been made available yet. If you will send me a complete list of all books for which invoices have been received I will check here and let you know which have arrived so far.

If you will check Agnes' letter against the list of questions I asked Father about, you will see that quite a few are left unanswered. Please ask her about them again.

I am studying both Spanish and French with the texts of the International Correspondence School. They are very good texts—the conversational system—but they are based on *records* which, alas, I do not have. With them I am sure any language can be learned better and quicker than by going to any school class. I am very glad that you are going to study Spanish. Here is my suggestion: Write the ICS at Scranton for their catalogue. Also shop around with Linguaphone and other *record* systems before you decide on the one to take. I am very anxious, also, to know if these records and texts can be bought secondhand. I will need both French and Spanish records to straighten out my pronunciation. Let me know what course you decide on finally and how much it costs. We can practice Spanish together before visiting Natalia.

I finished Aristotle's *Ethics* and have started his *History of Animals*. Also finished *How Green Was My Valley*. It is a beautiful, moving story, beautifully written too, but it took me more than a month to get through it. There is not much room for fiction in my schedule.

Glad to get the news about Marsh. I was on the point of asking Walta for news about him, especially about his health and activities outside the shop. Can't Lorna's orange allergy be cured by giving her small doses of juice, gradually increased until she builds up an immunity? She needs those vitamins. A whole summer in the sun will build her up. Is she going to be taught to swim this summer? She should get plenty of carrots and rutabagas until she is able to assimilate orange juice.

The news about George is not so good. Neither is the intimation that Frank may be leaving. I wonder what our people in the services and on the ships are studying. The NC should inquire about this, and supervise and aid the uninterrupted study-in-preparation-for-the-future of all our cadre people. They should *all* learn languages.

I am far more interested in your report about Darcy than Foster. Can you quote the *Daily Worker* item about him? Tell Evelyn to rest easy about the pardon petition. I don't want to be hurried about this business. It will come in due time.

So Usick wants to take some credit away from my Greeks about the "vacuum" theory. When I get the time and opportunity, I will explain this or any other question about the Greeks to anyone who wants to raise any point about them. I am—that is, I will be—an expert on the question.

What are we doing about the DeLorenzo case? This strikes me as *very important* for us to shout about.

LETTER 30

SANDSTONE, APRIL 10, 1944

This is Sunday morning and I am thinking of a breakfast of soft-boiled eggs with creamery butter, orange juice (iced), milk, crepes suzette and rightly made coffee with cream.

Then a cigar and a walk with my cane, Mick and Wong. (I have all this in imagination, which is almost as good.)

I have been reading the news about Wil. Their attention now should be called to the resolution and speech of our plenum held on the eve of our trial (October, 1941). This should help them to find a clear line in the new situation. Count everything up now and see how much we profited from the policy of this resolution!

I rather like the name "Revolutionary Communist Party." I winced a bit at Joe's reference to me as a "socialist." To be sure, the Stalinists have brought a great discredit to the name of communism, but in the popular conception its predominant connotation is that of proletarian revolution. The word "socialist," on the other hand, signifies to most a renunciation of revolutionary methods in the direction of reconciliation with bourgeois democracy. That also is the sense in which nearly all the renegades call themselves "socialist" but never "communist."

Note that the Shachtmanites, who are continually taking careful steps backward when they think no one is looking, have begun to speak of themselves as "socialists" in an offhand manner—as though it had always been so. This has a real political meaning in their case. I took notice of it some months ago. I told the comrades at the plenum of the Old Man's objection to "the compromising word 'socialist.'" This is an interesting question for our politicos, scholars and philosophers to mull over.

As I recall, it is possible to ship *unbound sheets* of Pioneer publications to England at a fraction of the postal charges on finished and bound books. Lillian should get all the information on this and then arrange with Wil to send as many copies of our books as they want (printed sheets). They can then bind them and sell them under their own imprint. For this, as for their publishing activities in general, they need their own *publishing company.*

In general, the work of Pioneer should be animated in this period by the same conception as that of our press and all other departments of our work: get more *volume* of distribution, by forced measures if necessary. Quotas to branches on all new publications should be *doubled* at least, and the National Office should put on the pressure to fulfill them. I believe the sub drive will convince everybody that the branches can easily stand the pressure to double all their normal distributions.

*

I finished the first reading of Aristotle's *History of Animals, On the Parts of Animals,* and *On the Generation of Animals.* I think I will read *Poetics* next. Today being Sunday, I will spend the day loafing, visiting friends, going to a movie and beginning Homer's *Iliad.*

I am waiting anxiously for further reports of the work of our cartoonist. It is so important to *brighten up* the paper, to make it more accessible to tired workers. Our artist should make up a number of sketches and drawings of revolutionary heroes and public figures of the day for half-column illustrations of articles appearing in the paper.

LETTER 31

SANDSTONE, APRIL 12, 1944

I think it is good to send Aunt Natalia extracts of our letters so that she can be kept informed of our work here and our plans for the future. The same can be done for various friends who may be interested.

I finished a first reading of Aristotle's *Poetics.* I wonder if he had Sandstone students in mind when he said: "To be learning something is the greatest of pleasures not only to the philosopher but also to the rest of mankind, however small their capacity for it." "Learning—gathering the meaning of things."

I wish you would send me the list of dates on the Calendar. Is the date of Marx's death, for example, on it? Wouldn't it be a good idea to present commemorative articles with illustrations?

Always keep in mind the new and young readers for whom the paper must be made attractive. This is where our cartoonist-artist comes in. She can play a great role in the popularization of the paper. I already heard that a good non-party critic—Farrell's mother—said the first cartoon was very good in her opinion. We hear nothing but praise of the paper—from all sides. They all say, "It is better than ever." Is the magazine getting enough attention and cooperative effort? We hear good things about it also, but I would like to feel sure that everybody is pitching on that sector.

My hours have been changed. Rise at 6:30; breakfast at 7:45; dinner at 11; supper at 3—that is, two o'clock by suntime, my old breakfast hour; lights out at 9:30.

*

I am thinking about the party school as an institution which organizes, directs and supervises the education of all party members from the new recruit to the NC member who is a candidate for active participation in international work. One department—one college in the university, so to speak—will be a full-time school for the training of candidates for professional party work and for party workers who require a broadening of their knowledge prior to their promotion to higher bodies and more responsible functions. Before completing my theses on this aspect of the school I would like to get some concrete information about the experiences of our predecessors and models, the Russian Bolsheviks. (We may be able to learn something also from the

Mensheviks—in a technical sense.)

I wish you would write Natalia and ask her what help she can give me on this problem—from her recollections, and her ideas in general. There have been many references to a school; at Capri, I think. What was it, how was it organized, how financed, what was its curriculum, etc.? Were there other schools? Ask Usick to see what he can find in the history of the Russians on this subject.

My thoughts on the school are inspired also by examples, anterior to the Russian. By Aristotle's "Lyceum," for example. We are going to train and educate a cadre whose task it will be not only to explain the world but, as Marx said, "to change it." Why shouldn't we put this work on an organized, systematic basis, do it right?

Our masters have provided us with ample material for our "textbooks," and we have qualified and worthy disciples who are fully capable of explaining them and making their wisdom more easily accessible to the untrained young militants. Along this line there is a question: Has the complete index of the Old Man's writings, long ago ordered by the PC, been put in final form yet? If not, shouldn't a time limit be set for the completion of the task?

LETTER 32

SANDSTONE, APRIL 14, 1944

There are two volumes short in Grote's *History:* 7 and 10. All three volumes of *Capital* and Hacker's *U.S. Since 1865* arrived. Why were some of the titles I sent included in the list submitted to Washington and not others? I would like my *History* included in the next list to be submitted. Gitlow's and Eastman's books are here. Did you get the catalogue of the Loeb Classical Library from Harvard yet? As

I explained before, titles not available elsewhere can most likely be gotten there. The price is a little higher.

I am hungry to read so many books on so many subjects but I must rigidly discipline myself to stick to my "rationed" list: Greek history and literature, philosophy, French and Spanish. I hope that by the middle of summer I can branch out a bit. I expect to have a good reading knowledge of French and Spanish by then. I have already been working at them assiduously for two and a half months, ever since I got out of quarantine.

When I get started to work again I want everything to be ready in a technical sense so that I can work up everything that remains from my past work into literary form and get it out of the way. I wish Sylvia—herself—to move in on my accumulated stuff and classify and index it all so that I can know any time 1) what is there—all of it—and 2) where it is filed. This will be the first condition for me to be able to take up work without unnecessary delay.

I have a rough idea of what I want to do with the stuff, but haven't the least idea of how much there is or where to find it. The most important material of all is the old *Internal* and *International Bulletins*. I need a complete file for some work I contemplate. With your and Usick's help Sylvia can ascertain what numbers are missing—too many, I fear—and then take steps to find the missing copies. A canvass of the old-timers is the best means for this. I hope Moish will allow Sylvia the necessary time for this work. I hope he is unloading some of the NO routine from her shoulders in any case. She should get a *real* vacation this summer, for instance. In addition to her annual trip home she could stay some weeks with you at Long Island and take Mick swimming.

*

We are all agog today waiting for George's visit tomorrow (Friday). From present indications he is going to see the whole fourteen. That is just what we have been hoping for. We won't have much to tell him but expect he will have many things to tell us.

If Usick still thinks my "Twenty Years" should be published, we can get at the job first thing when I return and get it out of the way in a few weeks. To facilitate this speedy operation my articles and speeches since 1940 should be collected and put in the appropriate folders ready for instant use. I don't think it needs to be typed. Newspaper and magazine articles can be pasted up on letterhead-sized sheets and the pamphlets can be filed as they are.

LETTER 33

SANDSTONE, APRIL 17, 1944

Received your Nos. 30 and 31. I heard indirectly that you don't understand something I wrote about but didn't hear what it is, so I am none the wiser. I don't intend anything I write in an ambiguous sense.

Friday was a big day for us. George had an hour's visit with all fourteen of us and then another half-hour with me and one other. It was a real treat for everybody. We were all preparing and looking forward to the visit like kids on Christmas Eve. It was good to get direct word from our world. We were busy rehashing the talk with George till bedtime. Then I got a letter from you; so, all told, Friday was a good day. George's visit made me realize fully, for the first time, what my visits to the forsaken men in prison in the old ILD days must have meant to them.

＊

The new rules say newspaper clippings can be enclosed in letters. I wish you would send me the clipping of Joe's piece from the magazine.

I still don't understand the proposal to run an exposure of Tito. Suppose it can be proved that he is a GPU agent? What does that prove except that he is a Stalinist? I would like to get clear on this point. I am suspicious of the slightest, most indirect concession to the Russophobes. In this connection the Italian manifesto is a danger signal. Do they call for the defense of the Soviet Union? Do they clearly and unambiguously characterize the Soviet Union as a workers' state? *If not, they are not our people!*

We must not permit our instinctive sympathy for any insurgent group fighting under such difficulties to betray us into political concilationism. Any group arising in Europe today which takes a false or ambiguous position on the Russian question can be nothing more than the artificers of a new, degenerated version of the POUM. I have even heard indirectly that we have people in Chicago who think we should give material aid to such politicians!

Was the manifesto printed without a merciless criticism of its attempt to cut corners on the principal question of the Russian Revolution? I believe we should make a clear declaration, right now, of where we stand, whom we go with and whom we fight in the European situation which seems to be opening up so rapidly. I think it is necessary also to have a complete and immediate understanding with Wil for joint action in these matters *which permit no delay.*

We read the German reports via Stockholm in the *Times.* (They should be fully reported in our paper, as the provincial press does not carry them.) From all indications there will be no lack of "Trotskyists" and "Fourth Internationalists" in Europe. Our task is to separate the genuine from the imposters and muddleheads. It seems to me that now is the time for the most energetic activity on this front on literary lines and also on the lines of Stuart's example.

Be very careful with the Darcy matter. Do not attack him,

Norman or Bill D. Make sure of your facts before printing anything more. The most important thing is to establish contact with Norman or Marguerite and try to get authentic information. You personally may be able to do this. Encourage them. They must represent an important movement in the ranks. That, at least, is the way I interpret Darcy's participation. He is shrewd in politics.

LETTER 34

SANDSTONE, APRIL 19, 1944

I got Walta's letter of April 14 with the snapshots. The baby still looks the same. I think Walta's method of teaching her to speak correctly is very good. Strangely enough, I have been thinking of the same thing and meant to write about it. I had noticed that she used the expression "I go" instead of the usual baby-talk "me go." How fortunate the baby will be if she is taught everything correctly at each stage of the development of her mentality and does not have to unlearn afterward.

I think often of the problem of educating her for "the good life" which Aristotle thought should be the aim of education, and of lifting her, even from her infancy, to the mental and spiritual attitudes befitting a citizen of the society she is destined to live in. As I pursue my studies of Greek history and legend I ponder ways and means of making this story available to her in such simplified forms as she can assimilate. Thus her education will begin to be molded in the classical form even before she starts to school and its influence will be always with her thereafter.

I believe classical education will have a great resurgence under communism, no longer for the few but for all. Mickey will have a head start. She will know all about Homer's heroes from her bedtime stories and begin her high-school studies with the impression of the Greeks' Golden Age already firmly fixed in her mind.

*

I finished a first reading of Aristotle's treatise *On the Soul* and am now reading *Politics*. Usick has brought a new element into the discussion of the origin of the theory of the vacuum. I will have to make further researches before continuing.

If Pioneer's new list is printed, I wish you would send me a copy. I want to check it over as a preliminary to some suggestions I intend to offer for an expansion of the publishing activity. One thing I have in mind is to start the project of a Pioneer classical library—new editions of the standard pamphlets of our masters with new introductions, and in some cases if necessary, new translations.

For example: our own edition of the *Communist Manifesto* with the Old Man's introduction written on the occasion of the ninetieth anniversary! The whole project should be planned as a whole before single ventures are started; all pamphlets in this series should conform to a single standard of page size, type, cover style, etc. I have some other ideas, but will leave them for later.

*

Check *Bill Haywood's Book* for his account of his prison days to see if all or part of it is suitable for republication in our paper now. I fancy it is—with a good *drawing* of Bill by our artist-cartoonist.

Lenin's concept of a *party* of professional revolutionists (in backward czarist Russia) is translated into the concept of a genuine professional party *staff* in America and other advanced countries. In this connection, ask Moish to ascertain the total number of full-time party workers (including the technical staff and non- and half-paid), check this total against the total party membership and determine the ratio of professionals.

I should like to hear the result of this calculation. It will aid me in the further development of some ideas I am working on in this regard.

LETTER 35

SANDSTONE, APRIL 21, 1944

If Lorna calls me "Little Bam" it translates into Italian as "bambino"—so a friend of that nationality here told me—and then if it is translated back into English it means "baby." Is that what she means to say?

✻

A number of new books have arrived. I will send you the titles in another letter so that you can check against the invoices. The new books are already being put to use.

The donation of $1,000 from a San Francisco friend, which you reported as an incidental item in your last letter, reminds me of another time when this amount in round figures entered into our calculations, or rather, into our wish-thinking, as the maximum needed, or even hoped for, at the time. When we were getting ready to open our fight and start publication of *The Militant* in 1928, we had a session devoted to the not unimportant question of how to finance the enterprise.

I went to see Max Eastman to ask if he could help. I remember confidently outlining my plans to do the thing right: publish a bi-weekly paper, open a headquarters, publish the *Criticism* in pamphlet form, finance a national tour, etc. "How much will all that cost?" he asked. "Have you figured it out?" I had. I said I could guarantee to get the new movement started in good shape and see it through for six months ahead if I could get my hands on $1,000. Needless to say, we didn't get the thousand, then or for many years afterward, but somehow or other we did what we started out to do.

You can tell the new donor that his gift aroused sympathetic appreciation in the Sandstone group. The news of it evoked a chain of reminiscences amongst us about various times we needed various amounts of money in the worst way. Strangely enough, nobody seems to remember our ever getting the money we needed. But we must have got some of it. Our memories, however, seem to stick on the money we always needed.

We all noted with satisfaction that George was looking very well, as though he is thriving on his arduous labors in our behalf. His work is deeply and genuinely appreciated by the comrades here. They speak of him very warmly, as they do also of the chairman of the Committee. I remarked in my polemic against Burnham that the worker-militants are very appreciative of intellectuals and only ask of them that they observe the excellent Arabian proverb: Shoot straight and tell the truth.

I have been reading the movie ads in the Minneapolis papers featuring the film *Jack London*. It is advertised as a Japanese horror picture and London is represented as a jingo-hero. (Nothing is even mentioned about his books.) It was sad to see the literary hero of my youth so dishonored. Yet, I had to admit that there is poetic justice in the spectacle. London indulged himself in the "white superiority" debauchery, and he sold his art for money to buy a ranch and play the rich fool.

LETTER 36

SANDSTONE, APRIL 24, 1944

I am just finishing Thucydides' *History of the Peloponnesian War*. It has been a great experience. In the final chapters, which I am reading today, one seems to be present, almost taking part, in the fatal events which toppled Athens to ruin from the heights of her power and glory. Thucydides, it is said, was the first critical historian. He reported what he had seen himself or carefully verified after the most scrupulous investigation. I am beginning now to get the feel of Greek history.

I wish you would include three or four French and Spanish readers, with vocabularies in the back, in the next list of books. Readers will make an easier transition from the textbook lessons to the novels.

*

Included in the historical information which we must make available to our new members and readers who have no political background is the history of the persecutions suffered by the men and the movements which preceded us. You will remember that we did this once before in the old *Labor Defender.*

The young generation of the present day is still further removed from the memory of the old events than were the young communists whom we enlightened in the twenties. But it is all the more important for us to show them the continuity of the movement, and also to do honor to the pioneers who endured persecution to make our present movement possible. We should also "recognize" their persecutors who set the pattern for their own successors.

Is there a place for Debs in your calendar? His Canton Speech, his imprisonment, first at Woodstock and then at Atlanta, and his death—these are dates which should be noted. I think the date of the Canton Speech should be observed by reprinting the speech with a good *drawing* of Gene by our artist-cartoonist. Our young militants need historical information. They also need heroes.

*

When I commended Walta's method of teaching the baby to speak correctly so that she will not have to unlearn anything later, I did not know that I would read in Aristotle the next day: "To unlearn is as hard as to learn." Would you infer from this that my understanding of Aristotle's method already enables me to anticipate what he is going to say?

The party school will be one of the most important mediums through which we will fulfill our principal obligation to the young generation: to tell them and teach them all we know!

*

The article on Aiken's speech seems to have missed the point. The seamen's losses which contrast with the super-profits of the owners are the *lives* lost; the bonus is a mere bagatelle in comparison.

I am very glad indeed that you found my fountain pen. I *missed* that little pen. It was given to me as a Christmas present by Sylvia and Lillian, it just fitted my hand, and besides all that I was used to it.

If Fred Beal is in a position to do so perhaps he can help the ILD—I mean CRDC.

The index of Trotsky's writings will not do any good unless it is completed and then mimeographed for all NC members.

LETTER 37

SANDSTONE, APRIL 26, 1944

Your April 18 came April 24. The delay in delivery was probably caused by the enclosure of the magazine clipping which was withheld from me on the ground of its length: "Articles of this length cannot be delivered to you and should not be sent in."

I saw a newspaper clipping of the Italian manifesto. It

strengthened the misgivings I mentioned in my previous letter. I think the editors, in their handling of this document, erred most grievously in relaxing the jealous vigilance and intransigence in regard to program which must dominate our approach to the newly developing events in Europe. The manifesto *is not* a Trotskyist manifesto; politically it would have been more in place in *Labor Action* or in Macdonald's *Politics.*

If the document was sent to our friends they should have subjected it to a merciless analysis and criticism. Whether this criticism should have been printed in the press, along with the manifesto, or conveyed by letter is a secondary question. This could be decided in dependence on another question: Do the authors really want to solidarize with us in full sincerity, or are they masquerading as Trotskyists and Fourth Internationalists in order to gain some credit for themselves as the Labor Actionists do?

It is wrong to attribute the manifesto to "Trotskyists" as the paper does. It is impermissible good nature to describe the paragraph on the Soviet Union as "vague and weak." This paragraph is *false to the core.* It has *nothing in common* with the program of the Fourth International. Its so-called vagueness appears to me to be a form of studied duplicity to avoid a straight answer to the question: Should the Russian workers support the war against Hitler, even though it is led by the Stalinist bureaucracy, or not?

The revolutionary workers of Italy as well as Russia and the whole world have instinctively answered this question in the affirmative. One who wants to deny such defense would naturally have to approach the question equivocally at first if he wants to get a hearing. This will most likely be the technique of all the neo-centrists in Europe at first. We must be on guard, militantly suspicious of every evasion or deviation. This will be far more useful to the Europeans than sentimental solidarity at the expense of clarity.

By this I do not mean to say that we should turn our backs on any new manifestation in the labor movement; in particular such manifestations in the CP as the Darcy movement in the U.S. or the group in Italy. But we must clearly define and distinguish between our *principled position* and our *tactical approach*. Our friends should try to *work within* any centristic movement that is open to them if it has sufficient numbers to promise fruitful results from such a tactic. But in order to make such tactics fruitful our ranks must be organizationally firm and programmatically irreconcilable.

No one should object that this maxim is ABC wisdom. The ABC's must be learned and applied over again in every new turn of events. It is precisely when new events strike that light-minded innovators tend to search for something "new." The tragic lessons of Spain are in my mind more than anything else these days. L.D. continually had to warn us not to let sympathy obscure political judgment.

LETTER 38

SANDSTONE, APRIL 28, 1944

Your April 22 came April 26.

I finished Thucydides. Also finished the first reading of Aristotle's *Politics* and his short physical treatises (*On Memory and Reminiscence, On Dreams*, and *On Prophesying by Dreams*). Have started to read *Metaphysics*.

I am studying Aristotle in the same way as French. In French I first see how the various grammatical constructions are actually *used* in sentences of living conversation, then I check back against the grammatical rules and memorize the formal conjugations *after* I have already seen them employed concretely. In this way I get to the essence of the matter much easier and better than if I first tried to learn the conjugations by rote, abstracted from life.

So also with Aristotle. In reading his treatises, one after the other, I can see more and more clearly that he has a method and see how he uses it in analyzing the various problems he attempts to solve. When I finally come to his treatises on logic—the formal exposition of his method—I think I will already understand it pretty well, and when I study the formal rules I will be thinking in terms of their concrete application. I believe this is the best way: to *learn*, rather than to *memorize*.

I will be out of Greece and ready to explore Rome by summer. As a starter on this subject, along with Rostovtzeff whose volumes have already been asked for, I would like to have Mommsen's *History of Rome* (4 vols., I think, in Everyman's Library).

＊

Your letter of April 22 strengthens the opinions about the Italian manifesto expressed in my last letter before this. When *Labor Action's* report says the Italian "working-man . . . has a lot of sympathy for Russia and cheers the victories of the Red Army," they unknowingly explain with crystal clarity why anyone wishing to offer them (the Italians) a treacherous formula on the Soviet-Nazi war has to begin with studiously "vague" circumlocutions.

The announced "center for the *construction* of the Fourth International" also employs a devious ruse intended, on the one hand, to exploit the sentiments of "the Italian working-man who cheers the Red Army" and no doubt also the name of Trotsky, and on the other hand to deny, by implication, the *existence* of any international organization known as the Fourth.

In my opinion the author of the Italian manifesto is not a revolutionary "Italian workingman" trying honestly to find his way but a slick rascal trying to deceive this work-ingman by palming himself off as some sort of Trotskyist or other. I believe the authentic Trotskyists will know how to deal with such imposters—there will be many of them—as the European events unfold.

Another giveaway expression in the *Labor Action* story is the representation that "Italians are heartily sick of any kind of dictatorship." This thoroughly dishonest, disingenu-ous locution—speaking of dictatorships "in general" without reference to their class content—is the bridge over which a large number of the petty-bourgeois opposition will try to sneak cautiously, while no one is looking, they imagine, to the formula of all the renegades who have taken off the mask: "Against all dictatorships, red, brown, or black."

To say the Italian worker is against "any form of dicta-torship" is to accuse him of renouncing the very thought of taking power into his own hands. I believe these people slander the Italian worker. I don't believe they represent any serious force. I think we should fight them openly.

May, 1944

SANDSTONE, MAY 1, 1944

The regular diet here finally caught up with me and I checked into the hospital last Friday. Here I was put on a bland diet with a liberal allowance of my favorite food-medicine—milk. The improvement was almost instantaneous. I have had no recurrence of the stomach pains since the first day, and in general I have been feeling much better the past two days. I guess the rest in bed has also helped.

I keep up my studies here without interruption. In a day or two I will have a thorough examination and some X-rays will be taken. You should not be alarmed at the "hospital" phase of my treatment. It is the routine method of treating every illness here until the precise nature of it is ascertained.

＊

I think Walta's "greater affinity" with me regarding the things she writes is due to the fact that we both believe in fairy tales. This may be at the bottom of the affair between me and Lorna too.

By the way, I notice that canned tomatoes have been taken off the ration-stamp list. Since you and Mick are both allergic to oranges this should be the signal for you both to substitute heavily with tomatoes. They are good, and good for you. You can tell Mick that cold tomatoes are ambrosia, the food of the Greek gods, and if she eats her share dutifully she also will someday see Mount Olympus.

Before you decide on which Spanish course to take you should get other catalogues. Two record-courses are advertised in the *Times* magazine or book review (classified ad section). You might also find others in the phone book. I am much interested in the records, also in whether they can be bought secondhand. I am convinced that any language can be learned best this way by people who have little time or opportunity to go to classes regularly. One can learn the language in the time spent in traveling to and from the classes, even if one is free enough to go regularly.

Why don't you take French instead of Spanish? It is harder, but after you learn French, Spanish will come easy. The main difficulty with French is the pronunciation. But the records appear to me to be the best solution of this problem.

I will probably have to wait till I come home to get the pronunciation straightened out by the records. But I feel that a reading knowledge of the language will soon be within my grasp. I made a letter-perfect translation of a 500-word French conversation last week.

Three of the NC members here are studying French and Spanish and another is studying French alone. Here is a question I would like Moish to inquire into and let me know the answer: 1) what foreign languages are known by what NC members, and 2) what NC members are now *studying* what foreign languages? We will be very troublesome about these questions in the future.

It will not do anyone any good to say in self-defense: "Cannon got along, in a fashion, with no language but English and not too much of that." That was in the primitive period of the party. The party leaders of the future must have a real world view and speak the world languages.

We saw the cartoon on Italy. Bravo!

LETTER 40

SANDSTONE, MAY 3, 1944

Your No. 36 came May 2. I will acknowledge your letters by number hereafter so that you can keep better track of their receipt here.

✱

This morning I had a "gastric analysis." This unique experience consisted of going without breakfast and having a tube pushed through a nostril down into my stomach. By means of this little device the doctor pumped out small samplings of my stomach contents at intervals of one-half hour over a total period of three hours. It felt very good when they got through.

Tomorrow morning I am to have what they call a "GI"—gastro-intestinal examination. In other words, they will take a number of X-rays—also of an empty stomach. Meantime, I am living on a "soft" diet, sleeping well and feeling OK, and keeping up with my studies.

✱

I received the clipping—a very interesting item from the *News* which I had not seen before. I also saw a picture of Farrell and Harry from *The Militant.* As far as I know there are no restrictions on the enclosure of clippings if they are not too long and, consequently, too much trouble for the censors to read. I would like to see a clipping of the sub campaign, but there had better be a good thermometer in it!

I have heard numerous reports of the sub campaign—all in the same vein. What do you think of the 3,000 goal now? Does it appear fantastic or realistic?

I am very glad to hear that Evelyn had such a good visit with our "Senator." The poor kid got the worst of it all the way around and we all have grieved for her. But at least she was not separated from us by her own decision. Thus we feel her to be with us in spirit and we all think of her warmly.

*

The school project is all pretty well outlined in my mind, and voluminous notes have been made. I could finish it up and send it to you if I had time to work on it concentratedly for a few days. It may seem ironic to say one "has no time" in prison, but that is the literal fact. My four studies devour both time and energy and fill every day till quitting time. Last night I heard the "lights out" signal with regret because I was just coming to the grand climax of Homer's *Iliad* and had hoped to finish it. This morning the medical examination robbed me of three hours. But I will catch up.

You can tell Evelyn that it was your report of her success that set me to thinking concretely about the school project in full scope and to discussing it with others as a major venture on a systematic basis never (apparently) thought of before and on a scale never even dreamed of. In my plenum speech I spoke, for the first time, of the element of consciousness which we have introduced into the selection and training of leaders. The school idea broadens and deepens the concept.

LETTER 41

SANDSTONE, MAY 5, 1944

This morning I had the last of the X-ray pictures taken. They were taken at intervals all day yesterday and again just before bedtime in order to get a sort of motion-picture sequence of my stomach's operations.

The doctor told me this morning that he had not yet studied the pictures closely in sequence but that a preliminary examination indicated the following: There appears to be no lesion in the duodenum, but there are indications of scar tissues remaining from a previous lesion. This has probably been irritated by the diet with its heavy accent on pork. I will probably leave the hospital this weekend and go on a "soft" diet for the future. Also: The doctor said the "gastric analysis"—the examination of my pumped-out stomach fluids—showed nothing abnormal. On the whole the preliminary reports are quite reassuring.

I don't mind some discomforts and inconveniences, but it would be quite awkward to be disabled with so much left to do. I am thankfully commending myself for the resolute decision I made in the summer of 1935 to "abstract" myself from the party fight with Muste and the Oehlerites while I nursed my ulcer with milk in the shack in Connecticut; for the long time afterward that I stuck to the monotonous diet of milk and bananas; and above all for taking things easier and letting worries take care of themselves during the past four years since the final settlement with the petty-bourgeois opposition.

Thanks to all that, I am still here and still able, I feel confident, to ward off this new threat with the aid of a conscientious doctor. I must admit, however, that this new attack shook me up a bit and put me on warning to be more careful of what I eat until I get home.

I read the press reports of the death of William Ellery Leonard with profound sorrow. This noble and valiant poet and man should be gratefully remembered by all who owe allegiance to truth and justice and fight for a better world. He should be honored all the more because he was a writer who did not lie to the people and a "professor" who was not a wretched coward.

I will never forget his Debs and Mooney poems—what they meant to us in the dark and heavy days when we were cut off and surrounded and harried from every side. He spoke out for Sacco and Vanzetti and served actively on the Trotsky Defense Committee despite the pressure brought to bear against him to withdraw. The good old man even wrote to the young secretary of the Committee, when the campaign to break up the Committee was at its height, bidding him to take heart and keep up the fight. I believe Amy has some material for you on this question.

In my opinion, *The Militant* should devote a big center page display article to the memory of William Ellery Leonard. The youth should be made acquainted with his beautiful, heroic life and learn to cherish him as one of their heroes. The Debs and Mooney poems should be printed with the article. Perhaps Frank should write it.

*

Natalia's May Day greetings to us were received with emotion. It was like her to remember us on our international holiday and to assure us that even here we are serving at a post of duty not unworthily. We all send our love to her. We thought of her on May Day.

LETTER 42

SANDSTONE, MAY 8, 1944

I was very glad to hear about the success of the May Day affair and your speech there. If you enjoy doing it, as nearly everyone does once the knack is mastered and communion with an audience is experienced, you will have a new activity to look forward to when your health is regained.

That is the most important thing—for the party and for all of us. I hope to hear in an early letter that you are all packed up for Long Island, the seashore and the sun with Lorna under one arm and Walta under the other. The baby is surely a child of the gods, endowed with the gift of humor, already spoofing her parents and her Nana about Bam. She and I are going to have a lot of fun cooking up jokes on the grown-ups. (I am trying to learn how to write with smaller letters so that I can crowd in more.)

＊

I finished the *Iliad* and have started the *Odyssey*.

I now have the doctor's final diagnosis. It is the same as his preliminary findings: the scar of a healed ulcer has been irritated by the regular diet. The prescription is soft diet, mainly milk and soft-boiled eggs, and no worrying, the main source of stomach ulcers. I responded immediately to this treatment and feel much better. Am remaining in the hospital another week for more rest and milk treatment. Then I will be put on the special-diet table for the rest of my stay here. I feel very good about the situation as I now know more precisely what the difficulty is, and that it is less than I feared. I have no doubt the rest here and then the permanent change in diet will keep me in shape from now on.

＊

I saw a clipping of the "Colonies" column and thought it a very good addition to the paper. The quotations from the *Progressive* were effectively used. This device is useful in more ways than one. Editors in New York sometimes forget that the great bulk of their readers never see such publications, nor the New York press.

The summarization of some old history about the Belgian Congo was another excellent feature of the column, both intrinsically and from the point of view of method. This information was once common knowledge; [King] Leopold's name had the connotation of infamy. I remember how skillfully Bill Haywood wove "the bloody Congo" into his speech to the Akron rubber strikers in 1913, merely by a few side remarks—his audience knew the story. The new generation of workers knows nothing, or next to nothing, about many things once familiar to their fathers. We must always bear this in mind; have the new generation in mind when we write, and *write for them*. The column about rubber did this very well.

Are you booming the sub campaign in the paper? I mean, by appealing to the readers to subscribe and help. This should be an important aspect of the campaign; the thousands of new readers should be appealed to. Special ads with sub blanks should be printed; the mailing list should be circularized.

Also: We should go in heavily now for the mailing of sample copies up to the limit allowed. I would send two or three sample copies to every name on our petition list, then follow up with a circular letter asking him to subscribe. That will cost money, but such promotional expenses are now more justifiable than ever, and they give more prospect of returns too.

I remarked before that New York should be a concentration point of double intensity in the campaign; we should be more lavish there than anywhere else. The reasons for this have already been given, as Aristotle would say. Our distributors and sub canvassers should swarm like bees at every labor and radical gathering, at union meetings, in the needle trades market, etc. We should now reappear at the colleges also. Our aim should be to *swamp* all relatively progressive articulate circles with the *volume* of our propaganda; to psychologize them with the impression of our energy and aggressiveness. This is a weapon.

Along the same line, if the CRDC can afford it and has not already done so, big ads should be placed in the liberal journals. It is a form of publicity and a way of putting indirect pressure on their editorial departments to notice the case.

Doesn't Haywood's memorial date come about this time of year? Or has it already passed? If it has passed, the date should be noted on the calendar for next year. If not, my memorial article (it is in the *Daily Worker* folder of my collected articles) could be reprinted. We must not let old Bill be forgotten.

I saw the second number of Dwight Macdonald's *Politics*. My impression: a little group of "fresh thinkers" thinking freshly out loud.

LETTER 43

SANDSTONE, MAY 10, 1944

We all want to see the cartoons. My health continues to improve. If I don't mention it again you may assume that I am all right.

I finally took three days off from my studies to put my thoughts on education into shape and herewith I am beginning to transmit them to you. I had to get the educational project out of the way because it was being imperiously crowded by another idea, to wit: the "Literary Secretariat" projected by Joe at the plenum last October. This idea has been burning a hole in my head and I found myself making notes about its composition, the comprehensive tasks it shall assume, its method of operation and certain projects upon which preliminary work may be done before I get home. I will write in detail about this matter later.

*

I have divided my thesis on education into four sections and numbered them for convenience in case you wish to comment on them. The first section is called:

1. *The Necessity of an Educational Plan* and reads as follows:

It is the historic task of the party to bring the element of consciousness into the spontaneous labor movement. The party, that is, the continuing organization of the vanguard, grows up to this task to the extent that it succeeds in introducing consciousness and plan into all phases of its own work. This takes place not automatically, and not all at once, but slowly and painfully as the party grows and learns from its mistakes and difficulties and gradually, in a long process of work and struggle, throws up a leadership which understands its tasks and knows how to plan and organize their study and execution.

At the October plenum it was remarked that our party, over a long period of years, has been animated by a conscious method in the selection and development of its leading cadre. The results have become clearly manifest. The superiority of our party's leading cadre over those of its historic predecessors, not even to mention its contemporary rivals, is as great as is the difference between our conscious method of selecting, training and developing our leading people and the unconscious and unplanned, hit-or-miss method or, better, lack of method, by which their leading people found themselves in unstable positions of authority. The difference is qualitative. It represents the conquest of method and design over laissez-faire in the most important question of the party, i.e., the question of the leadership.

Similarly, we have studied, planned and organized our trade-union work and the technical sides of party organization, of the publication and distribution of our press and of our books and pamphlets, although much remains yet to be done in these fields. Party education, however, has been handled in a slipshod, planless fashion. It is time now, and the party is fully ready, to make a revolutionary step forward by systematically planning and organizing the continuing education of the party membership as a whole, from the newest recruit to the members of the leading committees. An end must be made of hit-and-miss procedures in party education. The problem must be approached consciously.

The work must be organized from top to bottom under an all-embracing plan.

*

—I will write more on this subject Thursday. I remember McGuckin well and fondly, and have often thought of him through the years.

LETTER 44

SANDSTONE, MAY 12, 1944

The delay with my *History* makes me wonder what is going to happen to the Trotsky books we promised to publish in 1944. This is serious. The publication program appears to have a bottleneck on the production end.

*

Re education: The pioneers and outstanding militants of American Communism were mainly self-educated, that is, half-educated, workers who lacked adequate formal schooling and had only as much Marxism as they had managed to pick up on the fly in all-too-infrequent hours of leisure and freedom from duties and responsibilities. There was nobody to teach them; there were no schools where they might learn what to study, and how to study systematically; and they had very little time to learn for themselves, the hard way.

They were thrust into positions of leadership and overwhelmed with responsibilities without having previously acquired the necessary theoretical training and political experience to lead the party properly. As a consequence the early Communist Party made many egregious errors, devoured its energies in factional struggles which it was unable to resolve and finally, with the exception of a small nucleus, succumbed to the Stalinist degeneration.

The pioneers of American Trotskyism, standing on the shoulders of the antecedent movement, and aided and guided by Trotsky, did far better, and for the first time in the United States, built a political organization on solid Marxist foundations. The work of the pioneer American Trotskyists, however, while qualitatively superior to that of their immediate predecessors, was sadly deficient in some respects.

They made Marxist *politics* their study and did not do badly in this field, as results have shown. They developed the Leninist concepts of party organization and of the role of the party, and it may be said, made not unimportant contributions to the Leninist theory and practice of party organization.

Marxian *economic theories*, in contrast, have not had their due, either in study or in application. And the *philosophic method* of Marxism was regarded with such indifference that neo-revisionist attacks against Marxism, marching at first under the flag of philosophy, remained unanswered over a long period of years. Prancing intellectuals and academic tinhorns, preparing their migration to the imperialist camp, held the center of the stage. The sneering renunciation and belittlement of dialectical materialism was allowed to become the fashion. The party paid for this indifference with the factional explosion of the petty-bourgeois opposition which brought the party to the brink of disruption.

Moralistic quackery, another cloak under which desertion to the class enemy was prepared, long remained unnoticed and unexposed, and was even permitted to infect our ranks. The degeneration of the Soviet Union and the Comintern had produced a great wave of disillusionment, especially in intellectualistic circles. This took the form of a flight from Marxism. Revisionism, the first stage of class renegacy, was long on the offensive on the theoretical front. It remained for Trotsky to lead the defensive struggle of Marxism, first in *Their Morals and Ours* and, finally, in the great anti-Burnham polemics *(In Defense of Marxism).*

It must be acknowledged that the party leadership contributed very little to the historic battle in these respects. But the salutary experience of the struggle and the stimulating influence of Trotsky's valiant intervention awakened the party leaders to a new and deeper appreciation of the Marxist theoretical system as a whole, and impelled them to put themselves to school. More serious work is being undertaken in the theoretical field. Hereafter, it may be assumed, no kind of attack from any quarter on any phase of Marxist doctrine will go unrefuted. More on this subject in my next letter.

＊

Will you get along all right on Long Island without Karolyn?

LETTER 45

SANDSTONE, MAY 15, 1944

Here are more thoughts on education:

The further development of world events will certainly give rise to a new great wave of revolutionary insurgence. With it will most probably appear new manifestations of centrism in all colors of the rainbow. On our part, the new events must be the signal for the grand offensive of Marxism on all fronts. Trotsky predicted that Marxism will have its greatest flowering on American soil. That will be so if we plan and organize our study. Marxism will enter its heyday under the leadership of our party, and drive all opposing theories from the field.

The new generation of Trotskyists will grow up in a

party milieu characterized by the appreciation and glo-rification of learning in general and of Marxist erudition in particular. All the tasks of the oncoming generation of revolutionary militants will be made easier by what we have accomplished up to now. Thanks to these accomplish-ments, the new cadres will stand, *at the beginning* of their political work, as far above the ground where the pioneers stood at the foundation of the Trotskyist movement as the latter stood then above the first pioneers of American Communism.

The older generation must continue their studies, and continually deepen and broaden their knowledge. The cad-res of the new generation must be *inspired* to study by the general atmosphere of the party; they must be *required* to study in order to qualify for recognition in party work; they must be *aided and guided* in their studies in all stages of their development; and in preparation for their election or appointment to full-time party positions, the most talented young comrades who prove themselves to be resolute com-munists must be enabled *to devote full time to study* for an extended period *at the expense of the party*.

This comprehensive program, imposed upon the move-ment now by the stern necessities of the role assigned to us by destiny, is not in the least fantastic. Neither is it a vague perspective of the future. The program is rigidly realis-tic and is realizable now. The educational plan, once it has been discussed and decided upon, is to be put into opera-tion forthwith.

2. *The Party's Educational Plan.*

A National Educational Department shall be appointed by the NC, with an *Educational Director* who is to be a full-time executive officer of the NC. The National Educa-tional Department shall organize and direct the continu-ing education of all party members in all stages of their development. In the execution of this assignment the Educational Department shall:

1) Stimulate, aid and direct the organization of schools and study classes in party branches and locals; prepare study courses, outlines and all necessary materials for the conduct of such schools and classes; keep in constant contact with their instructors; receive regular reports from them; and aid and supervise their work.

2) Organize, in cooperation with local and branch educational committees, a corps of special tutors from the ranks of party members and sympathizers who have had advanced formal schooling, whose duty it will be to coach individual comrades and help them to make up educational deficiencies.

3) Prepare correspondence courses of study and give special assistance and direction by mail to individual comrades who wish to correct educational deficiencies by self study.

4) Ascertain, by questionnaire and personal consultation, the special educational requirements of party members who are obliged to be absent from party activities for long periods (political prisoners, sailors, etc.) and provide them with recommended study courses and reading lists adapted to their individual needs.

5) Prepare study courses, outlines and all necessary materials, and provide teachers for short-term, full-time training schools in party districts.

6) Organize and conduct a national long-term, full-time training school for party functionaries.

3. *The Aims and Methods of the Party Educational System.*

The educational plan, viewed as a whole, contemplates not a single school but rather a system of schools and study courses—a communist university. Its aim is to teach the party member what he needs to know in order to carry out his tasks efficiently at each stage of his development; to equip him for the post occupied today and to prepare him for more responsible work tomorrow. (More Tuesday.)

LETTER 46

I finished Aristotle's *Metaphysics* and have started on the Logical treatises. Also finished the first French book and started on the second. I now have a reading French vocabulary of a thousand words. We all want to know when my *History* book is coming out.

*

More on education: At the base of the school system is the basic-training class for beginners; at the apex is the national full-time training school for party functionaries which should rightly bear the name of the genius-teacher who founded our movement—*The Trotsky School.*

Those who go through the whole course of study, as hundreds and eventually thousands surely will, should have a rounded preparatory education in those subjects necessary for a working political leader, organizer, speaker and journalist. Naturally, the students' education will not end with their graduation from the Trotsky School. But they will have their necessary basic knowledge. They will have learned *how to study* and add to their knowledge the easy way in the course of their experiences in the political struggle.

By and large, they will be far better equipped than their political opponents of similar age trained in the bourgeois schools. That is bound to be so because our students in the main will be better material to start with, and they will learn nothing in our school system but scientific truth; nothing that has to be unlearned. These two great advantages will more than offset the material difficulties which hamper our work but which do not exist for the owning class and its pedagogical apologists.

Our school system will not be a poor imitation of the bourgeois schools, as so many pathetic adventures in "Workers

Education" sponsored by half-baked social workers have been, but something radically different from them, something rival and hostile to them. Everything that is good and necessary in the bourgeois educational systems will be taken over and made available for our students, either in school classes or in reading lists for supervised postgraduate study. All that is bad and false in bourgeois education, and that is plenty, will be rejected.

While studying and appropriating everything useful in standard pedagogical techniques, the Educational Department of the party will work out in practice its own unique pedagogical system to conform to the needs of the party membership. It will take each individual worker as he is and devise a way—by classes, by correspondence, by supervised reading courses, by special tutoring, or by a combination of these methods—to help him to learn more, progressively.

The first step toward this end will be to ascertain what his educational acquirements are to start with, for new learning can only proceed from what is known. There will be no need or occasion for anyone to hide his educational deficiencies or to pretend to know more than he does. There will be no shaming of ignorant workers who have been deprived by the social system of fair opportunities, but comradely help and direction in a friendly atmosphere.

While honoring and elevating Marxist learning, the party will wage an irreconcilable war against prigs, snobs and smart alecks who regard acquired knowledge as a private monopoly and a means of personal advantage rather than as an instrument of the cooperative struggle to be taught also to others. The knowledge of each individual must be shared with others and thereby multiplied for the general benefit of the party.

The party leaders who collectively have acquired a large fund of knowledge, both theoretical and practical, by dint of long study and experience, must make it their aim to teach their younger colleagues *all they know,* and the latter in turn must become teachers of others, and so on in an endless chain system of uninterrupted educational work to add to the collective knowledge of the party.

The main difficulty of the average militant worker is not his lack of adequate book-learning but the fact that he has never had time, free from worry and economic responsibilities, to study. He has not known what to study and in what order, and has not learned how to study systematically. The party will not be daunted by these obstacles. The main thing is the human material—young rebels with a burning desire to learn and to know and to put their knowledge to use in the class struggle.

The party will take them as they are, regardless of what their handicaps may have been, show them *what* to study and *how* to study and aid them through all their efforts by friendly supervision and direction. Following Lenin's injunction, the most promising and talented workers will, after a certain preparatory study, be taken out of the factory and sent to the Trotsky School and educated there for professional party work.

4. *The National Full-Time Training School.*

The party of the future will expect and require in its leading staff, along with skilled practical organizers and mass workers, people who are well educated in general and scholars in the field of Marxist theory. It is vain to hope that such leaders will be found by accident or that they will come to the party, ready-made, from the bourgeois universities. Experience has shown that it takes a long time and many tests to produce a serious revolutionary political leader. (More Thursday.)

LETTER 47

SANDSTONE, MAY 19, 1944

Your second No. 40 came May 17. Your first No. 40 was dated May 9. My letters are always written on schedule—

Sunday, Tuesday and Thursday—and dated the following day. I have not missed sending any. My notes show I wrote you under date of May 8. Check again. If you didn't get the letter I will have it traced from here.

Finished the *Odyssey*. I am awaiting detailed word from Stuart.

*

Here is more on education, taking up where I broke off in the middle of a paragraph:

Experience, all too painful and too fresh in memory, has likewise shown that the university intellectuals invariably bring with them a heavy excess baggage of petty-bourgeois prejudices, social attitudes and habits of life which must be unloaded, and false teachings which must be unlearned.

The party must train and educate out of its own ranks the future political leaders of a new type—the proletarian intellectuals. The two main schools out of which the proletarian intellectuals of the future will come are 1) the prisons, and 2) the Trotsky School, and many party leaders will pass through both. The persecutions of the class enemy will provide the first source. "The prisons of Czarist Russia were the university of the party" (Natalia Trotsky). This will be the case in "democratic" America also: the persecutions will be turned against their authors. The second source—*the Trotsky School*—will be deliberately organized by the party and supported and developed as its most cherished institution.

The Trotsky School will be a school of higher education directed to one end: the preparation of selected comrades for professional party work. Every aspect of the school—its curriculum, the selection of its student body, the organization of its faculty and its internal regime—will be decided with this single end in view.

The Trotsky School will be a unique institution bearing little resemblance to the bourgeois colleges, since it will be designed to serve different ends, and the quality of its teachings will be superior. The so-called liberal education provided by the bourgeois institutions of learning omits the study of modern man's most acute and unpostponable problem, the problem of the decaying social order and its revolutionary transformation, and the method of thinking whereby he can best understand the problem—the dialectical method of Marx and Engels.

The Trotsky School, in contrast, will build its curriculum precisely around those subjects. The bourgeois "liberal education" is a compound of knowledge, some useful and some worse than useless. It is tainted with evasions, equivocations and even with downright lies (its theories of history, its economics and its philosophy). The Trotsky School, in opposition to this, will evade no important problem and will equivocate about nothing. It will be dedicated to scientific truth and will engrave over its portals the commandment of Trotsky: "Thou Shalt Not Lie!"

All the existing schools of higher learning are class institutions, not only as regards their teachings but also in the composition of their student bodies. The academic atmosphere is poisonously hostile to the proletariat and its class interests. Their teachings are determined by the class bias of bourgeois politicians and wealthy patrons, and the professors trim their sails accordingly. Objective truth on any social question arousing "the Furies of private interest" is not permitted to be taught in the bourgeois universities. He who says otherwise is a liar. The sons and daughters of the working class, with rare exceptions, are automatically excluded by reason of their inability to pay tuition fees and maintain themselves.

The Trotsky School will likewise be a class institution, but of a different kind. It will frankly espouse the proletarian point of view; its student body will be chiefly proletarian; and the financial situation of prospective students will not affect their right to admission in any way whatever.

The first condition for matriculation in the Trotsky School will be that the candidate is regarded by his co-workers as a worthy communist who has already distinguished himself in party work and is prepared without reservation to devote his life to the party as a professional revolutionist. The students for each term will be selected by the NC from lists recommended by party organizations or trade-union fractions. Formal educational deficiencies will not bar the talented and ambitious worker from eventual enrollment. These deficiencies may be made up with the aid of special tutors assigned by the Educational Department prior to his coming to the school, or in some cases, during his attendance there.

It may be assumed that the average student, at the time of his enrollment, will be equipped with no more than a high-school education—in some cases even less—and may entertain, as is customary among deprived workers, an exaggerated notion of the importance of the "college education" sported by fortune-favored wiseacres.

This "mystery" will be dispelled in short order; a realistic view of the matter will be acquired at the outset. The student will easily convince himself that his failure to attend college is far less serious than he has imagined. His teachers will begin by explaining how much he has missed and precisely what it is, and how the essential things will be learned in the Trotsky School or in systematic, supervised study afterward. Those among the students who have previously attended the bourgeois colleges—and it is to be expected that there will be some—will have initial advantages in some respects and disadvantages in others, for they will have much to unlearn. That, as Aristotle said, is as hard as learning.

*

I will conclude what I have to say on this subject next time. Better wait till you have it all before showing it to others. Then get Sylvia to copy it for Moish and his friends.

LETTER 48

SANDSTONE, MAY 22, 1944

Be sure to check on the missing letter and let me know the date. They keep a record here and, I think, number the outgoing letters with a rubber stamp each week.

❋

The student body in the Trotsky School will no doubt greatly vary in its composition from one term to another. But one can visualize a typical class as being made up of a number of comrades now working as party functionaries, with one or more candidates nominated by each of the maritime, auto, steel and shipyard fractions, several others recommended by local party organizations, and some designated representatives of foreign parties.

Functionaries engaged in party work at the center may take one or more courses, and some field workers may be brought in for attendance at the school for limited periods of instruction. But the main body of students will devote their full time for the whole term in an atmosphere conducive to study and free from all party duties and personal financial responsibilities.

All expenses of the students during their attendance at the Trotsky School will be paid by the party out of special funds earmarked for the Educational Department. Food, lodging, laundry, textbooks, pocket money and medical and dental care will be provided. The student's sole responsibility will be to work and study conscientiously in preparation for his future party work.

The principal teachers of the Marxist courses on the faculty of the school will naturally be the party leaders. But for other subjects deemed necessary for the students and included in the curriculum—history, English composition and journalism, foreign languages, public speaking, etc.—the school will be able to draw on the services of party members and sympathizers who specialize in these fields. There is no room for doubt that the teaching staff will be fully adequate at the start and that it will expand with the expansion of the school.

The form taken by the school in its first experimental term will not be fixed and final. It will be changed, modified and expanded on the basis of experiences. The students will teach the faculty a great deal in this respect by showing what they lack, what they need most and what does them the most good.

From a modest beginning the Trotsky School will grow and develop into a great historic institution worthy of the name it bears. All other subdivisions of the overall plan of party education will be developed in proportion, each drawing upon and simultaneously supporting the others. All signs indicate that the conditions are present to launch the ambitious, rounded-out program outlined in the plan. The very fact that a *plan* of party education can now be projected and enthusiastically received demonstrates that the party has grown taller by a head.

The conjunction of the plan and the enthusiastic response it has called forth, with the assurance that the party can provide the necessary material means, is convincing evidence that the project is completely realistic and that the time is ripe to launch it.

The important thing is for the party to discuss the plan and adopt it as a whole, make a beginning with as many parts of the plan as possible, and set a date for the opening of the first term of the Trotsky School.

✳

This is all I have to say for the present on the subject of education. I am sorry that I could not cast it in better literary form, but the conditions here are not the most favorable for such work. I don't have Sylvia and "the Secretariat" here to help me, there are neither facilities nor time for copying, rewriting and polishing and I feel constrained by space limitations to squeeze everything into the smallest possible compass. Perhaps Usick can edit it a bit. Please send a copy to Natalia; I should like to hear her comments on the project.

We received a set of pictures taken of all of us, at Minneapolis, in small groups and one of the whole group, just before our departure. They would make a very good page spread for the paper. The extra two pages permits us to indulge in such extravagances, and they in turn make the paper lighter and more attractive for the new, politically unsophisticated workers who—we must always remember—are now the *great majority* of our readers. The cartoons get better.

LETTER 49

SANDSTONE, MAY 24, 1944

I have been reading the new book about language study, *The Loom of Language*. It is very good, especially useful for one who is studying several languages simultaneously. It strongly recommends the phonograph-record system for self-students.

Don't forget the tenth anniversary of the Minneapolis strike this July. Natalia would surely like a set of the Minneapolis pictures I mentioned in my last letter. I would like to see the "Militant Army" column given more space to print more letters from the field, especially those giving ideas. I think there should also be a new column: "Pioneer Publishers' Notes." I will write soon some reflections on the special sub campaign and make some suggestions about next steps.

I see that the U.S. Supreme Court has decided to review both the AP case and the case of the convicted Bundists. Have the CRDC and *The Militant* taken note of these decisions?

Is anyone in charge of the work of collecting the various movie films the party has and weaving them together?

Some of the new books have begun to come in. On the next list put three or four *German* readers and Marx's *Poverty of Philosophy* and *The German Ideology* (in English).

I am very much interested in the plan to prepare material for a song book. I had been thinking of the same thing and meant to write you about it later. I hope the work will proceed. I will contribute some ideas and suggestions in another letter.

*

I hope Sam's report on his visit [to London] will not be too long delayed and too laconic. I am deeply interested in this question. The future of the unification depends a great deal on how it started. The new events reported in *The Militant* should act to cement the unity, but persecution alone is by far not enough to hold a party together. One only needs to recall the early days of American Communism to be convinced of this. However, I think the new experiences will tend to help the new party and get it off to a new start. They have great opportunities and a bright future prospect.

My thoughts about the advisability of a plenum have expanded into the idea that an Active Workers Conference would be timely now. There would be an adequate agenda for such a gathering: a political review; the educational program; a report on the special sub campaign and new projects along this line; and an international report. It would be a real triumph for the party to hold a successful conference in our absence. That would crown all the other achievements.

On the sub campaign I have in mind a rather novel method of presenting the question. A general statistical and analytical report from the PC and then, as the principal feature, reports from the branch delegates as to how they did it in each case. I, for one, would surely like to listen to such a discussion. It surely would be both informative and stimulating. It is about

time, don't you think, that our wonderful rank-and-file workers be really *given the floor* at a national gathering. Does the
"dissolution" of the CP give our friends any new ideas?

LETTER 50

SANDSTONE, MAY 26, 1944

I note your increasingly favorable impression of the new
place with great interest. A good summer for you all there
will make mine easier here. Is there a yard—I mean, with a
fence around it, where the dog could stretch his legs?

You say the prospect is ideal for me, but you do not mention a creek to put my bare toes in. Where is it? And are
there some woods in walking distance where Usick and I can
cut some new walking sticks? And is there a climbable hill
with an old deserted farm at the top and another one where
an old single-track railroad used to run? And a pine grove
with a soft carpet of pine needles underfoot? And a wood
stove in a comfortable kitchen with an oven that can bake
potatoes and have them ready at 12 noon on the dot?

Have you ever seen two white deer fawns in the moon-
light there? Is auto traffic limited by law to three cars per
day? Are there apple trees which bear red apples with white
worms in them? And a sink in the kitchen with ever-running
water piped from a spring on the hill to keep the beer cool?
And wood for the new man to chop and carry while the old-
timers with seniority rights sit on the porch and tell him
how to swing the axe? Are you really sure you have found
the ideal place for me?

＊

I wish you and Walta to get green sunshades (eye-shades)
from the dime store; get one also for Mick and tell her I sent

it for her. I look forward to her happy splashing in the water and visualize her first swimming lesson. I can see her feeling her way cautiously at first and then, gaining confidence, plunging boldly in. She has the first virtue: courage.

＊

Your reference to "old activists from England" is not clear to me. I do not recall and cannot identify this group. I surmised the makeup of the Italian group just about as you reported it. It is clear that the authors of the wretched manifesto do not represent any genuine current in the working class, but are only vestigial survivals of old artificial cliques. One thing should always be kept clearly in mind: Trotskyist politics are always *serious*, directed toward the working class and real currents within it. We do not *play* at politics as all the artificial groups—sectarians, Shachtmanites, etc.—do, and *we do not play with them.*

Why? Because they have no importance. They represent neither serious people nor serious ideas. Their political life is only literary, not real. I think "conciliationism" is too dignified a political term to apply to one who orients himself upon such sterile cliques. It should rather be said that he misunderstands *the meaning* and *the task* of Marxist class politics.

LETTER 51

SANDSTONE, MAY 29, 1944

Walta's letter of May 22 came May 25. Tell her to use a larger size of paper next time as she is only permitted, under the rules, to use two sheets.

I think she is quite wrong to be cross with little Mick for crying. The poor child is only trying to strengthen her lungs. When I come home, tell her, she can come to my office and cry all she wants to. I am waiting for more news about how you all are getting settled in the new place, what company you are having, etc. You still haven't told me what kind of heating the house has and what kind of a bathroom and shower.

*

I stayed two weeks in the hospital. The diet and rest did me a lot of good. I was more tired than I had realized. Since leaving the hospital I have been on a special diet—soft-boiled eggs, toast and milk three times a day—and have felt no trace of ulcer trouble. Besides that, I feel very much better, so much so that I have taken on a new study: German.

Finished the first reading of all of Aristotle's treatises on logic and started *On Generation and Corruption.* Finished the first volume of Grote's *History of Greece* and started on the second. (I forgot to mention that your May 20 came May 24.)

*

The two speeches of the week—Churchill's and Browder's—must have given our editors plenty to write about. Did our cartoonist take a hand in the comment? We thought of an idea for a cartoon: Churchill and Franco and Browder and Morgan rolling merrily down the street singing "It's always fair weather when good fellows get together."

Here is a suggestion for the cartoonist's benefit. Get a number of the collected cartoon books which have been published in the past from time to time—Ellis', Burck's, Art Young's, etc.—and work over some of the ideas. They were mostly all borrowed from others so there is no harm in borrowing from them. If she has any qualms about "plagiarism" she should read Kipling's poem on the subject. Do you know it?

When 'Omer smote 'is bloomin' lyre
'E'd 'eard men sing on land and sea,
And what 'e thought 'e might require
'E went and took the same as me.
The dancing girls and fishermen,
The shepherds and the sailors too,
They 'eard old songs creep up again
And kept it quiet same as you.
'E knew they knew
They knowed 'e knowed
They didn't cry or make a fuss,
But winked at 'Omer down the road
And 'e winked back the same as us.

*

I am anxiously waiting to hear that you have taken steps to get started on your Spanish. Get the records, by all means. Even if they are rather expensive, they should be considered as an investment by the party for the use of one after another of the leading comrades engaged in the study of the language. Marvel, who is studying Spanish, can use them; and I will surely want them, as well as another here who is studying with me, when we come home. Also please ask Reba to check on the number and hours of *foreign-language broadcasts*. I would like to know what I can look forward to in this respect for practice.

June, 1944

Your May 26 came May 29. What is the book reviewed by Harry in the *FI*? By checking against the calendar you can easily tell whether you have received all my letters and eliminate all guesswork. I write invariably on Sunday, Tuesday and Thursday and date the letters the following day. I hope to hear soon that your new cold, and Mick's too, have yielded to the Long Island sunshine. I doubt, however, whether it is as hot and steady as ours.

*

I think my letters on education should be sent to our "Senator," to Murry, George Clarke, and I would like to know their comments. I would like to hear from them, through you, on other matters too.

If you have McGuckin's address I wish you would send him a set of my published stuff, including the *History* book if and when it comes out, to give him an idea of what I have been doing in my spare time since I saw him last. I liked Mc. a great deal. He and I were good friends in the old [IWW] days. He was a fine singer. If you had him around you wouldn't need to worry about getting the comrades to sing. I would like to know what Mc. has been doing all these years and how he is getting along.

*

The press role in the educational program can wait awhile. The first stage should be devoted to internal party orientation. The problem I specifically aimed to deal with is the orientation of the party toward consideration of the education of *our own cadres*. The *Internal Bulletin* is the right medium for that. The broader aspects of *mass education* should be treated as a special subject, in my opinion. I intend to write you some letters on this subject; have, in fact, already begun to make notes on the art of propaganda.

Also intend to write letters on the role of the "Literary Secretariat" and on the "New Stage in the Development of Pioneer Publishers." By this, I do not mean the *present* stage but the great work which must be undertaken as soon as the present oxcart methods are ruthlessly discarded, the program assigned by the last plenum is carried out, and the decks are cleared to put the work of Pioneer Publishers into harmony with the expanding activities of the movement in general.

Any talk about "patience" with the scandalous breakdown of the publishing program is sent to the wrong address, if it is meant for me. I feel that we are not making an inch of headway in the discussion of this subject because we are not talking the same language. You are talking to Usick and Lillian and they are talking about the idiosyncrasies of a printer. All that has nothing to do with the real question which I have tried to intimate in my letters.

I am talking about the *program of the plenum;* and the person responsible for its execution is the national secretary. He has been given the necessary means and authority and will not be asked about the small details which arise along the way. What difficulties arise and what drastic measures are needed to overcome them are solely matters for his decision. The only thing of general interest and concern is the result. I think you should invite Moish out for a discussion of this matter *in principle.*

We have an uneasy feeling that the affair of the publishing program does not stand alone but is rather a symptom of a fatal procedure that is very easy for a busy leadership to fall into. That is to measure work done by volume rather than by design; to fail to discriminate sufficiently between the primary and the secondary. I know very well that only so much can be done in a day. Some things have to wait. But let them be the little things, not the big ones.

LETTER 53

SANDSTONE, JUNE 2, 1944

Your May 28 came May 30. I expect further news tonight about this unreasonable cold that has overtaken you. As I told you in my previous letter, I am OK. By the way, I never had a single cold all winter. This is the first time I have had such luck for many years.

＊

Finished Aristotle's *On Generation and Corruption* (first reading) and started *On the Heavens.* Grote frequently quotes other historians and critics in his voluminous footnotes. I noticed for the first time today, not without a certain satisfaction, that I can make out the French quotations without much difficulty.

I was very glad to hear of the CRDC's action in taking full-page ads in the *Nation* and *New Republic* for the June 8 meeting. In politics everything depends on doing the right thing at the right *time.* The successes of the CRDC campaign and the sub campaign would seem to indicate that the response to our message is so much wider in its scope than we have known before as to be *qualitatively* different. If this is the case—I am not sure of it—we must take stock of the situation and *transform* all our work accordingly, according to a plan.

Have our friends discussed the results of their five-months work from this standpoint? I should like to hear their appraisal of the situation. We must always bear in mind, also, that international events make a strong wind for our sails and that it can only grow stronger and can hardly be expected to change its direction. All planning should be revised from the standpoint of *tempo* and *scale*—faster and bigger.

The very first preliminary survey of next tasks must indicate that the debacle of the publishing program is an anachronism that can no longer be indulged. Piddling reforms are of no use here. The wretched failure is not the result of external difficulties or lack of diligence but of a *false conception,* one suited to the unavoidable snail's pace of an isolated propaganda group but fatal for a dynamically expanding movement. The publishing logjam must be blown up with a charge of dynamite.

Do not send us *any* books unless we specifically ask for them! First, because we are reading and studying in definite fields and have no time for indiscriminate reading. The money spent on books on subjects outside our assigned studies will be wasted. Secondly, and still more important, we want to read *what we want* and not what someone else thinks we should want! Imprisonment consists of doing what others decide one should do and getting what others think one should have. Our little island of freedom consists of the privilege of asking the CRDC for the books *we want* and *getting what we ask for;* just that, no less and no more.

I appreciate the good will of the suggestions of friends, and so do all the others, but we want them to know that the only way they can help us is to give us what we ask for, not what is good for us. We have enough of that. If you will check my letters you will see that several books asked for do not appear on the list of May 24. What happened to them? *Dialogues of Plato* are here in the Modern Library edition. That is enough for the present.

Lying awake late last night I heard the whistle and rumble of a fast freight train highballing down the line. It reminded me nostalgically of my hobo days. That sound always gave me the foot-itch and got me ready for another trip.

LETTER 54

SANDSTONE, JUNE 5, 1944

Finished the second volume of Grote's *History of Greece* and started the third. Finished Aristotle's *On the Heavens* (first reading) and started his *Physics.*

Marked a milestone last night in my French study. The French reader sent in by our CRDC arrived and I began to *read* it. The *hard* part of French study is now already behind me. All that remains now is to read and build up vocabulary and then to learn the real *sound* of the spoken language from records when I come home. I cannot praise the French reader too highly. It is *just* what I needed and I hope the Spanish and German readers will be of the same type, that is, with an adult vocabulary suitable for adults, not childrens' stories as so many readers are.

Please add Schiller's poems to the book of Heine's poems which I previously requested. Be sure, if possible, to get all the language books *with vocabularies in the back* if possible. I think the bookstores have them in special college editions.

I am having a lot of fun these days speculating as to which foreign language I will teach to Mickey first. I will probably be most facile in German, but don't you think vivacious French would express her personality better?

I read with interest what both you and Evelyn have to say about the merits of the Long Island place, but you leave out one very important detail. Where is the crick for me and Mickus to cool our piggies in?

I am waiting, and have been waiting, for the first install-ment of Stuart's report. It need not be condensed too much. Remember, I am entitled to receive *seven* letters each week. However, I want you to ask Sylvia and Evelyn to do the typ-ing for you. I am afraid the exertion of typing is not good for you during your convalescence. If you get Sylvia to do the routine typing of office news and reports it will ease the task of letter-writing.

I note that the SP is holding a convention and that the CP just concluded one. Evidently they found a way to sur-mount the travel difficulties and the other wartime restric-tions. Perhaps our committee can do the same. But then, I imagine, they are worried by another question: what to tell the conference about the publishing program of the last plenum? Our people have been taught to be impatient for results and intolerant of excuses.

The "virtue of patience," mistakenly *recommended* by Usick, represents a political deviation on his part, although I would never think of accusing him of *practicing* it. This "patience" is a *soft*, i.e., a Menshevik virtue. It is all right for people who are not going anywhere in particular, and it may be good for cows to chew their cuds with. But it is no good for executive leaders, traffic managers, etc. If the traffic manager of the New York Central were afflicted with patience and its maudlin twin, good nature, the Twentieth Century Limited would never reach Chicago on schedule. It would be hopelessly blocked in a traffic jam somewhere be-tween Buffalo and Cleveland, keeping company with slow freights, milk trains and loose boxcars and empty gondolas which some sleepy yard clerk forgot to route to any par-ticular destination.

I learn with pain that Lillian is ill. I was afraid that would happen. That is why I proposed months ago that she be given some assistance and *not permitted* to overdo herself with two full-time jobs. Pioneer Publishers and David are both growing bigger and in need of more and more attention. What became of the Literary Secretariat?

LETTER 55

SANDSTONE, JUNE 7, 1944

Your Monday letter didn't arrive last night, delayed I suppose by the heavy storms in this part of the country. If possible I would like to have the German and Spanish readers graduated so that each succeeding one has a larger vocabulary than the preceding. I think the stores have college readers graduated in this way. I will soon be ready for the German and Spanish and for another French, rather, several more.

Can you clip and send me the cartoons and the "Militant Army" columns? I would especially like to get the May Day cartoon about which I have heard.

Here is a suggestion for the sub campaign which is liked here: Write a special circular to the *new readers* gained in the campaign enclosing four prepaid sub cards in each letter and asking them, if they like the paper, to sell them to four friends and remit the dollar. This would involve the printing of 20,000 new cards, but in my opinion it would be worth the investment. Perhaps you can leave off the postage stamp as that would cost $200, and instead enclose an envelope for mailing the cards.

It may seem strange to propose to trust strangers with prepaid sub cards—they might sell them and keep the money—but my experience in similar ventures has shown that the risk is very small and worth taking. Even in the worst case, if some cards are sold and not paid for, you will have some new readers to show for it and still be the gainer. It is really worthwhile to try to involve the new trial subscribers in the campaign and it will be a very great gain, and well worth the expense, if some of them respond. We must keep trying, by new and extraordinary measures, to expand and push out the boundaries of our active supporters.

Include in the letter greeting the new subscribers some questions: 1) How do they like the paper; 2) If they like it what features do they like best; 3) What are their criticisms and suggestions. I believe you will get some interesting replies which can be printed in the "Army" column. This column should be enlarged anyway. We shouldn't hesitate at the expense of this circularization. We must train ourselves to think in terms of ever bigger actions involving more thousands of people.

Perhaps you can kill two birds with one stone by enclosing a list and order blank of Pioneer Publishers. It will be interesting to see what response this will bring also. We don't know what the new people are thinking and should make every effort to find out.

Two more suggestions: Send a copy of my letter on education to Grandizo and ask for his comments. Ask Don to get addresses of Spanish refugees and others in Mexico and put them on the free list of the paper and magazine.

I hear that Dwight Macdonald, in the course of his independent thinking, has made the interesting discovery that Sandstone is a very funny place and that the trip here was quite ridiculous; also that it was a breach of etiquette for a proletarian revolutionist to question the moral conduct of the leading ideologist and philosopher of democratic capitalism. Well, we shall see about that. I intend to write you about this matter; not for his benefit but for the benefit of any in our ranks, if such there be, who are inclined to be influenced by what philistines have to say about us.

LETTER 56

I haven't heard from you since a week ago today, but I am not worrying about it, as I have convinced myself that there is some trouble and delay with the mail.

I hear that Joe Hansen's article in the February issue of *Fourth International,* written on the occasion of our departure, has elicited comment in *Politics,* the new-thought magazine edited by Dwight Macdonald. In commenting on the comment I am impelled first of all to congratulate the author on the equanimity with which he is enduring our imprisonment. Evidently he has read and taken to heart the advice Rose Karsner gave to the women in her speech at the farewell dinner: "Don't mope while the men are away."

Macdonald is clearly determined not to let our troubles get him down. From this hard-boiled point of view he takes Joe to task for dwelling on the trivial details of our departure— the leave-takings, the mementos, etc. The doughty Macdonald will have none of this sentimentality. He is a brass-tacks chap—no nonsense, chins up and all that sort of thing.

Perhaps he is right on this point. I, at least, can understand and sympathize, to a certain extent, with this matter-of-fact attitude. I am somewhat of a stoic myself—my mother taught me not to cry when I get hurt—and I appreciate the trait in others. I am ready to admit also that Macdonald is not motivated by personal malice or jealousy, as others who write in the same vein usually are, for I believe that he is sincerely stupid and is only guilty, at the most, of indulging his cultivated knack for misunderstanding things and his faunlike impulse to play pranks on inappropriate occasions.

In any case, this part of the quarrel between Macdonald and Hansen is not very important. After all it is a matter of taste and emotion; and as long as freedom and democracy prevail everyone has the right to his own taste and his own emotion.

The other parts of the editorial in *Politics* raise more serious questions. One concerns the attitude of a man of politics toward his own ideas. The other concerns morality. Both are questions of exceptional importance at the present time.

The editorial indicts our party as a "sectarian group" afflicted with "arrogance—which verges on paranoia." As evidence he cites Vincent Dunne's statement that "our movement is historic" and Joe Hansen's assertion that "the files of Trotskyist publications" represent more important material for future historians than the Roosevelt minutiae filed away at Hyde Park. These remarks impress Macdonald as the expression of a presumptuousness belonging to the domain of "political pathology."

One cannot make an offhand decision as to the merits of the dispute, for neither position is right or wrong *per se*. We are confronted here not with facts immediately verifiable but with a conflict of opinions regarding future developments. Consequently, in order to arrive at a reasoned judgment of the respective merits of the contending opinions, one must approach the dispute with a criterion, a point of view of his own, about contemporary society and its prospective further development.

The majority—those who line up with American capitalism and its war program—believe that capitalism has a long and stable future before it. If their assumption is correct, or only half-correct, they can very consistently and logically conclude that Dunne and Hansen, and all the rest of us Trotskyists, have fantastic delusions about the way history will some day be written. We, the minority, on the other hand, are completely convinced that capitalism, having outlived its progressive historic role—and a great role it was—is already doomed, is even now in its death agony and must make way for socialism. (More.)

LETTER 57

SANDSTONE, JUNE 12, 1944

Your Nos. 46 and 47 came June 8. Walta's letter came June 9. The news was most welcome. I will answer the letters when I finish telling you what I think of "The Tribe of the Philistines." Make the following corrections in my last letter when you copy it for Frank [for publication in *The Militant*]: In the first sentence change "I learn from correspondence" to "I see," and change "our departure" to "the departure of the Trotskyist leaders." Change the second reference to "our departure" to "the departure."

*

Continuing: If our assumption is correct, we can with no less logic and consistency conclude that the heralds of the new society, the pioneer militants of the revolutionary party, have far more historic importance than the representatives of the dying system and that this will be the judgment of the historians of the future. If our assumption is correct, it is the representatives and apologists of the outmoded social system who entertain delusions about the future.

Now, what are the premises, and what are the conclusions of Macdonald and the politico-literary species which he typifies? The magazine *Politics*—as far as one can make out from a cursory reading—is published to inform the world that the editor and his associated independent thinkers are somewhat dubious of the future of capitalism and are committed, more or less, to the socialist alternative. Yet Macdonald says—no, he doesn't say, he takes for granted as self-evident—that the contemporary statesmen of capitalism are the important and significant men of today and that they will be so regarded in the historical tomorrow.

Hansen's idea, for example, that historical research will

not center around the personality of Roosevelt, strikes him as too funny for words. Then, having made his joke, he goes on to say that his convictions—he calls them convictions—are in many respects the same as the Trotskyists ("The Cannon group stand for many of my own convictions"). In spite of that, he instinctively and automatically brands our party's confidence in the historic vindication of these same convictions as pathologic arrogance.

The significance of this *non sequitur* is quite clear. Macdonald's pen ran away with him. The intended lampoon of the Trotskyists turned out to be a document of unintended self-revelation. It is the portrait of a man who does not take his own ideas seriously and has no faith in their future. Such people are not worth very much. Their "convictions" are on the side of the proletarian revolution but all their deep-rooted instincts, feelings and spontaneous reactions—their heart and soul—are in the other camp. Hence their simultaneous "agreement" with the convictions of the Trotskyists and their amazement when we act on these convictions and draw them out to their logical conclusion.

Similarly, when the question of bourgeois and proletarian morality—"their morals and ours"—is mentioned in our press, the jackass ears of the philistine are pointed upward and forward in alarm. And when we calmly assert that our morals are better than theirs, that we are "the only really moral people"—among the conscious, articulate political elements, that is—Macdonald splutters like a society matron who has been insulted by a truck driver for snarling traffic.

Joe Hansen's report of a casual conversation with Cannon about John Dewey and the Moscow Trials causes Macdonald to break out in a moralistic sweat. And "words almost fail" him at Cannon's "nerve" in pointing out a flaw, from the standpoint of "strict morality," in Dewey's conduct of the office of chairman of the Commission of Inquiry on the Moscow Trials. (More on this subject Tuesday.)

LETTER 58

SANDSTONE, JUNE 14, 1944

Your Nos. 48 and 49 of June 9 and 10 came June 12.

The reports of the activities of our wonderful party help greatly to make our days lighter here. Such a party is worth being in prison for. In my last letter I spoke of the Dewey Commission.

Continuing: Here also Macdonald mixes up a small matter with a big one. The small point can easily be disposed of. He accuses us of trying to rob the respected Commission of Inquiry chairman of the "credit" due him for his services in that capacity. This is a misapprehension on his part; and we are ready to concede anything he demands in order to set the thing straight, even though we do not attach the same weight as he to the matter of "credit."

His accusation springs from his inability to read our press with an understanding of our standards and our sense of values. When we say that a man was moved to intervene in a great historic case by an appeal to his sense of justice we have meant to pay him the highest compliment we can possibly pay to a man who is not of our party and class. By his action in heading the Commission of Inquiry, Dewey became the chief instrument in the investigation and exposure of the greatest frame-up in history. We are grateful to him for that, and he will be remembered gratefully by all lovers of truth and justice in time to come.

It makes no difference whether Dewey's action was taken on his own initiative or was suggested to him by others. That is only a small collateral detail of the history of the affair. Dewey's credit flows from the deed itself, and we who believe in giving everyone his just due would be the last to underrate it in the slightest degree. Dewey must be honored for his courageous action all the more because he might justifiably have asked for exemption for reasons of age and ill health. He must be doubly honored because, of all the great public men of present-day America, he alone felt it necessary "to do something for justice."

But when all that is said, the fact remains that Dewey, in making public in a radio speech the report of the Commission of Inquiry which found Trotsky not guilty of the crimes alleged against him, took advantage of the occasion to denounce the political doctrines of the defendant. (See the report of Dewey's radio speech in the *New York Times*, December 14, 1937.) There are no two ways about it, that was "a departure from strict morality," which comes under the heading of *abuse of power*. By our standards of morality that is a serious offense, and we want somebody to tell us by what moral standards it is justifiable.

Macdonald's readiness to defend Dewey's misuse of his office of judge to turn advocate, on the ground that Trotsky, the defendant, also expounded his views before the Commission, will not satisfy anyone who seriously wants to face the moral issue we have raised. Trotsky had been accused of crimes alleged to flow from his doctrines, and was asked by the Commission of Inquiry to give an exposition of these doctrines as evidence in the case. In the same manner the defendants in the Minneapolis Trial were permitted to expound their views in court.

But Dewey, as chairman of the Commission, had assumed the office of *judge,* and with it the obligation, after hearing the evidence, to say truly whether the defendant was guilty or innocent of the crimes charged against him. So much and no more is a judge permitted to say when rendering the verdict of his tribunal, according to our standards of morality.

Macdonald's attempt to defend Dewey's moral lapse on this occasion only demonstrates how flexible his own moral standards are. His bad experience should warn all petty-bourgeois critics of the Trotskyists to confine their moralistic sweatings to eternal abstractions and keep away from the discussion of concrete cases. "Morality" is not their strong point—when you get down to cases.

*

This is all I have to say for the time being about the tribe of the philistines and their "morality." Now I can return with a feeling of real satisfaction to my interrupted study of the modes and tenses of the Spanish verb *hacer*—"to do," "to make." That is a Bolshevik verb. Macdonald and his ilk wouldn't know how to conjugate it in any language.

I am glad to finish with this disagreeable subject. Thursday I will answer your letters and write on other subjects.

LETTER 59

SANDSTONE, JUNE 16, 1944

In my German lesson today I studied a poem which Heine wrote for little Mick:

> Du bist wie eine Blume
> So hold und schön und rein;
> Ich schau' dich an, und Wehmut
> Schleicht mir ins Herz hinein.

Tell Evelyn to send on the pardon applications to all the eighteen. We will fill them out and send them back promptly. All the decisions in regard to time, method of presentation, etc., should be made in New York without further reference to us, once you have received the petitions. Needless to say, we are anxious to receive *The Militant* and *FI*. The Jehovah's Witnesses here get their organ, the *Watch Tower*.

I think the comrades in New York should decide what

kind of a national gathering to have. I am definite on one point: It would be a mistake to *promise* a convention next spring. That is too far away to make definite commitments about, and the future is too uncertain. After thinking over your letter of June 9 it seems to me and others that there is no plausible objection to a convention. Certainly we here can have none.

It must be borne in mind, however, that a convention is a more formal assembly and must be more carefully prepared. The main thing is the political resolution. Work should be started on it right away as you must allow sixty days for discussion after it has passed the NC and been published in the *Internal Bulletin*. Once the political resolution has been approved, the rest of the convention preparations will be easily taken care of.

We are especially interested in your report that Wheeler is being brought to New York for work in the publications department. It just happened that he was in my mind the same week. We have to think actively now of heavier responsibilities for the present professionals in the near future and keep canvassing the field for those next in line to step into the vacated places. We are most anxious to know more about the circumstances of Wheeler's appointment. We thought he was "frozen" in his job. We hope he was not released because of serious illness or injury at work. Please let us know about this.

Once the publication program is put at the top of the agenda for concentrated attention, I think the problem, for the present, can be solved without very drastic actions. It must be resolved to publish *two* more books this year besides the *History*. The difficulties with the present shop can perhaps be solved by letting them have one job while the other is farmed out to another shop. Or some other half measures may suffice for this year. The time for drastic and fundamental decisions will come when we elaborate "The Five Year Plan" of Pioneer Publishers and lay out the schedule for 1945.

The first stage of the educational program will also work out rather simply. I will write about that concretely soon.

I am very glad that you keep going to the doctor for checkups so that you always know exactly where you stand. I have strong hopes in the curative powers of the Long Island sun.

LETTER 60

SANDSTONE, JUNE 19, 1944

Finished Volume 3 of Grote and started on 4. Finished Aristotle's *Physics* and with it the whole volume—1,487 pages. I will now let Aristotle soak in for a while before returning to a closer study of his logical treatises.

This is Sunday, my rest day, and I am having a good time loafing and debating leisurely in my mind the only decision I have to worry about at present—whether to devote the Aristotle study period to French or history or just to take that time off for a while. Moish must envy a fellow who has no more serious decisions to make than that. Would he like, sometimes, to be in jail with us?

I saw the cartoon about Stalin and [Eric] Johnston. I think it is the best yet from the standpoint of technique. The lines are stronger and bolder, a very important feature of cartoons, and the artist's ironic sense laughs right out of the drawing. I recommend, above all, that she study attentively the old cartoons of Minor, the best of the "power" line cartoonists and the *master* of them all.

The political idea of the Stalin-Johnston cartoon was not so good, however. The fact that Browder takes his line from Stalin is funny from the standpoint of the bourgeois press, now that Stalin's line suits them very well, and of the Social-

Democratic philistines who take nothing really seriously. (They thought they could "kid" Hitler out of existence.) But for us the line of Stalin, and consequently of Browder, is too deadly, too ghastly, for jests. When I write my thesis on the rules of revolutionary political propaganda I will lay it down as an axiom: One cannot laugh at a murderous power!

Furthermore, now that we have organized our own party, rival and hostile to the Stalinist party, it is not very dignified for us to make a big point of the Stalinist organizational techniques, methods of transmitting and executing decisions, etc. Leave that barren occupation also to the Social-Democrats and such essentially parasitic political groupings as the Shachtmanites whose "politics" consists in buzzing and gossiping about other people's parties and their methods. As for us, we tend to our own affairs in this respect and let others alone.

We were concerned with the bureaucratic methods of Stalinism as long as we held ourselves to be a faction of the Comintern striving for its *reform*. Now, as irreconcilable opponents of the Stalinist organization, we concentrate our fire on its *policies* and don't chatter about their method of arriving at them and carrying them out.

Shachtman, four years after he hastily organized an independent "party" of his own, thereby renouncing the attempt to reform our party, is still worried most of all about our "organizational methods," our "leader cult" and other details of our own private housekeeping. If Shachtman were to stop to think and ask himself the elementary political question: "What is the WP anyway, an independent party or a faction of the SWP?"—he might begin to understand why in trying to be both he cannot succeed in either. But if Shachtman had ever learned how to stop and think he wouldn't be a kibitzer in politics.

Keller's [Art Preis] article on the new Stalinist campaign was excellent—well written with the right tone and the right note. The idea of running the cartoon as illustration of the article is also very good—I vote for this combination with both hands. We must remind ourselves over and over again that the majority of our readers are new people and that we must brighten up and lighten up the paper for them.

But my vote for the cartoon illustration on an inside page has a string tied to it: It must not be a substitute for the front-page cartoon! If the editor thinks he has some headline more important than the front-page cartoon the solution is simple. Don't argue with him but tie him up till the girls in the shop make up the paper properly. Then turn him loose and tell him it was all meant in fun; but repeat the process the next week, and make it a weekly routine until he comes to his senses and changes his ways.

We are proud of Keller's article, but thought the headline incorrect on two counts: 1) It is the Stalinist *political organization*, not its police agency, the GPU, that organizes the preparatory political campaigns. The GPU is an executory organ. It is important not to lump the two functions together indiscriminately. 2) Our new readers (the majority) probably don't know what "GPU" means. The fifteen-year habit of writing for the politically initiated hangs heavily on us all. But we seem to be entering a new period.

LETTER 61

SANDSTONE, JUNE 21, 1944

My notes on things I want to write about keep piling up faster than my letters can incorporate them. Three letters a week, to which I am limited, don't give me enough space. Now I must write about the pardon application. We had a disagreement on procedure.

I proposed that we say nothing in the application except that we ask for unconditional pardon on the ground of constitutional rights, adding only this: "In presenting my application for unconditional pardon on the above grounds I wish to make it clear that I have not changed any of the views for which I have been imprisoned, as expressed by me and other defendants at our trial." Goldman proposed to include a statement of views in the pardon application with the object of publishing it in leaflet form, and submitted a draft. I disagreed with the draft, but since we opposed any statement, that question (the draft) was not discussed.

My motion carried nine to five. For my motion: Cannon, Dunne, Dobbs, Coover, Skoglund, DeBoer, Geldman, Palmquist, Hansen. For the G. motion: Goldman, Morrow, Hudson, Cooper, Hamel. A second motion by me was then carried to the effect that each individual may put any statement he wishes on his own application, and that the other defendants in the case be notified of our decision.

In my opinion the issue is not important enough to debate at any great length. I will state my views briefly:

1) The campaign around the pardon demand is going along very well, is being conducted properly on the correct line of policy which makes the broadest appeal, and is meeting with gratifying successes.

2) I view the signing of the pardon application as a mere formality, nothing more, which we go through only because it is mandatory under the rules in order for our friends to secure a hearing on the case. Otherwise, I would consider it best for us to sign nothing and say nothing while the campaign is in progress.

3) There is no need for us to intrude in the campaign with another statement of views. Our position has been made clear enough in the trial pamphlets and the pamphlet of farewell speeches. Silence now on our part while our friends conduct our campaign is a way of speaking that is most effective under the circumstances. Everybody knows we are

in prison for our views. Every resolution adopted by trade unions in our behalf stresses this fact. So does every comment on the case in the labor press which I have seen. We reaffirmed these views quite emphatically in our farewell speeches, and nobody has accused us of changing them since our departure. Another statement from us is not called for at the present time; would not add anything to what is already known, and consequently could not attract very much attention; would not broaden the pardon campaign or help it in any way, and might possibly injure it.

4) The important thing now is not what we say but what others say and do in our behalf. Attention should be centered on this. The fact that we have gone through the formality of signing the pardon application should not even be mentioned in the press. The petitions presented in the names of the others are what counts. At the time of the formal presentation of these petitions to the President all publicity should be devoted to the new and essentially important fact that trade unions representing one and a half million workers and many prominent individuals have formally demanded our liberation. Tactically, this is the most effective way to proceed. It is out of the question even to speak of any principle being involved in this difference of approach to the specific problem of the moment.

✳

I am deeply sorry that my proposal to give a suitable notice to the death of William Ellery Leonard was not accepted. I believe that if I had been in New York a proposal of mine urged with such earnestness as I tried to put into my letter would not have been so lightly disregarded. I cannot demand that any specific proposal of mine be agreed to, but I do expect every one to be taken seriously. I also expect them to be answered promptly, and I think I am entitled to hear serious reasons for rejection so that I may know what has happened to my motions and why. I don't like to "fight City Hall." Our friends "in the office" should remind themselves that I am "in the field" now. I wrote about this question in my polemic against Burnham—the chapter on "bureaucratism," I think. I am still a field worker at heart.

LETTER 62

SANDSTONE, JUNE 23, 1944

I am glad you finally got started on your Spanish, but I can't understand why you don't use the record system. I am sure it is much easier and more interesting. Your impression of the weather here is somewhat exaggerated. It has been very cool all spring with the exception of a very few days. Even then the nights were cool enough. I am told that summer nights here are always cool enough to sleep under a blanket. We are all sleeping under *three* so far. The climate here, in fact, is very good, although one cannot say much for the scenery. It is the wide-open prairie, and close enough to Lake Superior to get the benefit of some of its cool breezes. (I remember the summer I spent in Duluth years ago.) The air here is rather dry and seems to be good for me, but I will be ready enough to exchange it for the bad air of New York when the time comes—seven months from tomorrow.

I am sorry to hear that the comrades are not making more use of the beach accommodations. They should remember that there are many tasks yet to come and that they should save some energy for them. Moish should see to it, at any rate, that the PC passes a motion formally providing for two-week vacations for each member of the staff in all departments. This has been our procedure for many years, but they may think a new motion necessary. Sylvia's annual visit to Chicago should not be counted out of her two weeks. Let

that be taken out of my vacation time. Tell Moish to be sure
and not let any of the girls skip or skimp on their vacations
on the theory that there is too much to be done. That condition will never be remedied. Meantime people must live
and have something besides work in their lives.

I have been thinking of Wheeler as party organizer in
Chicago. It should be easier to find someone for the technical
work you have in mind for him. From a political viewpoint
Chicago is the weakest branch in the party and it doesn't get
better while we sleep on it. Quite the contrary. The reports
I hear are far from reassuring, and the conviction is growing on me that the Chicago sickness can't cure itself. It requires national intervention—and a correct diagnosis. The
Chicago manifestations and similar ones we noticed in the
past year or so are nothing but echoes of the petty-bourgeois
opposition. The sooner we frankly recognize this and quit
pampering it, the better for the party.

I wish you and the other correspondents could organize
your clipping service a bit. I usually see two, three or four
copies of the same article.

Your report that you are feeling much better does me good.
It also strengthens my confidence in the curative powers of
the Long Island sun, although I personally never expect to
overindulge myself in it. I am waiting to hear that Mick
has taken her first swimming stroke; nothing will stop her
after that. It seems to me that both you and Walta are ex-
aggerating the negative sides of the baby's reactions to the
ordeal of cutting her last teeth. She shouldn't be expected to
laugh and dance when she is in pain, and should be allowed
an occasional sniffle. I don't like to hear bad reports about
my favorites; I don't believe them anyway.

The action of the ILGWU convention on our case represents a great achievement for the CRDC. Did Tobin really
try to prevent it? The fact that it is an AF of L organization makes the action especially significant in the circum-

stances. I hope this is being pointed out in the press. And by the way, while we are lambasting the Stalinists on the case I hope we are not neglecting Tobin and the shameful deal between him and Roosevelt and Biddle. Don't let this get lost in the shuffle!

I am all ready to start the Spanish and German readers when they come. The French reader is fine, I am reading it every day.

LETTER 63

SANDSTONE, JUNE 26, 1944

Finished the first Spanish study book and started the second. The German word *hold* means "lovely," "charming." *Wehmut* is "sadness."

Your report about the visit of Wong made me very homesick. This is a beautiful Minnesota Sunday and I am thinking what a fine day it would be for a leisurely walk with Wong and Mickus down to the creek and up the hill to the old abandoned farm. I think it is well established that dogs understand the meaning of certain sounds—that is, that they can be so trained. I remember Dave's dog obeying his order to "go upstairs and get Grandma" for dinner. My mother often told me that our dog named "Fritzie" understood and carried out her instruction to "mind the baby" (me) while she was washing on the porch. That is, he would sit on my dress and keep me from exploring the edges of the porch. That was quite a while ago.

I hope the apartment question can be settled satisfactorily; plans for future work depend on it. What I need and will insist on having under all circumstances is a workroom which is not considered part of the "house" and does not encroach on your living quarters; which is *provided for me by the party* and fitted up with all the facilities necessary for my work—desk, library, dictaphone, typewriter, etc. It must be exclusively an *office*, not combined with the sitting room, bedroom or dining room, and in using it this way it must not be considered that I am taking special privileges or monopolizing a disproportionate share of the house.

In short, I want a place to work that is indisputably mine. I need it if I am to do efficient work and I think I am entitled to it. According to plans we have discussed here I will not work in the party office any more—I have served my full time at that desk!—but will devote my time, on a regular schedule, to literary work and study in a separate office, either at home or in some other place.

The place where we lived on Eleventh Street suited me in this respect during the last period after the front room was converted into an office only. That alone made it possible for me to finish the *History* book. If that place doesn't suit you I have no objection to your finding another, but be sure to find a place which appeals to you as adequate for "living" purposes *without including* the workroom.

The place under Walta would be very congenial and attractive but you have to think of it with one of the rooms sealed off and nonexistent as far as our living quarters are concerned. Take another good survey of the place from this point of view. Would there be room enough then? Or would you like to live there and let me have a workroom somewhere else? The only thing I am absolutely intransigent about is the workroom. That I intend to have at any cost. Once that point is settled and out of the way any decision you may make about the apartment will be agreeable to me.

I will write more about the school. It is simpler and more feasible than it looks. The problem, at first, is not the teaching staff but the student body. But that also can be solved if resolute decisions are made. My view is that the first student group should be small, perhaps six, and should consist entirely, almost entirely, of people now on the staff of the party. The problem is how to replace them. Here we must make bold experiments.

I hear that some rather wise people in Chicago consider the educational thesis "utopian." It all depends on the premise. Is the party facing a period of expansion, contraction or stagnation? All our work must be planned in dependence on the answer we give to this question. To object to a plan itself is to manifest a sickness, from which unfortunately our party is not entirely free, which should be called organizational nihilism. To *organize* means first to *plan;* and planning requires perspective and realizable goals. I have the advantage over these critics in that I thought about these things before I wrote my thesis.

LETTER 64

SANDSTONE, JUNE 28, 1944

The news about Moish's summary of the subscription campaign and the projected new campaign of literature distribution is well received. The report is one of the many things I will have to read later.

I am waiting for a comprehensive report from George about his impressions of the branches. One question we wish to put is, why is Los Angeles so slow in getting started in the campaigns?

I have started to read *John Dewey's Philosophy*—the "Modern Library Giant" edition of his selected writings. It is a big book of 1,069 pages, 241 of which are taken up by a comprehensive introduction by the editor Joseph Ratner. I had planned to read all the ancients first, but I began to get impatient to see what arguments (reasons) the moderns give for rejecting the dialectical materialist method of Marx and Engels.

I have read one hundred pages of Ratner's introduction and haven't found anything yet. (I have more than a strong suspicion that I won't find anything in this entire book—or any other book—but I intend to keep on the trail until I come to the very end of it.) Oh, yes, Ratner tries to dismiss dialectic materialism in a flippant footnote, somewhat after the method of Burnham and company. They will have to do better than that! I'm from Missouri and they have to show me.

I was well satisfied to hear from our Chilean friend. I think Moish should keep in contact with him, send him party circulars, etc. I also think it timely now to put into effect the plan we once adopted, and then postponed for financial reasons, to invite a Chilean to come to New York for a period to work with Gerland. I suggest that Moish discuss it with him.

*

The educational thesis can be broken into parts if it is so desired. The second section (the concrete plan) can stand alone as a proposition to be voted on, amended, etc. The other parts could be called "Comments on the Educational Plan" or something like that. Some comrades agreeable to the plan might object to some of the comments and motivations. Others who are skeptical of the plan might select debatable sections of the comment for the main discussion. I am ready to debate the motivations, etc., in the "comments"—and there is plenty more where that came from—but the concrete proposal should stand by itself for *decision* and not get swamped in a discussion of the merits of the bourgeois universities, methods of pedagogy, subjects we should teach, etc.

I find that I have to study pedagogy also, and I intend to do it, so that our educational system can be conducted in the most efficient manner in *method* as well as in curriculum. I am getting madder every minute at *how little* the college people have given to the movement, not only in comparison to their pretensions but in general. What in the devil did they learn in all the years they spent as adults in school with nothing in the world to do but study?

Perhaps the fault belongs to the teachers. Be that as it may, we Sandstone intellectuals are going to look into their pedagogical methods as well as their philosophy and their history.

LETTER 65

SANDSTONE, JUNE 30, 1944

You forgot to include the May Day cartoon in your No. 59.

The decision about the convention, as about everything else, must be made by the NC solely from the standpoint of what the NC considers to be the party's needs and interests. For *our* part, as I think I wrote before, we have no objection to a convention—in fact, we tend more and more to favor it—but the action, whatever it may be, should not be taken on our motion.

I speak only from the standpoint of those who supported the decisions of the last plenum and who see no need for revising them. The others must speak for themselves and should be consulted directly through their correspondents. I think it should be a matter of indifference to the PC whether the post-plenum document is submitted to the pre-convention discussion. Let the author decide that. We are inclined to think the discussion would be a good thing; and a second discussion, if necessary, after our return a still better thing. We feel no need to participate in the pre-convention discussion; we are well content to leave it to those who participated in the adoption of the plenum resolution and know very well how to defend it.

This job was easy enough at the plenum and will be still easier now after a lapse of nine months or so. This is one of the most attractive sides of politics: time comes to the aid of the correct policy. The events of the recent months in Europe also argue in favor of sticking firmly to tested principles when drafting party resolutions. Such documents don't have to be changed or rewritten every year.

I think the main political task of the convention is to pass on the line of policy followed by the NC since the last convention and to adopt a resolution summarizing what has happened *since the plenum.* In order that there be no ambiguity, no possibility of misunderstanding, the proposed convention resolution should begin by explicitly endorsing the policy of the plenum resolution and proceed from there to analyze subsequent developments from the same fundamental standpoint.

Pre-convention and convention discussion should not be restricted to the *policy* of the NC; it should not be restricted at all. Those who feel disposed to criticize should have their aims facilitated by the presentation of a special subordinate resolution dealing with the *work* of the party and the *state* of the party since the last convention. This will give everybody a point on the agenda under which they may freely discuss the question whether the party has been conducted properly and is being built properly or not.

You can see from the foregoing suggestions that I am not of the opinion "that every discussion disturbs the party." That is a slanderous echo of the petty-bourgeois opposition. To be sure, I am not very much in favor of kibitzing which leads to nothing but more of the same and drives serious workers away, and I am not very much in favor of pampering chronic kickers and windbags. But I am strongly in favor of full discussion which leads to a decision by the party whenever different viewpoints are presented in the proper season. The pre-convention period is the season.

*

I don't think I will want to make a visit to Florida when I come home. Indeed, I don't think I will want to visit anyone for a while. After thirteen months here it will probably take some time for me to return to normal ways of living, and I will probably want most to be alone with you somewhere for a while to accustom myself gradually to a natural life of freedom, as a sandhog or deep-sea diver must spend a period in a decompression chamber before entering open air.

July, 1944

SANDSTONE, JULY 3, 1944

This has been a bad week for us. We have waited in dread for news of Henry's [Schultz] condition. When we got a telegram Saturday morning stating that he had undergone a second operation we were in despair. Now that twenty-four hours have elapsed we are permitting ourselves to hope that Henry's fighting spirit, plus the best obtainable medical care, will pull him through.

We take it for granted that Moish is keeping in communication with Minneapolis by telephone and sparing no expense to provide Henry with the best of everything. The movement is indestructible, but the individual humans who make it and build it are so fragile! Yet it is these few individuals whose lives are so insecure, threatened by so many unknown hazards and liable to instantaneous destruction by some blow in the dark, who are preparing the great new world of the future.

＊

Do you remember our first "program of expansion"? It is recorded in the old *Militant*—in the spring or summer of 1932 I think. We are of the opinion that the time is ripe now for the NC to propose a new program of expansion to the forthcoming convention, and offer the following concrete plan:

A $? Program of Expansion Fund to be related to our release on January 23, with that date as the deadline of the campaign. The program to consist of four points:

1) An eight-page, $1-a-year *Militant* with a bigger staff, new features, two cartoons and more pictures.

2) Set up the Educational Department with a full-time director and start the full-time National Training School.

3) Subsidize the publication of four new books by Pioneer Publishers.

4) Put eight more organizers in the field. (Chicago, Philadelphia, Flint, Boston, San Francisco, Ohio, New Jersey, Buffalo.)

The plan may appear to be somewhat ambitious, but we are sure that it is completely realistic. The fund and the forces needed to carry out the program will both be provided by the party without hesitation. It is only necessary for the leadership to ask for them. In this case, as in all our other experiences, the rank and file of the party will show more enthusiasm, energy and capacity than we expect of them.

Besides being realistic, and more than that, absolutely necessary now, it should be noted that the proposed program is *balanced*. The bigger, cheaper, more popular *Militant* for the benefit of newly awakened workers is balanced against the Training School for the education of party leaders. The publication of four more important books for the political and theoretical improvement of the party is balanced against a revolutionary step forward in the expansion of the organizing staff.

Differing opinions have been expressed here as to the amount of the fund to be asked for, but no one doubts that enough can be raised to execute the program. Here are the suggestions that have been made: Ask for the same amount as last time, $15,000; ask for $18,000—one thousand for each of the eighteen; ask for $23,000 to be raised by January 23; set $25,000 as the goal. In any case, the final decision will naturally be made by the convention—the program should issue from the convention—but the NC should go to the convention with a definite proposal.

There is no doubt that the proposal to give an eight-page *Militant* for a dollar a year will strike fire in the party ranks as it has here at the Sandstone branch. One comrade said this morning: "I am willing to do a year in prison for an eight-page *Militant* at a buck a year."

Are they working on the political resolution?

LETTER 67

SANDSTONE, JULY 5, 1944

I am writing this on the blessed Fourth of July. This is hardly the ideal place to celebrate our twentieth anniversary, but by adding the memory of the nineteenth and the prospect of the twenty-first I manage to make it do.

Monday is usually our heaviest mail day. Last night we were all waiting for the mail with exceptional eagerness to learn the final score on the sub campaign. We were all disappointed; there must have been a delay in the mail at this end.

Your proposal to invite our cartoonist to Long Island for the summer is all right as far as it goes, but if she is seriously ill we are in favor of more drastic measures. You and Moish should speak to your doctor about the matter, arrange for a thoroughgoing examination and follow his directions for treatment. If he prescribes a change of climate or a period of treatment at a sanitorium, we should take the financial responsibility for it without hesitation. We must do everything we can to save this precious talent.

I think I wrote you before that I would like to hear from Larry [Turner], George [Clarke] and Murry [Weiss]. Did you write to them?

I am anxious to hear what plans the New York organization is making to utilize the two thousand new *Militant* readers. This new contact and mailing list gives Local New York something to work on in the creation of a new periphery. As I wrote before, I think it is more urgently necessary than anywhere else to push out boldly and build a new base in New York.

*

I am looking forward to July 12. On that day we pass the first half of our sentence; the rest of the time we will be coasting downhill. By that date also I will finish the second French study book. Then I intend to lay the language studies aside and take a two-week "vacation." It will be the end of a "semester" so to speak. I have been driving away at the study every day for five solid months and I am a bit fagged. I have started to read *A Treasury of Science*. Perhaps I will continue with it on my vacation. However, I am not obligating myself to read anything or do anything except my routine duties here.

Who got the highest number of subs in the campaign nationally? Who were the three highest? How did the new members show up in the drive? I think a cost-accounting job should be done on the overall cost of the new subs, the amount received and the net subsidy required to fill them out. Can you send these figures to me when you get them?

The book situation here is quite satisfactory as far as we are concerned. The books already received, plus those approved and ordered, will keep us occupied for some time. It is not likely that we will ask for many more. I am most eager to get the language readers—three or four, graduated in difficulty and vocabulary, in French, Spanish and German—and I understand they have been approved and ordered. The first volume of Sean O'Casey's autobiography (*I Knock at the Door*) came some time ago, but there is a second volume—*Pictures in the Hallway*—which I would like to get.

I am glad so many of the comrades are getting some good out of the seashore place and that you are having a houseful for the long weekend of the Fourth. But how can they keep the beer cold without having a spring running through the kitchen? I must admit that the steady bombardment of praise for the new place is beginning to wear down my resistance. How did Wong like it?

LETTER 68

SANDSTONE, JULY 7, 1944

I am still waiting for my first letter this week but I suppose it will turn up eventually. We are all feeling better today after hearing the first definite news of Henry's improvement. We are beginning to feel confident now that the Dutchman will fight his way through. It is a great satisfaction to us also to know that Moish has been on top of this situation which affected us so deeply.

We believe the "eight new field organizers" is a realizable goal for the NC to set for itself but it might be wiser not to specify that number definitely in the program. It is bad to make promises to the party if there is a reasonable doubt of being able to fulfill them. It might be best for this point of the expansion program to be limited to a more general provision to "strengthen the organizing staff in the field."

❋

Someone may question my statement in a previous letter that the Chicago branch is the weakest branch in the party "from a political" standpoint, and think I am intentionally overstating the case. No, I mean it literally. I disregard the

arguments of those who consider Chicago the "best branch"—
we do not measure by the same political criterion—and confine my explanations to those who may say that a small, new
branch of politically uneducated militants is at least politically inferior to the highly "political" Chicago branch.

This assumption is incorrect. To be sure, the *uneducated*
militants must learn, but the *miseducated* people in Chicago must *unlearn*. That is much harder. Usick has correctly pointed out that Aristotle's formula in this respect
requires amendment under modern conditions of education
and miseducation.

The Chicago branch is a *diseased* branch. The disease is
in part an inheritance from the past. The Abern clique did
not dominate the Chicago organization for so many years
in vain. In part the sickness is the product of the sentiments,
moods, prejudices and half-formed ideas which were exhibited
at the last party plenum. The Chicago branch is the unfortunate guinea pig upon whom this unwholesome mixture
has been tried out. The same results could be guaranteed
anywhere. But once we recognize that the medicine is poison
I think it is our duty, under the Pure Food and Drugs Law,
to put a proper label on it, warn the party at large against it,
and take remedial measures in the branch which is suffer-
ing from an overdose of the Menshevik dope.

I am interested in the new Negro columnist. Who is he?
Where did he come from? What is his age, educational and
political background? How and where was he recruited? The
"Shop Talks on Socialism" are very popular with us. It did my
heart good to see the "Letter of a Steel Worker to his Son,"
especially with the illustration. I am beginning to feel that
we are really learning how to talk to the workers and make
a paper interesting to them. That is the big task now—to
talk to the workers without "writing down"; to have elementary propaganda for the new workers without eliminating
the more serious political material for the more advanced

workers. That is why we need a bigger paper.

Our thoughts are turning more and more to the idea of a big national weekly, subsidized by the party and sold at a cheap price, instead of a daily as the next step in our forward development.

I read [James T.] Farrell's piece on Ring Lardner in the *Times Book Review*. He is a good critic as well as creator, a combination not seen too often. I wonder if Jim doesn't read more consciousness and design into Lardner than Lardner knew about. I recall the baseball stories as rich humor.

LETTER 69

SANDSTONE, JULY 10, 1944

Finished my second French study book a few days ahead of schedule and started my two-week vacation (from language studies) Saturday afternoon. I am taking this vacation partly because I think it will do me good and partly as an example to my hard-working colleagues on the party staff. Please add Lenin's *Materialism and Empirio-Criticism* to the next book list.

I am especially pleased to hear that you are gaining weight steadily. Please keep me informed of your progress. So Mickey mistakes [Senator] Bricker for me? She isn't turning Republican, is she? Maybe we had better send her to the Trotsky School for indoctrination.

We liked Harry's book review. His remarks on the trade-union question were especially perspicacious. The review had the right tone and the right note; that is the way to write *about* renegades always; not to reason sweetly with them as Morrison did in his article about Hook in the *FI* last year. The longer I live the more I become convinced that "the style is the man."

I am glad you are going to get the Spanish records, as I am quite sure that this is the easiest and best way to learn a foreign language by self-study. We finally got the books we ordered long ago: *The Loom of Language* and a good French and a good Spanish dictionary. We will know a lot about self-study of foreign languages before we leave here.

I seem to be fated to learn everything the hard way. That is one reason I am so anxious to help others find the easier way. This will be the case with language study by comrades in the future. They will profit by our experiences and hard work. We will see to it that the party educational system scraps all obsolete pedagogical methods in this field and helps comrades to learn languages the best, quickest and easiest way.

✻

We learn that our vigilant Control Commission has uncovered some cases of organizational disloyalty in New York and is investigating the matter further. We are not surprised, and we will not be surprised if investigation discloses similar actions in Chicago. It is important to analyze this new phenomenon closely and not to proceed to the necessary organizational steps prematurely.

Politically, the new manifestation may be diagnosed in medical terms as a small pus pocket left over from the abscess which we drained in the split of the petty-bourgeois opposition. The source of the infection—politically and spiritually—is not in the New York branch and not in the Chicago branch, but in a higher organ, namely, the NC. This was shown for all to see at the plenum. Our patience and forbearance on that occasion, and our adopted motion to confine the dispute to NC members, gave the proponents of neo-Menshevism a good opportunity, which they didn't deserve, to retreat and save themselves from discredit and disgrace before the party membership.

They are evidently not satisfied with these opportunities to cure themselves. They want to let their unattractive disease run its course. More than that, they want to communicate it to new young members who have not been previously inoculated.

We cannot allow that. That would undermine and destroy all the good results of the great constructive work the party is carrying forward. As far as we are concerned a state of war exists, and we intend to carry this war to a conclusion as soon as we are in a position to do so, freely and in the open. Meantime, the press must be guarded against the ideological smuggling operations which such political tendencies always attempt.

LETTER 70

SANDSTONE, JULY 12, 1944

We get full reports about Henry. Sunday he sent word by Marvel: "Tell those guys at Sandstone, you can't kill a Dutchman." So he seems to be getting back to normal. It is now most important that he doesn't go back to work until he is fully recovered. We are depending on Moish to see to that.

✳

I have been making use of a part of my vacation time to sort out and classify my notes. So far I have run across three separate notes marked "Bermuda" and I am far from the bottom of the pile. I think travel conditions in the West Atlantic will loosen up sooner or later. You know I never did have any faith in Hitler's victory, and there is not much ground to start believing now. To be sure, I also have very little faith in Roosevelt's victory and still less in his "historical" position, but he will outlast Hitler at any rate.

Of course, we do not insist on sending Wheeler to Chicago. There is more than one good reason to have him in the center for a while, and even longer. But the reasons given for not sending Wheeler or someone else to Chicago are not very reassuring. An activist organizer is not our prescription for such a politically sick branch. It is something like trying to cure a boil on the neck by taking physical-culture exercises. I am more in favor of a surgeon's lance to open the boil and let the pus drain out.

I am becoming quite convinced that 1) either I was asleep for the past year or two, or 2) we did not get correct and adequate reports of the state of affairs in Chicago. An observant rank-and-file member, reporting the meeting of the Chicago branch where the question of demanding a financial accounting from the National Office was discussed, comments: "I'll tell you one thing. The petty-bourgeois elements have not left this branch yet. And some of them are very sensitive to the criticisms of the minorityites and the Social-Democrats."

I wish to make two suggestions in the handling of the same manifestations in New York. 1) Question all concerned in the evidences of disloyalty over and over again and keep a record of all the statements. Track down every lead relentlessly until you get all the information possible. Take no organization measures until the investigation is fully completed, and make it clear to any individual involved who may sincerely wish to remain in the party that his chances depend on his cooperation with the Control Commission in protecting the party against treachery. Keep in mind all the time that this is a political question upon which the party must be fully informed at the proper time and upon which the convention must finally act. Keep probing until you find out definitely whether New York has connections in other cities, especially Chicago.

2) Do not allow *any* discussion of disputed questions in the press, no matter who may "demand" it, but provide for the fullest discussion in the pre-convention *Internal Bulletin*. Everybody will be satisfied with this procedure except those who want to appeal to petty-bourgeois public opinion and justify themselves before it. There is another reason for our proposal. We must put a stop to all attempts to "smuggle" a revisionist change of our fundamental positions into the press before the party has had a chance to pass judgment on them.

We have tolerated too much of this already under the mistaken assumption that we were confronted only with isolated individual aberrations. We are confronted with a tendency which does not feel at home in a Bolshevik party. But we must show these people that *this* Bolshevik party still knows how to protect itself.

LETTER 71

SANDSTONE, JULY 14, 1944

Your No. 66 came July 12 with the next-to-the-last scoreboard.

The news of our wonderful party makes us do our time easier; or more correctly makes it less difficult, for there is no such thing as "easy time." How badly we all underestimated the energies of our membership and the new responsiveness of the workers to a paper that tells the truth!

Our defense campaign is a remarkable achievement. I never expected that anybody outside our close circle would trouble themselves about us so soon, or that there would be anything more than the adoption of formal resolutions by a few small unions. Contrary to that, the campaign in our behalf has penetrated more deeply into the official trade-union

JULY, 1944 / 163

movement than any *political* case ever reached before.

The Roosevelt gang can have good reason to be glad that our case will be off their hands in another six months by expiration of the sentences. They never dreamed that there would be so much fuss about the imprisonment of a group of Trotskyists in wartime, with the U.S. Government allied with Stalin into the bargain. To be sure, much of the official support is little more than formal. But that is nearly always the case in the first stages. The great mass protest movements of the past began with formal, more or less perfunctory resolutions which the dynamic small minority of militants pushed through in one way or another. These formal resolutions, in turn, became factors in the acceleration of the genuine mass movement.

The first conclusion one should draw from the results of our defense campaign up to date is that considerable sections of the organized labor movement are alert and apprehensive of threatening encroachments on their basic rights and, from the beginning, have recognized the case of the Trotskyist "reds" as a *labor* case. This never happened before in America. I think it is the most important development. Next in significance to be noted is the emergence of the CRDC as a genuine labor defense organization widely supported and universally trusted and certified as legitimate. This is also something new.

The pioneer communist defense committees never became anything more than narrow party formations denied access to the official labor movement and depending on party members and sympathizers for everything, including funds. The ILD, much broader in its concepts and methods, suffered from the general indifference of the labor movement to the fate of radicals here or elsewhere. Except for the Sacco-Vanzetti case—which was considered a miscarriage of justice in a criminal, not a political, case—the scope of the ILD was quite narrowly restricted.

The CRDC has raised the theory and practice of labor defense work to new heights. Its general concepts and policy appear to be completely correct, and its organizing work is beyond praise. No one can know and appreciate better than I that the flow of protest resolutions which is becoming a flood did not originate spontaneously or by accident. In each case there is the background of arduous work—from the plans and directions of the National Office to the countlessly multiplied individual exertions in the ranks. We see that work behind every resolution reported to us, and we appreciate it with all our hearts.

That is the way great mass movements are made, not otherwise. We are proud of our CRDC and grateful to it. We believe it will not cease to exist with the ending of our case but remain as the permanent defense organization of the advanced workers' movement.

[LETTER 72]

SANDSTONE, JULY 17, 1944

I just had my ingrown toenails operated on and am writing this from the hospital. That is why it lacks a number; I don't remember the number of the last one. Walta's letter of July 11 came last night, July 15. Her reports about the beneficial effects on both you and Mick were good to hear. I hope she also is benefiting and that the others are having good weekends. I wish you would write more about the weekend guests and parties. It does us good to hear that they are having a good time. I am beginning to soften up on the L.I. place.

In your questions about a place when I return, you do not make it clear whether you are referring to a permanent place or a special place for a temporary vacation. If you mean the latter, I think it best to do nothing about it. The main thing I will want—if present feelings are any indication—will be complete freedom in all respects. I don't want to be tied down in advance to anything definite that I have to do or any special place where I have to go. Above all I don't want to be obligated to visit anybody. I want to be free.

If your reference is to a permanent place to live, I think you should decide and settle that with only two requirements in mind. First, be sure that the living quarters suit you. Second, provide for a workroom for me which is separate and which does not push your living quarters into a dark corner. I want to make it clear once more that my workroom is to be considered as an auxiliary office to be provided for by the party and not at the expense of your living space.

Take this up with the party secretariat before you decide on a place. I don't want to have any possible misunderstanding on this point, which by the way is strongly insisted on by my colleagues here. (They think they will be able to get more work out of me by this arrangement.) I would also greatly prefer to have this place selected and fitted up before I return so that valuable time will not be lost looking around afterwards. But if the party secretariat is not agreeable to this proposition, let the whole matter rest until I get home; and get an apartment that suits you without an extra room for my office and library. Please let me know what decision you make—after you have closed the deal with the landlord, not before.

The assignment of Wheeler is agreeable to us, all the more so since we had just about come to the same conclusion. We note with satisfaction that separate phases of the educational program are already in progress. That is the way it naturally works out, as I view it. To adopt a general plan does not necessarily mean that every detail of the plan must be put into operation at once. But a plan is necessary now to give symmetry to the development of the educational work and a goal to aim at.

I repeat again that the project of the Trotsky School is much simpler than it may appear. The main problem is the students, not the faculty. Indeed, this is no problem at all. As for the students, I think we should apply our tested organizational principle: Use the material at hand. That means, in this case, to constitute the first student body out of people whom *we already know* as more or less qualified party leaders before we begin to experiment. We will do that later— and no doubt get some surprising results, both good and bad—when we are richer and have more people. Almost every member of the present staff should be considered as a candidate for the school. Who shall be the first six?—that is the only question.

[LETTER 73]

SANDSTONE, JULY 19, 1944

I am still in the hospital nursing my sore toes. I am assured, however, that for my trouble I will be free from ingrown toenails in the future. The operating technique was to burn the sides of the nail down to the roots with an electric needle. It has turned out to be less fun than I expected. It has been an awkward and painful business and the toes are still sore, but you can assure Macdonald that I am taking a nonchalant, chins-up attitude toward it, even though they are my own toes.

It has been a very cool summer here, the coolest I remember since my summer in Duluth with Frank Little in 1913. We haven't suffered a bit from the heat, so you can put your apprehensions on that score at rest. Since your health is improving so well at the beach it seems foolish to jeopardize it by a strenuous train trip here, especially under the bad and crowded conditions of the trains these days. Why not take it easy where you are and build up your strength for a trip we can make together later on under better conditions?

I think it is all right for little Mick to think of me as a Christmas tree. That is what I always want to be for her. It seems to me that she should be allowed to continue her association of my return with Christmas right up to the end. That can easily be done by pushing the date of *her* Christmas back for one month. It would be nice to come home to a Christmas tree. I will bring her a ring and something else, and she can begin to save up for her presents to me. You can tell her that what I would like best are a special pipe, a box of Edgeworth tobacco and a special pair of slippers to keep at her house and use only when I visit her.

I am glad but not surprised that you invited Dorothy [Schultz] to send on little Ann. She is such a little thing she couldn't be much trouble. She should make a good playmate for Mick, but if she happened to get her Dutch up at the same time Mick got her Irish up there might be some fireworks. A still better idea, I think, is to invite the whole Schultz family. Dorothy could visit Grace, and Henry could rest up on the seashore from his battle with the croakers. Besides, there Henry would be under the direct, physical control of the NC and couldn't go back to the N.P. Railroad without formal permission.

*

It seems to us that the paper is handling the strike question somewhat too defensively. We suggest that the stories on the Stalinist campaign and the story about the alleged protest of a naval unit about a strike be examined again from this point of view. We have to be doubly careful all the time to make no concessions to bourgeois public sentiment even by implication. I have written before about the significance of terminology in this respect.

I don't have the clippings here and therefore cannot make

exact quotations. But as I recall the points we discussed, the Stalinist accusations that the Trotskyists fomented a number of strikes in Mexico were called "slanders" and the AP navy story was called a "smear." Uninitiated readers—and they are now the majority—can get false impressions of our policy from these inadvertent expressions. We must not yield an inch, even by implication, to the bourgeois-Social-Democratic-Stalinist thesis that strikes are intrinsically wrong.

It is good to hear that thoughts in New York are shaping up along the same line as ours on a big national weekly as the next step. But what is the idea of changing the format? Very good and convincing reasons must be given for such a proposal. I am especially sensitive on this point just now because I am reading Engels' *Dialectics of Nature* simultaneously with *John Dewey's Philosophy*, and experimentalism isn't faring very well. What is the matter with the present format?

[LETTER 74]

SANDSTONE, JULY 21, 1944

We received the paper and magazine yesterday. I read the scoreboard first. Poor Buffalo! They tried so hard, and we were all rooting for them. But they were nosed out of first place in the final score by worthy rivals and they needn't feel too bad about it. Newark really astonished us. This branch has been hit so hard by the double draft—of the army and the party—that we would have been well satisfied with a modest score of 100 percent on their part. Instead of that they bounce back with a score of 657 percent! I think we are just beginning to get a rough idea of the real quality of this party.

The paper looks very bright and lively with the new departments, illustrations and "rubrics." I read the "Militant Army" notes second. Now that the scoreboard is finished for the time being, I think the "Army" column should be enlarged. The most important thing is to print extracts from letters. I read the Negro column and part of the "Trade Union Notes" next. Then the editorial on the "7,614 New Readers." Then the "Workers' Forum" and the front-page story about the Stalinist campaign. Then the CRDC page and "Ten Years Ago in *The Militant*." Next Kovalesky's article and "Pioneer Paragraphs" under the attractive new rubric, and the squib about "Browder's Diet."

I haven't mentioned the cartoons, but I looked at them first of all, as I suppose everyone else does. I put off reading the longer articles till the last in order to take more time to soak them in. I imagine most people read the paper somewhat in this order, especially the new readers. The features, short squibs and illustrations are very important. They lead one very easily into the deeper parts of the paper.

The magazine keeps up a good standard. So far I have read the manager's notes, the editors' "Review of the Month," the English report and the French piece. I think the editors' review should be headed by the signature "By the Editors."

I would like to get more complete and precise information about the report of the Control Commission. Who were the four involved? How was their activity discovered? With whom did they meet? How many times? What did they discuss? Who were the abstentionists on the vote? Why didn't the leaders take the floor? Precisely what was the parliamentary incident at the close of the meeting?

What estimate do the leaders make of the whole affair and what are their further plans in regard to it? Has the political resolution for the convention been prepared? I keep mentioning this without eliciting any response, but convention preparations cannot even be started nor can a date even be set until the resolution is ready for adoption. On the other hand, once the resolution is out of the way, all the other convention preparations can be reduced to easy routine work.

I don't seem to have any definite opinions on how the CRDC should proceed organizationally—except that they should not think of folding up January 23. There will be plenty of work for them to do from now on!

*

I am still in the hospital. There is nothing the matter with me except sore toes. I will probably be discharged from the hospital tomorrow or Saturday, but I will have to wear cut-out shoes and step around carefully for two or three weeks thereafter. I am taking it easy on my "vacation" here, sleeping a lot and reading at random. I still know how to loaf. I think that is the main reason I have lived so long and feel like living longer. I just finished reading *The Deputy Sheriff of Comanche County* which was recommended to me as "a great book." It was terrific, if you know what I mean.

[LETTER 75]

SANDSTONE, JULY 24, 1944

I am gradually getting better, but my toes are still plenty sore and I am still in the hospital. This is to keep the weight off my feet and give them a better chance to heal. Ask Sweetums to put a sympathetic bandage on her big toe to help mine to get better quicker.

*

The Irisher's comment about the "Dog Days" chapter of our *History* reminds me that I hesitated a long time over that title, fearing that it might be considered too slangy. If you hear anyone make this objection, however, you can assure them that, far from being an expression of American slang, "dog days" is a *classical* term. Aristotle used it frequently to describe the period of summer heat and stagnation. I couldn't think of a better term to cover that chapter of the development of our movement without using the title which it really deserves and which I have no doubt the future historians will employ: The Heroic Period of American Communism.

I still take my reports of Chicago seriously despite the assurances that everything is OK there, because my informant gives facts. The interpretation of the reports is my own. It coincides, however, with that of my informant who, by the way, makes some very shrewd observations in regard to the Chicago phenomena and their causes. In regard to the optimistic assurances you sent me, he remarked: "I'm glad Rose wrote and made the comments she did. I think they reflect the attitude of the National Office. That has been the attitude the NO has taken all along. They want Chicago to solve the problem themselves. Fine! But it is about time that some of these people realized that instead of solving this problem by recruitment, the workers vote with their feet."

This last remark expresses what I meant to say in a previous letter about the type of organizer needed in Chicago. He says it better, and more succinctly. The principal reason why I am less tolerant now than before of the "kibitzers' club" theories of organization is precisely the good prospect of an influx of new, politically inexperienced worker-militants. I know that such workers will not stay in a kibitzers' club. They won't talk back to the articulate smart alecks, and they won't write letters to the NO either. They "vote with their feet." But the new workers are more important than the old incorrigibles who think the party is a hospital for sick souls and a forum for unrestricted and unlimited self-expression. This is the essence of the problem in New York as well as in Chicago. I hope the leadership sees it this way and utilizes the pre-convention discussion period, and the convention itself, for a salutary pedagogical campaign.

The prejudices against leadership and the fear of discipline are characteristics of the petty bourgeois who doesn't want to be tied down to anything definite. To the militant worker, however, who has an instinct for organized struggle, strong leadership and firm discipline are the most attractive features of a party. Such a party, in his eyes, is serious, it means business—and that is what he wants.

Lenin wrote on these subjects in *What Is To Be Done?* and *The Left Sickness.* I hope the forthcoming discussion will produce some instructive articles which go to the very root of the new criticisms and help the new workers in the party learn what is involved and why. I am sorry I cannot participate. There is at least one more pamphlet on this question in my system.

[LETTER 76]

SANDSTONE, JULY 26, 1944

I imagine your apprehension about my being in the hospital—I am still here but will probably get out tomorrow—springs from the usual association of "hospital" with serious illness. That is not necessarily the case in a place like this where everything from a cold to an appendectomy is treated in the hospital. I am still on my diet of soft-boiled eggs and milk three times a day, seven days a week, except about twice a month when I get beef stew for dinner. I have had no recurrence of stomach trouble; and as far as

I know there is nothing physically the matter with me but sore toes which are healing satisfactorily, if slowly, with no sign of infection.

*

I would like to hear how the class on historical materialism is going. Would like to attend it, in fact, as I am deeply interested in this subject. We have many discussions about it here in connection with our historical studies, American and Greek. Historical materialism takes the mystery out of history and gives the reader a unique advantage over the historians, enabling him to see the grand causation of the events which the historians only relate in chronological order. The superiority of the Marxist conception in the study of history is not less than that of the X-ray camera over a dollar Kodak for the clinical examination of the human organism.

*

I don't think you need to be alarmed about putting on a little weight. The clothes question can easily be solved by cutting up my Hollywood suit and making two out of it—one for you and one for me. I am hoping you retain a protective layer of fat about your bones. Perhaps it will keep you warm next winter and shield you from the annual plague of colds.

The only argument I can see against keeping the old apartment is the poor heating service. But I don't think the coal shortage will last longer than another winter; perhaps not that long. Meanwhile I think you should resolutely decide to counteract the chill of the apartment by getting a *good* electric heater as soon as you move back to town. I am sure the Secretariat will allow this little extra expense in the budget; and you should not hesitate to ask for it. Remember that our old bones have at least a traditional value to the party and should be kept warm on that account alone, if for no other reason.

One of my pals here is quite sensitive on this point and keeps bringing it up in conversation. Every time he sees a new copy of *The Militant* or hears a new report of party progress in our absence he renews his proposal. His idea is that the party should buy the Pennsylvania farm. By this, he says, two birds can be killed with one stone. The party will thus be able 1) to take care of poor old Jim in appreciation of his past services, and 2) keep him out of the way of the young leaders who seem to do so much better without him. You can write and tell Evie [DeBoer] that this is the kind of idea her husband cooks up when he gets away from her influence.

The second issue of *The Militant* arrived Saturday. We have to thank the comrades for making this possible by sending it by first-class mail. It is a great treat to have the paper to read over Sunday. By reading the paper at this distance and with such a perspective we are best able to appreciate what a great paper it is; by far the best this country has ever seen. I hope the "Diary of a Steel Worker" will become a permanent feature. It is just right and just the right length to help *The Militant* become what the Old Man wanted: a paper *of* the workers.

You haven't yet told me what kind of a heating system the Long Island place has. So "Snow" Larsen is going to get married—and to one of our office girls at that. The party raises them, marries them off and struggles to assure a better world for their children. Still, the party itself remains ever young and keeps alive the spirit of youth in those who serve it faithfully.

My "vacation" ended Monday and I should have returned to my routine studies of languages, history and philosophy. Instead of that I have continued loafing and reading *A Treasury of Science*. It is a magnificent and fascinating book. Man's achievements are great, but only a faint intimation of what they will be.

[LETTER 77]

SANDSTONE, JULY 28, 1944

I read a volume of short stories reprinted from the *New Yorker* and Norman Thomas' new book, *What is Our Destiny?* From this you can see that I am still *loafing*, resting mind as well as body. It would be hard for me to say which book is the more empty. The *New Yorker* stories at least present a picture of the futility and decay of the middle-class sophisticates. But a very little of that goes a long way with me. It is repulsive to read about them. What must it be to live among them and know no other milieu?

Some people don't appreciate the intellectual and spiritual qualities of the proletarian revolutionists. They don't seem to know how fortunate they are to be permitted to live in such circles.

I heard via Henry Schultz that George [Clarke] was on his way to New York. I am still waiting to hear from him— about himself, the Seattle branch, his views on independent thinking, iconoclasm, etc.

❋

"Iconoclasm" is not, as its devotees imagine, an intellectual but rather a spiritual quality. It is a form of skepticism which, in turn, is a form of capitulation before the triumphant lie of capitalism; an inability to believe, that is, to really believe in anything to take its place. It is the product of feeling, not of thinking, independent or otherwise. It is good only to disorganize and demoralize a movement, never to build one.

Our movement is based on definite adherence to a body of ideas which were not thought out originally and independently by ourselves but by others who went before us. They are not our creation but our heritage. To be sure, we had to study them critically and assimilate them and thus make them our own. But our common membership in the party presupposes that we have definitely agreed upon them and that we proceed from there to their application in life. Naturally, nobody is obligated to agree with us in regard to these ideas. Anybody has a right to dispute them, reject them or "iconoclize" them to his heart's content. But it is a very poor exercise to recommend to the party members. They cannot fight for a program unless they believe in it. Those who have doubts about the program ought to stay home until they have made up their minds. There is no inspiration in their lugubrious soliloquies. And without inspiration it is impossible to build a fighting movement.

✳

I received Walta's letter. You all seem to be doing a pretty good, organized job of boosting the Long Island real estate. But it is still only an idea presented by you to me. I did not think it out independently. Therefore I must approach the question critically and cautiously and think, think, think for myself, not be a hand-raiser. Then I feel that I ought to see the place for myself, touch it, feel it, sleep in it—in short, submit it to an empirical test.

Then I ought to compare notes with little Mick; I know she always thinks for herself and says what she thinks. Then there is Wong. He doesn't say much but he has a way of letting it be known what he likes or doesn't like. If all three of us come to the same conclusion we will go in with you. If I finally make up my mind to join, you can depend on two things: 1) I won't go around hobnobbing with real-estate agents who are knocking your beach in favor of another. 2) I won't commune with lost souls who wonder whether Long Island exists or not.

LETTER 78

SANDSTONE, JULY 31, 1944

I got out of the hospital Friday and can now start numbering my letters again. I didn't have my records with me there. My toes are still sore but gradually healing. I don't think I would recommend such a drastic operation to anyone else afflicted with ingrown toenails. Better to clip them periodically and risk a recurrence of the trouble than to go through so much misery and inconvenience.

＊

I wish you would send me Morrison's comments on the educational thesis. If it is too long to include in one letter, send it in installments. From the single paragraph you sent me it is clear that his conception of the method and purpose of party education is different from mine. I think I told you that, in presenting the matter to the convention, the *program* should be separated from the comments of Martin [Cannon]. That part, with such amendments as the NC thinks needed, is what should be acted upon by the convention. Nevertheless the discussion of conception and methods can serve a useful pedagogical purpose, and should be encouraged.

＊

We hear with considerable dissatisfaction that Usick again has the flu. People who are in good shape shouldn't get sick in the summertime. Perhaps the NC will have to set up its own Board of Health with both discretionary and disciplinary powers to invade the private lives of the staff members and see to it that lazy people like me don't loaf too much and super-industrious people like Usick don't work too much.

Now that George [Clarke] is there—which is a good thing in itself—we think a concrete emergency measure should be put into effect about as follows: Let Frank or Warde be responsible for the magazine and George take Usick's place on *The Militant* staff while Usick recuperates on Long Island—put him and Wong in the room that would be mine—and devotes himself to self-development as an original, free, fresh and independent thinker.

*

We received the July *FI* Saturday, but to our great disappointment *The Militant* did not come. The mails are very undependable these days. Besides that, we hear there was a wreck on the road from Minneapolis and that this delayed some trains. I have read only part of the magazine so far; we have to share it around. Stuart's report on Cuba was very welcome. We think there are too many subheads in the editorial section. The quotation, "Without revolutionary theory there is no revolutionary action," should be checked for accuracy. I think it should read "movement" instead of "action." Two subheads per page are enough. On page 220 the third line up from the subhead in the second column belongs as the seventh line from the bottom.

And what did Trotsky have in mind in the words (last paragraph, page 221): "This is similar to someone who values original people setting himself the task of becoming original himself—naturally, he would not attain anything except the most wretched monkeyshines"? I think he meant to say that if God neglects to endow a person with originality, i.e., genius, he cannot make up the deficiency by banding together with kindred unfortunates to protest against the state of affairs in the party. I think he meant to say: "We had the same trouble but in spite of that we made a revolution. Just cheer up and do the best you can."

August, 1944

Received your No. 73 and No. 74, with the list of books ordered. It is not necessary to send Homer's *Iliad*; there is a copy here. Not necessary to bother with Schiller's poems if it is out of print; we have his *Wilhelm Tell*, that is enough. As soon as I get a chance I will make a complete check of all books received here and send you the list.

I don't think Mick and I will be disappointed with each other when we meet again next Christmas. We will both be a year older. That always makes some change. I am anxious to hear about her progress with her swimming lessons. I feel sorry for the poor kid—having to make her first acquaintance with the water in the big, impersonal ocean. Turkey Creek, where I learned to swim, was an intimate, friendly place with cool mud on the bottom to sink your toes in. It felt good. Besides that, we had a soft mud bank with a groove cut in it for a slide into the water. It was nice and slippery when we kept it wet.

*

Please let me know: 1) What was decided about our proposed expansion program; 2) What has been decided about the convention. It is quite important to give the practical program and the fund a *name*. The more I think about it the more my mind sets on $18,000 as the fund goal. That is quite a large sum to ask of the party. It is best not to ask too much, and better to err on the side of conservatism in financial matters.

I think the Chicago inquiry on finances should be handled fundamentally. The answer should be made to the party as a whole at the convention. It is a good opportunity to explain again the budget system of National Office accounting. Thanks to this, the party functions better in a business sense than nine-tenths of the projects of "free enterprise"; keeps out of debt; enables all the departments to develop symmetrically; makes it possible to plan work ahead and to avoid sudden crises and emergency appeals.

These are new features in the organization of the radical workers' movement in America; most likely elsewhere too. This introduction of planning, system and discipline into the financial management of the party was not attained all at once, and not without effort. We first had to cleanse the party of the petty-bourgeois opposition before we could overcome the irresponsible bohemianism which they expressed in all fields, from politics to housekeeping. Purposeful Bolsheviks, on the other hand, cannot tolerate any kind of sloppiness or hit-and-miss drifting and waiting for something to turn up.

Neat, clean and well-ordered headquarters and offices and well-managed finances are by-products of the political victory of Trotskyism in the historic party struggle, and not unimportant ones either. The Chicago inquiry offers a good occasion to explain our financial system once again to the party, and the party members will gladly hear it. Like all serious workers they appreciate good management. They will readily understand why the British trial expenses, which were not provided for in the budget, had to be met by a special fund in order not to upset the budget and interfere with coordinated plans based on it.

The convention should receive a roundup financial report of party finances in general and of the fifteenth anniversary fund in particular. A breakdown of this fund into its various allocations and the way it was used by the various departments—an exposition of their work in terms of dollars and cents—would be a good introduction to the proposal for a new expansion fund.

LETTER 80

SANDSTONE, AUGUST 4, 1944

The following two books are requested: 1) *Citizen Tom Paine* and 2) *A Rebel in Thought* by Mrs. Colvin (Island Press). This latter is the autobiography of a St. Paul woman, friend of Grace, etc.

*

A small item from the Associated Press reports the filing of the pardon petition in today's *Minneapolis Tribune*. I suppose we will get further information.

We all want to know who is Kovalesky.

The front-page cartoon this week (July 29) was not so well liked but the inside-page cartoon of the donkey and the elephant is thought to be *perfect*. Perhaps the artist can explain to us why we reacted so differently to the two cartoons.

R.J. Thomas, in his letter to Kay, says the National CIO supports our case. Has there been some official declaration to this effect? It seems to me that this lead should be followed up by making *indirect* inquiries first. A *direct* inquiry to Murray might bring an unfavorable answer.

I am deep in the study of *The Loom of Language*. It is going to be a great help to me in my further studies of languages. A very good book on its subject which, incidentally, contributes a useful item to my contemplated study of pedagogy in general.

The financial report of the CRDC is very interesting. When we were first indicted we didn't dream that people would pay $40,000 for us.

I got the snapshot of you on the porch and am waiting for the others you promised in your letter of July 24.

I think I suggested once before that *The Militant* and *FI* should be sent to the radical emigré groups in Mexico. It would be advantageous for our press to be widely circulated in these circles. Has anything been done about it?

＊

The excellent reports from Seattle about the Stalinists and the Quakers came in the midst of a discussion we have been conducting on the subject of *broadening* the news treatment of *The Militant*. This arose from the project of developing *The Militant* as a really big national weekly dominating the progressive labor field. We should print *news* about all progressive, dissident tendencies and be alert to publicize all infringements on democratic rights. The reports from Seattle seemed to punctuate our discussion.

We think it would be feasible to print now some round-up informational articles on the conscientious objectors in this war; how many in jail; what opinions and tendencies they represent; what their experiences and demands are; etc. Muste, at the Fellowship of Reconciliation, could give you or put you on the track of all the necessary information. Such reports should be written objectively, as a matter of news of interest to many progressive-minded people, without polemics against them—in the articles, I mean.

Our propaganda, in my opinion, can be more effective if it is a bit more subtle in some respects. It should be our aim to make *The Militant* the recognized leader and best and most reliable source of *news* of general interest to dissident and generally progressive circles.

I think we should also take up the case of Jehovah's Witnesses. Run a series of informative articles about this persecuted sect which has *hundreds and hundreds* of its young men in prison in the U.S. The *statistical* side of this story alone is well worth telling. All other papers neglect them.

LETTER 81

SANDSTONE, AUGUST 7, 1944

I received your No. 75 and No. 76 with the snapshots. It is a good picture of a trio plumply pulchritudinous, at ease. I didn't recognize you in the dim light and wondered who the rather ample, well-contoured dame in the corner might be—I am still mildly interested in such things—until I read the letter and then scrutinized the picture more closely. Mick looks like a sun-baked gypsy, and Walta looks like her mother and your daughter.

＊

I wish you would make arrangements with Sylvia to copy my letters so that I can have them for easy reference when I come home. My space is so limited that it is hardly possible to elaborate any idea properly in these letters. Most of my thoughts can only be expressed as brief and inadequate notes. Many of them I will want to develop further when I have more time and space. I don't want my numerous proposals and suggestions to the party to be lost, either.

In a discussion this morning we were remarking that our thinking here is a rather complicated process which ends in midair. One first goes to the trouble of thinking and formulating an idea on a given subject. Then it is discussed with others and perhaps changed, modified or supplemented as a result of the discussion. Then one takes the trouble to write it down in a letter—and that, as a rule, is the last we ever hear of it. It is something like dropping a stone in a void and waiting to hear it hit bottom.

*

When Joe gets back from his present trip I wish you would ask him and Usick how they feel about going in with me on the "secretariat" project. If they are agreeable, I will write in detail my conception of the functions of this institution and its methods of work as a literary factory based on cooperative labor, and will suggest some undertakings upon which preliminary work can be started. The method I will propose represents a big advance over handicraft production.

In my opinion the pre-convention period must be the occasion for a real, that is, a Bolshevik discussion. In other words, a full and free discussion which leads to a decision by the party. The leadership should not only welcome and encourage the free expression of dissenting and critical views; it must not tolerate the game of avoiding discussion of disputed points at convention time in order to keep it going the rest of the year. In such cases the NC should take the initiative.

*

I understand that the Chicago branch has become a forum for unrestrained criticism of our "trade-union policy." I don't think their criticism has any merit, but it can serve very well as the takeoff point for a thoroughgoing pedagogical exposition of this question which can be very useful to the party, especially to the new members. It appears that more clarification is needed.

We must begin with precise definitions, distinguishing between our trade-union *policy* in the broad sense and our methods of work in the *tactical application* of the policy under illegal or semi-legal conditions in the trade unions.

Most of the criticism directed ostensibly against our policy is really aimed at our methods of work under present conditions in the unions, at the strict regulations and restraints imposed by the party on its fractions in the unions. The discussion will be all the more illuminating if we can agree in determining the nature and the limits of the disagreement. As far as I know, no one has challenged the broad lines of our trade-union policy in wartime—attitude toward the war, the government, the bureaucracy and the employers; AF of L and CIO; strikes, etc. (More Tuesday.)

LETTER 82

SANDSTONE, AUGUST 9, 1944

I can't find any error in my numbering. Check back a little and see if I didn't use the same number twice.

Again we liked the inside-page cartoon better than the front-page one. Can it be that the artist feels more at home in dealing with national politics?

❋

Who is the "J.M." who writes from Chicago about the two-party system? Just judging by his lack of manners alone I would take him to be an over-educated college boy who "majored" in "iconoclasm."

There are differences in the Republican and Democratic parties, in my opinion, though not in the sense that J.M. takes as his point of departure—that the Republicans are more "reactionary" than the Democrats. This is an illusion entertained by many workers and fostered by the bulk of the labor bureaucracy, the Social-Democrats, and the Stalinists. *The Militant* does well to center its fire on this illusion; this is the main point, and should be the burden of our agitation. Big capital rules through the mechanism of the two parties as far as fundamental issues are concerned, but not always directly in response to their unanimous commands.

There are deep conflicts of interest as well as differences of opinion in the ranks of the capitalists. The two parties, which are in reality two big factions of a unique two-party system united on fundamentals, and the numerous factions and cross-currents within them, reflect these conflicts and differences. The big capitalists on the whole are more class conscious than the workers, but they are by no means omniscient in judging their own political interests. They don't always know what is best for them; and as *The Militant* correctly observes, they are not notably grateful to politicians who have served them best in a given situation.

These Oliver Twists always cry for more with an animal instinct. And they are not a bit squeamish about their methods of getting it. Their ruthless criticism, obstruction and sabotage of the Roosevelt administration—undeterred by the plaintive bleats of the "liberals" and labor fakers that they were hurting the "war effort"—have to be understood as methods of pressure to compel Roosevelt & Co. to do things their way.

It is not an unreasoning "opposition," as the labor fakers represent it. Results have shown that their brutal "opposition," which put Roosevelt in his place as their servant, has been far more effective than the lackey-like support of the labor leaders offered to Roosevelt as the master. Why should he pay for support that he can get for nothing?

The classes are not homogeneous, and neither are the two big class parties. There are differences of origin—this ought to be the starting point in the analysis of every organism—differences of tradition, composition, sectional interests, political machines with their own special interests to serve, different techniques and methods of demagogy to hold various strata of the population in line. These are important factors worthy of notice by the political analyst. But one can lose his bearing entirely if he does not recognize their secondary character.

They complicate the political situation in which the big capitalists have to manipulate the masses in order to assure their firm rule. But in the absence of an independent class opposition on the political field they will continue, as in the past, to solve the problem without too much difficulty.

What is their fundamental method? It is the *two-party system*. Which party do they support? They support *both*. And what is even more important, both parties support them in all *fundamental* questions. It could not be otherwise under the present political scheme.

The petty bourgeoisie (including the farmers) *cannot* play an independent role in politics; and the workers—under the Murray-Green policy—have *renounced* it. In this situation the presidential election becomes a diversion and a safety valve, not a class fight. I would like to see this question treated in an *FI* article.

LETTER 83

SANDSTONE, AUGUST 11, 1944

Continuing from August 7 letter: Our first dispute over tactical methods of working in the trade unions was with some Detroit comrades. The last convention settled that quite definitely. While some sectarian tendencies and a rather formalistic approach were to be discerned in the position taken by the Detroit comrades, the main point at issue was the estimation of the temper of the masses and the immediate perspectives, as well as the strength of the reaction, in the first period of the war.

They took too lightly the general *acquiescence* of the workers to the policy of Washington, even though their support lacked enthusiasm, and the strength of the combination arrayed against them—the government, employers, bureaucracy and Stalinists. The masses sensed much more accurately what they were up against and moved much more slowly and cautiously than the Detroiters expected. It is easy to see now how severely the party cadres would have suffered had they not been restrained by the party leadership from premature, self-isolating actions. The Buffalo experience alone is sufficient proof of that.

At first glance some comrades may have been inclined to identify the Detroit criticisms with the tactical line recommended to us by the WP, and practiced by them in certain instances where they have some members in transit through unions. In my opinion there is not much basis for such a comparison. Sectarian radicalism is not in the nature of petty-bourgeois oppositionists where action is concerned. And as for such things as reasoned perspectives and a serious analysis of the relation of forces—these have not yet entered into the thinking of the *Labor Action* exponents of journalistic trade unionism.

Their so-called trade-union policy is simply the expression of the impatient moods of visitors who don't expect to stay long and sink roots in the unions, and want to make a splurge and provide some newspaper copy before they are thrown out. It is a policy of irresponsible adventurism which is good only to sacrifice militants needlessly and thus to facilitate the work of the bureaucracy in housebreaking the unions.

Lately we have heard a third criticism of our trade-union tactics and practical methods of work emanating from a section of our Chicago branch. It would be false to identify this criticism with that made by the Detroit comrades prior to the last convention. In my opinion it borrows rather from the jitterbug philosophy of the WP; is, in fact, an echo of it. Their demand that we "do something" without specifying precisely what, and their complaint that "our policy is not consistent," show that they have not bothered to analyze the problem which presents itself in different forms in different unions and which must be worked out concretely in each case.

Our general trade-union policy, as unfolded in full scope in our press, has been completely consistent since December 7, 1941. And, as far as I can see, it has been 100 percent correct. It could not be applied in practical work uniformly in every union because each and every union presented different practical problems. The "law of uneven development" works in this field also.

The demand for "consistency" is the demand for a universal formula that will not work out in real life. We must keep our broad general conception in mind as a guiding line and apply it as best we can in each situation. (More of these notes later.)

LETTER 84

SANDSTONE, AUGUST 14, 1944

I did not receive your No. 79. This must have contained the information about the Cassidy document which we have been awaiting. Please check and see that I get this. I don't mean for you to send quotations from others as a substitute for your own letters. Write more.

❋

We have read and discussed O'Neal's and Morrison's letters in relation to the ideological struggle which seems to be taking shape rapidly. It seems that inexorable social impulses are once again driving some people blindly to a break with us. So strong are these impulses that they do not permit their captives to halt, to think and consider the objective logic and the unavoidable consequences of their course. On the contrary, they seem to be impelled, without even waiting for our return, to precipitate the conflict in the party ranks artificially and prematurely over issues and incidents which, in themselves, must impress the membership as rather trivial.

How unthinkingly they appear to follow on the path previously taken by Burnham and Shachtman! The last party plenum, with the sudden intrusion of an unheard-of issue, was a reenactment of the famous "July Convention" of 1939. The present manifestations, coinciding with the windup of the present war in Europe, parallel the hysterical outburst which greeted us at its inception. If we have learned anything from the past experiences, we may anticipate the early submersion of the incidental disputes which appear so uncalled for, so puzzling in their irrationality and violence, so difficult for the uninitiated party member to understand— in a thoroughgoing ideological struggle over the most basic principles, which will be clear to all.

The task of the responsible party leadership is to think the problem through to the end; to see what is coming and prepare for it. Before making decisions on single and incidental questions which arise, we must come to an understanding and agreement on our analysis and lay out a broad line of strategy which looks ahead. The day-to-day decisions will easily fall into place once the nature of the problem and the objective we are aiming at are agreed upon.

Every decision must be made politically, with cold deliberation. We are thinking about the problem in its most fundamental aspects, and will transmit our views in a number of letters. We believe Moish and his friends should do the same. Let us have a clear mutual understanding on what the situation is and what we want.

Since you asked me to answer concretely about the O'Neal letter, I will digress from the main theme to give you our views. This letter lays the whole absurdity of the latest reaction against Bolshevism wide open, starkly and crudely. It is a temptation to publish the document and utilize the occasion to restate some fundamentals. At first, we were inclined to this procedure. More thorough consideration induced us to change our opinion. The recommendation which we have agreed upon in this case proceeds from our general concept of the problem as a whole and the best road to its solution. This, in our opinion, dictates the following decisions:

1) We should firmly resolve to settle this fight *inside the party*, as we did the last one, and not permit any outside interference or pressure to influence us. Still less should we tolerate the absurd presumption of anyone, inside the party or out, to "umpire" the struggle. We aim at a contest *in the party*, pedagogical in character, and an eventual decision *by the party*.

2) Our small, persecuted party, surrounded by enemies, must carefully guard its internal solidarity, the fierce, uncompromising loyalty and patriotism of its rank and file. Our party, in the present circumstances, can serve its own interests best by confining the discussion, especially in the first stages, to the *Internal Bulletin* and branch debates. This is also in the interest of any loyal opposition; a public discussion would serve to compromise them publicly and, perhaps, cut off their retreat.

3) The O'Neal letter, written without doubt at Cassidy's instigation, is such a painfully literal transcription of the documents of Morrison and Cassidy that the publication of his letter in our press, with the answer it deserves, would appear as, and would in effect be, a public attack on the views of our internal opposition. They could be expected to follow with a demand that their documents be published in

the press—an opposition of this kind instinctively and invariably seeks "public" support against the "rigidity" of the Bolshevik party membership—and, in the circumstances, some party members might sympathize with their demand. (I will continue from here Tuesday.)

LETTER 85

SANDSTONE, AUGUST 16, 1944

You and Grace will both be interested to learn that the allergy fakers finally got their hooks into me. Last Saturday night I started to take some sulfa tablets at the doctor's direction to speed up the too slow healing of my poor toes. Sunday afternoon I broke out in a rash which looked like the measles and by Sunday night I had a high fever with chills, shortness of breath and general debilitation and demoralization.

I checked into the hospital Sunday night and am still here. The treatment is rest in bed and a liquid diet—with plenty of water in addition. The fever is gone and the rash is abating. But I still don't feel very good. And my general state of mind is not improved by the bland explanation: "You are *allergic* to sulfa." How can that be if I don't believe in allergy?

*

To resume where I left off Sunday:

It is best to avoid this kind of an issue by deciding resolutely at the start to confine the discussion to internal channels, at least until our return. (We expect the discussion to be started in our absence and finished after we get back.)

4) From these considerations the O'Neal letter should be refused publication in our press. He should be told that we are discussing some of the questions internally and do

not want to anticipate the convention decision. His letter contains an implied threat to publish his letter elsewhere. In truth, it would not be at all out of place in the WP press. Let him publish it there if he wants to, and have no qualms about it.

The publication of the letter could not hurt us, but it could deal a nasty blow to O'Neal's own reputation. I should not like to see that if it can be avoided. From this point of view you may, if you see fit, tell him that I personally advise him to withhold his letter from publication for the time being. He should think it over a while longer and wait to see what our party looks like when we return. And you can tell him also that I offer him this advice out of friendship. (It is always sad to see a friend make a fool of himself as the dupe of others. But it might offend O'Neal's vanity to tell him I added this postscript.)

Now a word as to the two articles which ostensibly—but not really—have caused all the hullabaloo. We haven't seen Joe's article; only a few short quotations out of context have been available to us. But from the type of criticism which it has elicited, which cannot impress a Bolshevik seriously, we are inclined to judge that the article was all right *for the occasion*. When we see a fight going on we always take the side of the Bolshevik first and inquire about the formal causes later. That puts us in Joe's corner.

Frankel's article we have seen and carefully reread and studied since receiving O'Neal's criticism which, by the way, we heard before. (The trade-union part is Cassidy's invention.) We are ready to sign our names to every line of this article. It is an excellent employment of the Marxist method in the analysis and exposure of a politico-literary fake. Frankel's remarks on the trade-union question represent a most interesting and valuable extension of Trotsky's illuminating "trade-union analogy" which Shachtman unthinkingly adopted without realizing what a hole he was digging for himself.

This part of Frankel's article is a good example of critical and independent thinking which we recommend to the attention of all comrades, especially the youth, who wish to cultivate this valuable quality. In addition, we appreciate the *tone* of the article. That is the *right* way to write about renegades and charlatans. Our dispute with them is not a polite exchange of views between friends but a class fight. The tone is the man, as well as the style.

LETTER 86

SANDSTONE, AUGUST 17, 1944

I am grieved to hear about little Mick's sore foot. I think Walta was right to go in to have the doctor check it. Let me know further developments on this front. Tell Sweetums that I am wearing a sympathy bandage around my foot until hers gets well.

I am writing this from the hospital, but will go out tomorrow. My toes made good headway and are now in pretty good shape. So it seems that I got some good out of the otherwise unpleasant experiment with the sulfa. My philosophy teachers will be very disappointed with me, but on the toenail question I am a crass empiricist. I am convinced that burning ingrown nails with the electric needle is no good. How do I know? Because I tried it myself! I suppose Usick and Warde will shake their heads sadly at this deviation, but they will never be able to straighten me out as far as toenails are concerned. This boy from Kansas knows what he knows whether he learned it the right way or not.

Tell George not to bother about writing to me. From what you write I judge he is losing his sense of humor and proportion and did not understand that I was spoofing him about "independent thinking." Most revolutionists, I have sadly observed, get out of step with me when they begin to get old.

From what you have written to me, I gather that several of the others who used to have a certain spiritual communion with me and therefore knew the difference between irony and anger, are also beginning to get hardening of the arteries. When I get back to New York I am afraid I will have to cultivate a new group of friends among the younger members of the party. I can't stand old people. They give me the willies.

*

I received your letters No. 82 and No. 83. This clears up the mystery of the missing letter. Your numbering system is a good check, I must admit. However, I was disappointed not to get some factual information about the missing document—what theory of the affair is held and what investigation is contemplated—in which I am greatly interested, instead of the quotations from Shachtman—in which I am interested not at all. My opinion about the way to "answer" this great revelation follows logically from the general premise laid down in last Sunday's letter. That leaves no possible room to notice the incident in our press, still less to "answer" Shachtman there.

A good politician must think *first* of his own party, *first* straighten out things there and *then* speak to the outside world *in the name of the party*. Or, as Moish would put it: When you are in hot water you should first pull in your horns, settle the question in your own ranks, then speak to external enemies in the name of the party and unfurl your banner while standing on solid ground. Let Joe straighten out those metaphors, if he can.

*

I don't think it is feasible to send the resolution to me and then wait for our opinions, etc. That will take too much time. We are too far removed from events and our writing facilities are too circumscribed, and time is drawing short. The convention has already been delayed too long to extract the maximum value from its two greatest advantages: the enthusiasm of the party over the great sub campaign, and the *fact* that a convention is held in our absence.

The thing to do now is to finish the resolution, set the convention date and open the discussion before the idea of holding a convention before our return begins to lose its point. We don't need to see the resolution. All we care about is that it be written in the tradition which we have established with respect to party documents since August, 1940, when we had to go on our own, and that it be programmatically firm and written with *complete* political objectivity.

LETTER 87

SANDSTONE, AUGUST 20, 1944

Dear Walta,

If I were superstitious like my paternal grandmother, I would say that I was warned of Lorna's foot trouble by a bad dream the night before Rose's letter came. I dreamed that I had a sad homecoming. Rose and the baby met me at the station; I didn't see anyone else there. Rose looked very thin and sick, and Lorna was a bundled-up, sickly infant in her arms without the recognizable personality I know, and she didn't recognize me or seem interested in anything.

Not being superstitious, I attribute the dream to the distorted memory in my sleeping mind of a harrowing account I had just read of the famine days in Russia during the early thirties. Perhaps it is just that one should not be allowed to sleep forgetfully while there are hungry children in the world.

I am relieved to know that you took the baby to the doctor and that he prescribed a felt pad to shield her wound from the pressure of hard and rough surfaces. In addition, you should keep her off her feet, or at least try to, for a while. There is always danger of a "stone bruise" from a wound on the bottom of the foot. This was a rather common ailment amongst us when I was a boy, and it was never much fun.

We ran barefooted from the last day of school in the spring until the new term in the fall. That was fun, but we ran into plenty of foot trouble running wild over all kinds of rough territory. My boyhood memories are pretty well dominated by the recollection of running rusty nails in my feet, and stepping on thorns—there were plenty of real thorn trees on the Rosedale hills and they always seemed to grow best on the sides of paths through the woods; and stubbed toes—that is a mean business; and cutting my feet on broken bottles and tin cans in the alley; and stone bruises.

Modern city-raised kids miss most of that. But they miss some good things too, such as walking in bare feet on cool dirt paths in the shade; or walking on the hot rails of the railroad track to the swimming hole until the soles of the feet are almost cooked, and then jumping into the creek and letting the toes sink down into the cool slimy mud at the bottom. That was good; it feels good even now to think of it.

We never had a doctor for any of our minor troubles. I can't remember *ever* having a doctor throughout my entire childhood except the time they cut my thumb off. I remember sharply the time I had a bad stone bruise on my heel, caused, I presume, by running around on rough roads and rocks with the pressure of my weight on some unhealed sore or other. My mother put a flaxseed poultice on it, which was supposed to "draw out" the pain, and kept me in the house, that is, on the porch, for a few days.

I remember that it was very painful and kept me awake one night. This meant also that it kept my mother awake changing the poultice and reassuring me that the pain came not from the wound but from the poultice "drawing" it. I remember hearing her tell the neighbors next day, proudly, how bravely I had endured the pain without a whimper. She said she knew it must have hurt me because she heard me moaning in my sleep after I dropped off. That was a pedagogical trick of hers—to praise me for virtues she *wanted* me to have; first of all, stoicism.

LETTER 88

SANDSTONE, AUGUST 22, 1944

I wanted to add two more points to my comments on Frankel's article but ran out of space. There is never enough space to develop a thought properly.

1) It could have been shown that Shachtman's conception of dialectical materialism as of no special use in politics led him into error on the "trade-union analogy" he employed, just as it did originally in the fundamental question of the analysis of the Soviet state. To a certain extent this is implied in Harry's criticism, but an explicit elucidation would aid the education of the readers on the mainspring of Marxism—dialectics.

Journalistic impressionists, who are simply empiricists of the pen, habitually judge everything as it appears to them at the moment, in isolation from everything else and from its own past and future. This is all right for feuilletons, and is even entertaining at times, but for political analysis a more serious method is needed. Marxists begin the study of a social organism, such as a trade union, with its *origin* and then follow the process of its development, whether progressive or retrogressive, and note all quantitative changes which may have taken place in order to determine whether quantity has been transformed into quality. To be sure, this is a somewhat more difficult procedure—thinking, in general, is more complicated and slower than guessing and feeling—but in return it gives more serious results, especially in complicated political questions.

If Shachtman had learned to respect his dialectical method of thinking, he never would have ventured to apply the same superficial criterion to trade unions, which originate as class organizations of the workers, and Robert Ley's "Labor Front," which originated as the fascist substitute for trade unions which have already been destroyed by the fascists. Trade unions may be compared to each other; or the Soviet state, "a trade union which has taken power," may be compared to trade unions existing in more elementary stages of development; and this analogy, as long as it remains an analogy and not an identification, can yield fruitful results as an aid to thinking out and determining the present status and character of both. With the example of a trade union in mind we can trace the development of the Soviet state from its starting point and ask ourselves whether the changes remain quantitative or have become qualitative.

2) From that follows the next question, and the answer to it: Is destruction of the organism necessary or is reform possible? With the example of the degenerated workers' state in mind we can turn to such degenerated trade unions as the Hod Carriers and the Stalinist UE and ask the same questions. The answers to the questions in each case depend on the accuracy of the analysis. But the method of dealing with the problem is unassailable.

Shachtman is a stranger to this method, and thereby to the heart and core of Marxism. That is what induced him to *first* arrive at a negative position on the defense of the Soviet state and then, later, try to bolster it up by a *retroactive* "analysis" of the character of the state. He employs the same superficial method in his approach to the trade-union side of the "trade-union analogy." The results cannot be any better.

*

My space is up again. We are profoundly disturbed by the editorial on Warsaw. I earnestly hope it is an incidental error, not a new program.

LETTER 89

SANDSTONE, AUGUST 24, 1944

I received your No. 85 and No. 86 last night after a lapse of one week. Your No. 84, to which you seem to make reference in No. 85, was not received. I am still taking it easy and feeling not bad physically. My weight now is 163. This is twenty pounds less than I weighed at the time of the trial. I was down to 154 but began to gain again after I started the new diet.

*

I hope the comrades are arranging for a good and thoroughgoing discussion which will demonstrate once again that ours is the most democratic party in the world. At the same time the occasion must be utilized for the teacherly instruction of the new members in the principles and methods of Bolshevism.

By now we should understand the dialectic of factional struggles, and that they contain both good and evil. They always interrupt constructive work to a certain extent and discourage some people. On the other hand, if they are conducted properly, new people learn faster and more firmly in factional conflicts than at any other time or in any other way. If you bear down heavily on the educational side and try to reduce the negative features to a minimum, the party on the whole will gain from the experience, regardless of the further course of some of the individuals involved.

This was shown by the results of the fight with the petty-bourgeois opposition, which I believe was a model, despite the fact that it cost us nearly half of the membership and nearly half of the leadership, too. The party gained greatly in health and energy and self-confidence. Moreover, the improvement was noticeable from the first day after the split. This proves rather conclusively that the opposition of that time, despite its large size, was not really a part of the party organism but a parasitic tumor upon it.

I believe the present opposition is the same kind of a tumor, but a smaller one which may even be cured by lancing and draining without more drastic surgery. At any rate, the party is strong enough to try this experiment first, and to take plenty of time with it. At every test the party demonstrates that it is stronger than even we think, and we think it is pretty strong.

＊

I will not try to take part in the discussion, but I will continue to send you notes on certain points which others may put to some use. This is the first time in my experience that I have been compelled, or permitted, to stand at a distance from a party struggle and comment on it as an observer. This role has certain advantages and compensations but it is not ideally suited to my "temperament."

You may not know it, but all the [critical] letters which you refer to and quote from are circulated in Chicago; in other places also, I presume. Too bad the NC has no representative in Chicago upon whom it could rely to send accurate information and defend its point of view. It seems to me that there is still too much reliance on the "independent thinking" of the Chicago rank-and-file comrades to keep them straight, and an underestimation of the prejudicial effects of one-sided propaganda. Even Michaels, I hear, has been infected by the "free-thought" revelation. I think Kugie should be made a correspondent and provided with full information. (Your No. 84 just arrived.)

I saw the editorial in *Il Proletario* of Bari reprinted in *La Parola* (New York) August 19. This appears to be the authentic voice of the revolutionary opposition in the Italian CP. The Fourth International should turn its attention to them. There are its future cadres, not in the moth-eaten cliques of Russophobes. Without a correct position on Russia it would be impossible even to talk to these workers.

LETTER 90

SANDSTONE, AUGUST 27, 1944

I received your No. 89. If Mick's foot begins to hurt her, Walta should put a hot flaxseed poultice on it.

＊

The *FI* came yesterday evening. We opened the package eagerly, and found—the *July* issue! What a letdown! How could such a mistake have happened? I hope the *August* issue will come without too much delay. The paper comes sometimes on Saturday but more often on Mondays. It is the greatest convenience to get the paper Saturday to read over the weekend. Ask Reba to experiment with first-class *airmail*. Perhaps if the papers are mailed that way as soon as they come from the press we can count on getting them Saturday.

＊

On the convention: 1) I think the convention call should refer to it as the *eleventh* and that term should be used in all references to it. 2) To allow for thorough discussion of the *constructive side* of the convention as well as the disputed questions, be sure to allow enough time, perhaps by providing for four days instead of the usual three.

I have some more notes on the trade-union question but don't know when I will get to them. Did you read Lewis' article in *Collier's* about a month ago? It is interesting as showing a similarity between Lewis and Stalin. Lewis condemns strikes, and at least inferentially the high wages of the war-industry workers. It is a good example of the narrow-minded bureaucrat fiercely defending his own position, and in his own way, the interests of the labor organization (the UMWA) which he heads and on which his position is based, against the capitalists, while showing indifference and even hostility to other labor organizations. One could judge from his article that he is making an offer to the capitalists to sacrifice the interests of fifty million other workers if they will let his own union alone and grant it a few concessions which are necessary to maintain the position of the UMWA bureaucracy.

Stalin likewise offers to sell out the workers of all other countries, and even to collaborate with the imperialists against them, in return for a truce with the Soviet Union. The nationalist, Stalin, is *Soviet Union*-minded; the provincial Lewis is *mine union*-minded. There is a certain difference, of course, but the analogy is clear. I think Frankel could write an interesting article on this theme for the *FI*.

❋

The "educational" counterthesis is not interesting to me, as it is all negation except for the insistence on independent and critical thinking. Since I myself have always been since my earliest childhood as independent as a hog on ice, and since the beginning of my conscious life strongly inclined to critical thinking, I cannot have any objection to anyone indulging these traits and recommending them to others. It is my opinion, however, that the example of our champions of independent and critical thinking lags far behind their precept.

They are so pathetically *dependent* on external pressures and influences that it is painful to observe. Perhaps without realizing it, they slavishly repeat what has been said by politically demoralized people before them, without even any independent variations, without a trace of originality.

To state the brutal truth, they only think they think. Their complaints and formulas are not the product of thought at all, independent or otherwise, but of moods and sentiments induced by intestinal and cardiac disturbances. These moods and sentiments impel them to blame others for their own weakness, their morbid pessimism and fear of the future.

LETTER 91

SANDSTONE, AUGUST 29, 1944

What was ever done about the expansion program we proposed many weeks ago? I am just going through your August letters to see if I neglected to note and answer anything before I file them away.

＊

If you can, dig up Trotsky's letter criticizing the old *Socialist Appeal* for its too literary brilliance and its lack of real worker writing (1939, I think). I wish you would send a copy of it to Kovalesky, and tell him I think the Old Man would approve of his column. Ask him, also, what he thinks of my thesis on party education. I am especially anxious to learn how my thesis has been received by the worker-communists. I don't care much what the educated people think about it.

It was not written for them, but for the ambitious workers who have been deprived of their rightful opportunities; a manifesto in their behalf.

I regret that Ruth Johnson's otherwise excellent article on Sacco and Vanzetti neglected to say that they were anarchists. The implication is left that they were communists. I think it very important for *The Militant* to take special care to be scrupulously fair and objective in relating the facts about any subject it deals with. This becomes all the more important as we strive to make *The Militant* the leading organ of progressive labor opinion and the recognized authoritative source of accurate information on all questions of general interest to this wide audience.

While Henry [Schultz] is in New York, Moish should talk to him about the project we discussed with him before our departure—the possibility of him replacing Don on the Southern assignment.

LETTER 92

SANDSTONE AUGUST 31, 1944

As soon as I finish sending some notes for Moish I will send my proposals on the "Literary Secretariat."

We are greatly relieved by the reassurance on the Warsaw editorial.

The news from Italy is most interesting, also most instructive. It confirms us in the opinions we held before:

1) The workers are a thousand times more revolutionary than the moth-eaten cliques of Russophobes who masquerade as "Trotskyists."

2) It is impossible to find an approach to the revolutionary workers without a correct position on the Russian question.

3) It is permissible to work with or even inside these cliques only long enough to consolidate a firm nucleus of our own.

4) *Unity* with any group that does not accept our position on the Russian question is a crime.

5) *Conciliationism* toward the petty-bourgeois opposition (in the U.S. or any other country) is a manifestation of political degeneration. Irreconcilable war must be declared against this tendency which, unfortunately, is beginning to make its appearance in our ranks.

6) It is most important to inform the [British] RCP fully of our opinions and secure their complete collaboration in all future developments in Europe.

*

I am eager to hear all about the branch expressions on the educational proposals. It is good to see the pre-convention discussion begin on this constructive line. This program, along with the rest of the expansion program and the proud record of achievements since our departure, gives the NC a great advantage over the defeatists and calamity howlers who want to blame the party for their own bellyaches. But it seems that the NC does not see the political implications of the new opposition as clearly as we do.

These people are burning their bridges behind them. They may not be fully conscious of it; they may not have thought it out—the trouble with professional independent thinkers generally is that they don't know how to think things out to the end—but the logic of the steps they have already taken and of the positions they have already committed themselves to is leading them directly to a break with us. We must be prepared for that and concentrate on the strategical aim of reducing the damage they can do us to the minimum.

The Chicago branch needs more attention from this point of view. I think Moish should plan to visit Chicago and camp there for a week or two, conduct some thoroughgoing discussions in the branch and prepare the solid elements for all possible eventualities. The Chicago comrades have been subjected to a solid barrage of one-sided propaganda for the program of leaderphobia, Menshevik concepts of organization, and conciliationism toward the petty-bourgeois opposition. It is time for them to hear the other side of these questions before they become so poisoned with prejudice and gossip that they will not listen.

The defection of Mike Michaels is a warning signal that the Chicago atmosphere is really unhealthy. It is wrong to assume that it is the same old Chicago situation. It is the old Chicago tendency enormously magnified and stimulated by direct encouragement from elements in the national leadership.

We should like to have a full report on the Michigan school when the New York delegates return. Also a report on the California school.

*

It is very chilly here today. Our brief summer is gone. This reminds me to remind you to be sure to get a good electric heater—not a little bathroom gadget, but a good one—and tell Moish to make early plans for National Office heating.

September, 1944

We received the August *FI* last night. It is a welcome gift for the weekend. It is a very good issue and properly dedicated to the memory of the Old Man. This makes up, in part, for the editors' "oversight" last year. I believe Natalia will approve of this issue. We are glad to see the "Review of the Month" signed by the editors. It is insufferable to think of the magazine, which is properly regarded as the theoretical guide of our world movement, appearing or even seeming to appear as the personal organ of an individual. Such monstrous pretenses must never be tolerated again.

I have read nearly all the articles already (Sunday morning). First of all, as usual, I read the "Manager's Column." This reminds me to make a suggestion I have been thinking of for sometime. A new feature, "Pioneer Publishers' Notes," should be started in *The Militant*. Party activists, and many others, appreciate all these departments which give them a picture of what is being done on a national scale and what others are doing.

*

Simmons' [Swabeck] article is very impressive, a thoughtful treatment of the contradictory problem now arising in full scope in Europe. I believe the editors, both of the magazine and the paper, could study this article with profit, if for no other reason than the fact that it deals with the *contradictory* nature of the European problem in general and of Stalinist policy in particular; problems which exclude one-sided, impressionistic and subjective appreciations of the situation.

Simmons does well to remind us of *dialectics*. One really cannot do without them if he wishes to rise above the level of a mere political feuilletonist. We are curious to know who Ann Vincent is. She is evidently well informed on the subject she treats.

What is the press run of the magazine now? Of *The Militant*?

*

Despite your reports that Mickey is becoming more talkative while I am more taciturn than ever, I have no doubt that we will continue to understand each other. I think of her and miss her all the time; partly for herself, I guess, and partly because she represents the future which will be better than the present.

*

I think your suggestion of a name for the fund is about right. But it should be amended to read: "$18,000 *Party* Expansion Fund"—to make it more precise and more rhythmical. The departments for which the fund is destined should be indicated, but the amounts should not be specified. The NC must keep a free hand to determine how the money is to be allocated.

Don't you think it would be a good idea to invite Simmons to participate in the preparatory work of the convention, especially in the discussion at Chicago, and in the convention itself? The Chicago situation continues to disturb us more than anything else. We are not thinking of "premature measures," or "measures" of any other kind—just the contrary—

but we think the situation there must be correctly appraised in order that the political struggle against an obviously unhealthy tendency may be properly organized.

Of course, it is not only, or even primarily, a question of Chicago alone. We have a *conciliationist* tendency crystallizing into a faction in the party, and also aiming at a similar crystallization in the International. In Chicago, this faction has created an organizational base and lined up some inexperienced comrades by the traditional methods of petty-bourgeois politiciandom: gossip, prejudice and the exploitation of personal grievances and frustrations. Left to itself, this situation will grow worse, not better.

LETTER 94

SANDSTONE, SEPTEMBER 5, 1944

I finally finished the fourth volume of Grote [*History of Greece*]. He is a very prolix writer and I get impatient with his meandering around so long before he comes to the point.

✳

I digressed awhile and did some undisciplined reading during the August "dog days." I read *The Dream We Lost*, Freda Utley's book about Russia which was touted so highly by all the disillusioned people. She is an educated Englishwoman with a British middle-class liberal background who became enamored of the Russian Revolution at the period when the Stalinist decline was already in full swing; married a Russian non-party "spetz" in the London "Arcos"; went to Russia; lived there about five years; had some very bad personal experiences during the first Five Year Plan—her husband was swallowed up in one of the purges—and then returned to Western civilization as a repentant British liberal.

She didn't know it, but that is all she ever was. She tells a harrowing story of hunger and terror. I don't doubt that every word of it is true, but she understands nothing fundamentally about the revolution or the causes of its decline. But a little detail like that couldn't stop her and hundreds of others from pontificating about it.

*

I read *Characters of the Inquisition* by a writer named Walsh. This is a Catholic apology for the "Holy Office" which dealt with dissenters by other means than prayer and good works 600–700 years ago. Those who expressed doubts about the infallibility of the Pope were simply arrested, starved in prison, tortured on the rack and then burned at the stake. I thought when I was reading this horrible book: What a hard way man has traveled, and has yet to travel, before he reaches the fraternal society of the free and equal for which he is destined!

*

Now I am back on my regular study schedule, and am slowly reading *My Life* [Trotsky's] in the brief periods of spare time I have. It is a political autobiography, but hardly a personal one. The Old Man is too reserved, too preoccupied with his struggle, to tell much about himself. One can get glimpses of Trotsky, the man, with his human contradiction, only by what he reads into the book; not by what is written there.

Strangely enough, nearly all those who came into personal relationship with him in the intimacy of his household feel impelled to write, more or less, in the same impersonal political way, as though bound by the pattern of Trotsky's own memoirs. In the brief contacts I had with him I sensed something of his personality as a man, something of his human weakness and need, of his overeagerness to seize upon anyone who might be able to lend a hand. Sooner or later, a biographer with real insight will undertake the task of writing the life of Trotsky, and he will not be content with the source material Trotsky himself has written (in *My Life*) nor with the appreciations of him written by others in the same impersonal spirit. I hope he will be able to find more of the other kind of material than we now know of.

*

I am afraid the way they ran things in the first days after the conquest of power, as reported in Chapter XXX, would not have met with the approval of the present critics of our NC, who don't understand any difference between leadership and the bureaucratic leader *cult*. Lenin and Trotsky always had their way. When they were agreed no one wanted to oppose them. "Not because the others were afraid to oppose us—at that time there was no sign of the present practice of keeping in line with your superiors and of the revolting fear of compromising yourself by an inappropriate word or vote—but because the less the bureaucratic subservience, the greater the authority of the leadership."

A leader *cult* cannot be maintained without *compulsion*. But real leadership has no need of it.

LETTER 95

SANDSTONE, SEPTEMBER 7, 1944

We have devoted quite a bit of discussion here to the question of how best to *begin* the necessary ideological struggle against the new opposition. We must keep in mind all the time that almost *one-half* of the present party membership have been recruited since the split with the petty-bourgeois opposition. This means that they have never had the experience of an internal party struggle; the great majority of the new members have had no previous political experience of any kind. On the other hand, the other half of the party are so familiar with the stale arguments of the opposition, and so hardened against them, that they may be impatient with the discussion. This sentiment, which would be quite understandable, could nevertheless lead us astray.

We must adapt ourselves to the other half—to the new members. The task there is to explain, or as Lenin would express it, to *patiently* explain. The task is pedagogical. We must show the new members what the fearsome "methods" of Bolshevism really look like in practice; how far removed they are in life from the way they are described by superficial critics; how organizational methods are made to serve political and pedagogical ends, not substituted for them.

In addition, we must remain acutely aware of the international movement. Here also we must teach the less experienced by example. We must not let the opposition have a single plausible ground to appeal for sympathy to foreign comrades on secondary issues. It should be our deliberate policy to remove each and every one of these minor grievances by sweeping concessions, in order to clear the way for a discussion of the political issues which are expressed or implied in the tentative platform of the opposition.

In Chicago, we are informed, where the discussion was opened without waiting for the formality of the convention call, the disciples of Morrison and Cassidy presented four grievances to prove the existence of bureaucratic tendencies in the leadership.

1) The censure of the four comrades in New York.
2) The suppression of an article by Gerland.
3) The suppression of an article by Morrison.
4) The hostile reaction of the National Office to their de-

mand for a financial accounting.

We believe this provides the occasion for the NC to issue a statement which will serve to force the discussion over onto broader grounds, somewhat as follows:

1) The NC will recommend to the New York local that it *rescind* its vote of censure of the four comrades in order to clear the road for a discussion of the *political* issues of party loyalty and party responsibility without the intrusion of organizational grievances.

2) It was previously decided to publish Gerland's article on *Capital* in the *Internal Bulletin*. However, in order to avoid a discussion which would divert attention from more important issues, the NC has reconsidered its decision and decided to publish the article in the next issue of the *FI*.

3) *All* controversial articles submitted by Morrison, Cassidy or any other party member will be promptly published in the *Internal Bulletin;* it is not in the party interest, *at the present time,* to conduct the discussion in our press.

4) A complete, detailed, financial report of the NC and of all party departments will be presented to the convention.

If the critics say, as they most likely will, that these decisions were "forced" by their criticisms, the answer is obvious: "These decisions are meant as *concessions* on the organizational side in order to clear the road for a discussion on the political side which will be more instructive for the membership. If you have any more 'grievances' let us know what they are. We will most probably concede them too."

We believe the Old Man would advise us to proceed somewhat along this line. The "censure" in New York served to start the debate on the wrong basis. We must first clear up the principle involved before resorting to disciplinary measures. The concessions will cut the ground from under the opposition. The new members will be reassured.

LETTER 96

SANDSTONE, SEPTEMBER 10, 1944

I guess I was so interested in the subject of my last letter that I forgot to mention that I wrote it from the hospital. This time it was for a head cold. After two days rest in bed I was turned out in pretty good shape. I am still sniffling a bit, but otherwise seem to be OK. The weather turned quite cold here.

I am glad you are able to stay on at the beach until the end of the month. Perhaps there is a curative power in the sun. I read some interesting chapters on this theme in a book by De Kruif at the hospital. I got plenty of sun in my early boyhood, but since then have been more or less a "shade-loving animal." Perhaps I stored up enough sunshine in the first thirteen years to carry me through the next forty-one of irregular living and artificial light. I think you all will like Ann. New York will be a new, strange world for her.

❋

We have to begin thinking concretely of relief for Don and De. Henry and Dorothy would be the best but they seem to have too many family obligations. It is a very difficult problem, but a way must be found to solve it.

I would like to get more detailed information about the school in Michigan. How was it financed? I hope we can get away from the tuition system in our educational work. Education should be *free* for party members. Also wish to know what the conference was about and what the *political* results were.

❋

I understood that the Bari paper was not ours. The thing that interested me was the report of an opposition

in the CP. The Bordigists are a very dogmatic, very sectarian group; at least, they were when I last heard of them
a dozen years ago. But still they are very probably much
better material than any European Shachtmanite group
could possibly be.

These people are not, and never were, genuine revolutionists. When they were associated with us, and bound to
a certain extent by that association, they were able at times
to exhibit a simulacrum of Bolshevism. But it was never in
their blood. Shachtman showed his real self in the split, as
he had shown it in the crisis ten years before; and as he had
always shown it in little things which are so often the surest test of character.

*

I hope the debate around the question of "democratic
centralism" is not allowed to *revolve* around the questions
of formal discipline and the right of comrades to "discuss"
with other people, including members of opponent parties,
which we allegedly are "afraid" to permit. The question is
the *concept of the party* and what flows from it. Democratic
centralism is not a method for any kind of an organization
but for one of a *specific* type; i.e., the Leninist *combat* party.
Such a party needs *discipline* and *loyalty.*

A discussion club has no need of discipline; it only needs
a subject for the current debate, and people who really want
that kind of a party should not pretend to be in favor of
discipline. For that matter, a discussion club has no need of
loyalty, either. The glaring contradictions in the position of
the freethinkers can be easily seen by the new members of
the party if the debate is not permitted to shift away from
the central proposition: *What kind of a party?*

Formal discipline by itself cannot make a Bolshevik out of
anybody. A voluntary party like ours can be held together
only by common agreement on program and the means to

realize it. At bottom, objections to discipline spring from disagreement or doubt on these two propositions.

LETTER 97

SANDSTONE, SEPTEMBER 12, 1944

The intervention of Morrison on the matter of the O'Neal letter marks a new stage in the development of this shining champion of "democracy" unlimited; more correctly, in the open manifestations of a basic attitude somewhat restrained heretofore by the pressure of party public opinion, tradition, etc. The real significance and logic of this new demand will not be lost by those party members who learned something in the past and remember what they learned. The doses of Morrison's medicine progressively increase in strength, like drugs to which the human body, reacting against an alien substance, must adjust itself by degrees.

First, we heard that the right of the party to know about and control the external political activity of its members does not apply in the case of formal discussions with traitors. That was a strong dose to start with, but we soon learned that it was only a starter. Next, we learned that any criticism of plenum decisions, even by one minority member, must be immediately communicated to the ranks and a discussion opened, regardless of any exceptional circumstances such as the departure of the previously functioning central leadership, the need of the substitute leadership for a little time to get their bearings and get acquainted with their tasks, etc. That was a still stronger dose of the new dope.

But right after that, we are now informed that our press *must* be opened, in the middle of an internal discussion, to the critical contributions of a non-member who has taken the most explicit pains in the past to make it clear to the public that he is "not a Trotskyist" and is quite obviously seeking a new pretext to give a new public demonstration of his freedom from that taint.

But what if the article in question is at bottom nothing but an attorney's brief for clients who are badly in need of a lawyer—the petty-bourgeois splitters who have had such poor success in their attempt to destroy our party? This presents no problem for Morrison. He simply labels the venomous attack of O'Neal "a friendly letter by a friend" and thinks that suffices for the likes of us. This is adding insult to injury. It is something like a cynical doctor saying in the presence of a patient who is still conscious, if somewhat groggy from previous "medications": "Give him a shot of arsenic this time. Tell him it's ambrosia and the damn fool won't know the difference."

Morrison's *demand* for the publication of the O'Neal letter puts the issue, as we have previously discussed it, on another footing. There was no good reason for us to publish the letter. But now the internal discussion is opened, and *Morrison* wants to publish it—with an endorsement of its "friendly" character. We have no reason to doubt that he will publish it in any case. That is his "right" in the pre-convention period. We cannot stop it. But, even more important, we should not even think of trying to stop it. We are confronted with an ideological and political conflict. Now is no time for us, of all people, to quibble with anybody about organizational forms, well-known rules, etc.

I hope we have all learned, and I hope we will teach others in this conflict, that organizational forms and methods must always be subordinated to and made to serve political ends. That is the only rule of organization we never change. The political end in this case is: education of the new members and hardening of the old in an absolutely free and unrestricted internal discussion. We favor printing O'Neal's article in the *Internal Bulletin* with a *note* saying it is published only because Morrison demands it, and printing his letter [making the demand]. I think the party will learn something from this episode.

LETTER 98

SANDSTONE, SEPTEMBER 14, 1944

Our opinion on the demand of Cassidy that you publish the various drafts of the plenum resolution is the same as our opinion on the latest demand of Morrison, which I stated in my last letter, and follows from the same premise. Of course, it is somewhat of an abuse of party democracy to demand the publication of preliminary *drafts* of resolutions as well as those finally adopted. Such a practice would tend to clutter up the *Internal Bulletins* and make it harder, not easier, for the members to get to the essence of the matter.

Almost every resolution undergoes some changes between its preliminary drafting by a subcommittee or a single individual of the PC and its final adoption in finished form by the full committee. There is nothing abnormal about that. Cassidy may not know it, but this is simply the practical result of the working of a democratic process in the collective leadership of the party.

By assigning to the NC as a whole the power to adopt resolutions, the party constitution provides the means for a subcommittee or an individual to accept correction and improvement in the preliminary draft, or in some cases, to change or modify opinions in the course of the debate. In that way we get better resolutions in the end. And that is also why the Leninist principle of democracy, *in the collective leadership* as well as in the ranks, gives better theoretical and political results than the Stalinist (and fascist) principle of one-man rule.

It is difficult to understand why anyone should demand the publication of all drafts as well as the final resolution unless he hopes to point out some errors or oversights for the purpose of discrediting the individual author or authors of the first drafts. I doubt very much that the party members will sympathize with such an attitude. They are apt to applaud rather than condemn an individual leader if it is shown that he learned something from the debate of the full plenum and finally voted for a better resolution than he was able to draft as an individual. Such a demonstration can only strengthen the party members in their confidence that the plenum of the NC really leads the party, and leads it more wisely than any individual or small group could.

The party has a great confidence, and I believe a not unjustified confidence, in its plenary leading staff and will look with disfavor upon any attempt to undermine it, to disrupt its solidarity, or to denigrate or disqualify individuals who demonstrate the capacity and the good will to work cooperatively.

*

We have no individual man or men of genius, but despite that we are strong. *Our strength is in our combination!* That is what the party members know and feel in their bones. That is why they have such great confidence in the leadership, a confidence which *no other party* even approximates. Let somebody break that combination if he can!

Cassidy, unfortunately, is not known amongst us either for his restraint or his capacity to think out and consider the consequences and implications of his proposals. In my opinion he is even lacking in that sense of scrupulous loyalty to communist colleagues which is the pride and glory of the leading cadre of our party and not the least source of its strength and solidarity.

In spite of that, we would let him have his way with this

exorbitant and unreasonable demand. Keep the debate on fundamental grounds; don't let it be shifted to side issues and trifles. Print everything he demands, even if it requires a special extra bulletin, but explain to the members *why* you are printing it and what you think about it.

LETTER 99

SANDSTONE, SEPTEMBER 17, 1944

We can agree to a compromise on our proposal for an eight-page *Militant* at $1.00 per year. If you will agree to make the eight-page paper a definite item of the expansion program, we can let the price of the paper remain unchanged until a further survey of the financial situation can be made after our return. To this sweeping concession on our part we add a small proviso: The proposal to change the format to that of a tabloid is to be ruled out of order and further discussion of the subject forbidden. Democracy is not anarchy, liberty is not license.

*

We have read Solly's encomiastic comments on Frank's work with mixed emotions. We have long had the opinion that Frank is a bright fellow. But is that any reason why he should be adulated? Isn't there a danger of the leader cult raising its ugly head? Besides that, shouldn't Frank himself come down with his heavy hand and put a stop to this chorus of praise before it ruins him?

Look at me. I was roundly abused, denounced and even slandered in print almost since the beginning of my political work, and seemed to thrive on it. Then a whimsical fellow named Hansen, tired of the monotony, decided to change the tune and wrote a few words of praise just for the hell of it.

And look at all the trouble it has caused me. I will probably never hear the end of it. It is always the unusual that attracts attention and makes news, as in the journalistic illustration, "man bites dog." Abuse is considered normal for a political leader and does him no harm, but praise can be fatal.

Take the case of Aristides, who was chosen archon of Athens in the year 480 B.C. because, as Grote tells it, "his exemplary uprightness in magisterial functions ensured to him lofty esteem from the general public." But his "incorruptible probity," says Grote, "procured for him, however, along with the general esteem, no inconsiderable amount of private enmity from jobbers whom he exposed, and even some jealousy from persons who heard it proclaimed with offensive ostentation. We are told that a rustic and unlettered citizen gave his ostracizing vote and expressed his dislike against Aristides, on the simple ground that he was tired of hearing him always called the Just."

The unfortunate Aristides was exiled from the country. Later he was allowed to return, but "he died very poor, and the state was obliged to lend aid to his children." I hope Frank will take this historical example to heart.

While I am on the subject of Frank, I will utilize the occasion to explain that my complaints against the failure to give memorial notice to the death of Professor Leonard were not directed at him personally, but at the editorial board. As a matter of fact, I had been under the impression from a letter received here that Frank was ill at the time. Also, by my reference to "fighting City Hall" I did not mean to offend my esteemed colleagues, and certainly not to identify them with the "office leaders" of odious memory.

I only meant to scare them by reference to a "horrible example," as the old temperance lecturers used to point to the rednosed drunkard, dying from hobnailed liver complicated with delirium tremens, in warning young men against the first drink. Perhaps my pedagogical methods are out of date. I learned them in an old school and they don't always work out under modern conditions. But even in such cases there is a way to retrieve the error. If I said too much I can always take a little back.

LETTER 100

I just finished reading *My Life* again. I get something new and interesting from every reading of this book.

＊

The pictures came out quite well. You and Mick look well, but Wong looks lonesome in one of the pictures.

I am deep in my studies again; the strict routine doesn't give me much time for anything else. I would like you to get French, Spanish and German records for me, also a *Cassell's German-English Dictionary,* so that I can continue my studies of the *spoken* languages without interruption when I return. (I have a French and a Spanish dictionary and will bring them home with me.)

Also—while I think of it—Mick should get a *calabash* pipe for me with a curved stem to smoke at her house. I never had a pipe of this kind, and always thought I would like to have one. I am going to bring her something nice— made in Sandstone.

＊

Naturally, free tuition for students at the summer schools cannot, at present at least, include free board. The point that interests me is whether the students at the Michigan school had to pay *extra* for tuition. My impressions of the *school* side of the Michigan affair are still quite vague. I would like to know the impressions of the educational director, but I seem to have great difficulty in getting any kind of direct, official and informative reports about anything.

Perhaps my annoyance springs from 1) my tendency toward critical thinking, my desire to *know* about things, what really happened and how, before forming definite opinions about them; 2) the fact that for a long time, when I was sitting in a different chair, I was accustomed to asking for reports of party activities and getting them promptly. Habits are not easy to break, for that requires *unlearning* which, as Aristotle and Wright say, is harder than learning.

*

The various proposals we submitted for the organization of the discussions naturally have to be taken as suggestions indicating an orientation, not as an ironclad program. The important thing is to see the implications of the issues that have been raised clear through to the end; to aim at a discussion that will educate and reeducate the party members and arm them for the future; and to realize that the cause of communist education can best be served by eliminating every possible obstruction, diversion and organizational side-issue from the discussion of the principles involved in the dispute. The detailed decisions must be made in New York to fit the circumstances.

I have no doubt that the pre-convention discussion is being well taken care of, and for that reason am content to stand aside from it. But there is no "meeting of minds" between us when you suggest that this may be a permanent role for me. You perhaps remember my favorite story about Gompers. The executive council of the AF of L once proposed to the old man that he retire from the presidency, with honors, and take it easy on a comfortable salary as editor-in-chief of the official magazine. "I'm not a writer," said Gompers, "I'm a fighter."

The old scoundrel *was* a fighter, that we must admit; and

died in harness as every fighter deserves to die. I showed your letter on this point to one of my pals here. His comment was even more laconic than that of Gompers. "No," he said. "That's against nature."

We haven't yet studied and discussed Natalia's letter very thoroughly. We will soon do so and give you our opinions. Perhaps we can make some suggestions useful for the *discussion* but not necessary in the *resolution*.

LETTER 101

SANDSTONE, SEPTEMBER 21, 1944

Has the CRDC made any inquiries yet about the unseemly delay in acting on our pardon application? Has *The Militant* yet taken notice of a series of incidents which may have a bearing on the case? These incidents which we have noted are 1) Tobin has lunch with the President, and his magazine then steps up its lynch campaign against us; 2) Biddle visits Minnesota and confers with Anderson, our prosecutor; 3) then he addresses the Minnesota State Federation of Labor Convention; 4) the convention adopts a resolution condemning the eighteen prisoners in the Minneapolis case.

✳

Point No. 50 in the resolution of the NC says Stalin has granted "state support" to the Greek Orthodox church. What is the meaning of this statement? We would like to know the authority for this statement. State support of a church has a definite meaning to us, and we are much interested to learn if some new concrete steps have been taken—we mean definite grants of state subsidy in one form or another, and similar material privileges to the clergy—which we have not heard about.

I hope, for our peace of mind, that the resolution is, on this point, based on fact and substance and is not simply loose journalistic expression without precise meaning. We *detest* "journalism" in general, and in political documents in particular, and we always boil with rage when we see any evidence of it in our press. (I hope, of course, that the report of "state support" is false.)

*

We read in *The Militant*, September 16, that the reports of the slaughter of 1,500,000 persons in one camp at Lublin "have been confirmed by *independent* observers." We have never doubted the inhuman brutality of Nazism, but we don't believe this story—the *1,500,000 part*, we mean— and we believe our press not only should treat any story coming from Stalinist sources with the utmost reserve, but also should look for the political implications of their lies. The atrocity propaganda in general must be regarded as the moral and political preparation for a harsh peace whereby the German masses will be indicted for Hitler's crimes.

We should not believe anything that is said in the war camps as long as we have no knowledge of the facts. Our task and our duty is to distrust all the propaganda of the enemies of mankind and to teach this distrust to the readers of our press. But what about the "independent observers"? I'll tell you what about it. To see such a queasy liberal journalist locution in *our* press just once had a bad effect on our blood pressure. We are bitterly opposed to the relaxation of standards even in an incidental article. We should never yield an inch to the slovenly mental habits which substitute impressionism for serious analysis and loose talk for precise statement.

Errors of this kind are perhaps unavoidable on the part of inexperienced writers—we are not blaming the author of the article in question—but *every* article should be ruthlessly edited from the standpoint of our established standards. Our terminological razor should be kept surgically clean.

While I am on this subject, let me mention that I saw the expression "management" used in a recent issue of *The Militant*. The right word is employers, or bosses, or blood-sucking exploiters. Terminology signifies *line*.

LETTER 102

SANDSTONE, SEPTEMBER 24, 1944

We waited anxiously for *The Militant's* account of the auto convention and were not disappointed when it came yesterday. It is uplifting to see one of our slogans [the sliding scale of wages] become the slogan of the masses, in this case the most dynamic section of the greatest power in the whole world—the American proletariat. Next will come the turn of the labor party slogan, and not long after that our military policy. It is difficult for one to be a pessimist when he sees the auto workers in convention. It is almost as difficult to have any patience with the critics of our trade-union policy when it begins to reveal its rightness.

The third paragraph of Art's [Preis] otherwise excellent report—a good model of *our* kind of journalism—contains a grave deviation on the grammatico-syntactical front. I refer to the elimination of the definite article at the beginning of the first sentence. For the sake of my personal relations with this estimable comrade who has lived right so far, I hope this is a printer's error and not an adventure in literary experimentalism on his part. Nowhere is it written—in no official resolution of the party or the Fourth International—that we demand either revolution or reform in the construction of the English sentence. All we want is the king's head; let the king's English alone.

Our artist's caricatures of the most prominent scoundrels are delightful. I only want to suggest one added touch to make the titles conform to the spirit of the drawings. The editors should omit the initials of the caricatured phonies and simply label them contemptuously by their last names, "Byrnes," "Curran," etc.

Also, that merciless caricature in last week's paper of some fathead pounding the air would make an excellent standing illustration for a weekly paragraph or so ironically reporting the alleged remarks of "Senator Mushmouth" or some such character. By the way, are you all taking good care of the health of our artist? She should be fed on milk and honey and put to sleep on balsam boughs.

*

We thought Stein's article a good thesis on the subject under discussion. His answer to Morrison will probably be conclusive for all those who have been educated in our tradition. It is really pathetic to see Morrison beginning *now* to formulate some "general rules" on organization procedure as if nothing had ever been thought or said on the subject before. But his new ideas are not at all new. They represent the conceptions of organization which were prevalent in the American radical movement prior to the First World War, that is, before any of the conflicting tendencies in the labor movement had been tested by war and revolution and before we had ever heard of Lenin and *his* theory of how to build a party. I will send you some notes on this and other related points.

For the half of our party members who have not learned and assimilated the methods of Bolshevism in fight, however, Moish's thesis—which takes much of this for granted—should be elaborated and explained in a number of separate articles. This discussion is a splendid opportunity to *educate* the new members and you must make the most of it.

All the leaders should contribute to this discussion. Let the discussion be a real one.

*

I think three days is too short a time for the convention. You need more time for the reports of practical work, for the organizational and financial report, and for detailed reports from the managers of the press and publications departments.

LETTER 103

SANDSTONE, SEPTEMBER 26, 1944

I finished Volume 5 of Grote and started on Volume 6. Am also reading O'Casey's *Pictures in the Hallway* and find it very interesting.

*

Aunt's [Natalia] letter draws attention to the accelerated pace of the Stalinist degeneration in the conduct of the war. The political policy of the bureaucracy is the most vulgar nationalism. There is abundant evidence on this side of the question, and the facts cited by Aunt add more concrete instances to fill out the picture whose outlines we have long known.

We do not know, however, what sentiments animate the Soviet masses in their unprecedented struggles and sacrifices. I personally am strongly convinced that the conquests and the memories of October play a bigger part than the Stalinist appeals to the past glories of czars and czarist generals. And I do not for a minute forget that the objective logic of the Red Army's achievements in the war against the Nazis, regardless of the officially declared aims, is profoundly revolutionary.

We know and we have always said that the Soviet Union cannot be carried through the transition period from capitalism to socialism without workers' democracy. That is the reason we call for the revolutionary overthrow of the bureaucracy and the reinstatement of workers' democracy. By this formula we sharply distinguish our position from that of the fetishists of democracy who regard it as an end. For us it is a means to an end, i.e., the construction of the socialist society by the creative efforts of the masses and international collaboration between them. We are no less convinced that the transitional period, which has assumed the form of a degenerating workers' state dominated by a nationalistic bureaucracy, cannot be "permanent" or even long-lived.

The fundamental alternative confronting the Soviet Union is and remains: Forward to socialism, or back to capitalism. By this formula we draw a line between ourselves and all the profound "theorists" of a new "bureaucratic class." We have less reason than ever to reconsider our conclusions on these two basic propositions. The bankrupt bureaucracy was capable of producing only the one evil which it promised to avoid, and to avoid which it sold out the international revolution—a war on Soviet soil. The "theory" of a new "bureaucratic class" interposing itself between defeated capitalism and unrealized socialism was given a certain superficial plausibility only by its bolder representatives, such as Bruno R., who assimilated the regimes of Mussolini, Hitler and Stalin into one homogeneous system.

The sorry fate of Italian and German fascism, after a brief rule of twenty years in one case and ten years in the other, seems to me to have knocked the props out from under Bruno R.'s "theory" of "La Bureaucratisme du *Monde*." It is not necessary even to speak of his halfhearted imitators and their anemic new, nationally limited "class of bureaucrats" in one country.

The national-reformist policy of the bureaucracy, in its degenerating course of reaction against the October Revolution, can only—unless the bureaucracy is overthrown—pile quantity upon quantity, and this in turn must at a certain point result in a qualitative change in the state inherited from the great revolution. I think we must look for signs of such a change in the field of Soviet economy. *Politically* the bureaucracy seems to have done all it can do to erase the revolution. By their politics they brought the Soviet economic system to the very brink of overthrow by Nazi militarism, and now leave it exposed, in a terribly weakened position, to the still mightier and as yet unspent military power of the Anglo-American bloc. (More later.)

LETTER 104-A

SANDSTONE, SEPTEMBER 28, 1944

Continuing: The same type of superficial thinking, characterized by the attempt to form political conclusions without reference to economics—the type of thinking which determined an attitude toward the Soviet Union in war without any prior estimation of its class character, which in another version lightmindedly assumed that the Stalin-Hitler Pact would be long-lasting because of the "affinity" of the two regimes—is now quite convinced of the durability of the Anglo-American-Soviet pact of Teheran. In reality, the irreconcilable conflict of economic systems completely excludes the possibility of an Anglo-American toleration of the Soviet economic system over one-sixth of the earth any longer than it is compulsory by reason of necessity, i.e., the relation of forces and the disunity in the imperialist camp.

If we leave aside the prospect of workers' revolutions in the capitalist states or such a state of unrest and insurgence as that which followed the First World War—and it is just these details that are omitted in all varieties of literary politics—then there is no room to doubt that an economic and, if necessary, a military offensive of the allies against the Soviet Union is predetermined as soon as accounts are finally settled with the Nazis and the Japanese; perhaps even before.

Of course, there are all kinds of difficulties and complications. But—again, if we eliminate the detail of workers' revolution—the only serious question is whether the required economic concession, opening up the Russian market to Anglo-American exploitation and thereby the overthrow of the Soviet economic system, is to be accomplished by war or by economic pressure and threats of war. Have such fatal concessions already been tentatively agreed upon? What was the real meaning of Eric Johnston's visit to the Soviet Union? There is ample ground for the deepest suspicion flowing from the inexorable logic of the situation, even if we disregard such surface indications. But so far we do not *know* of any basic infringements on the Soviet economic system made during the war, and we therefore have no reason to change our attitude toward it in its relation to the capitalist world.

On the other hand, we do know that the nationalized property system, permitting state planning and control (even though it is monstrously distorted and crippled by bureaucratic mismanagement and privilege), revealed an enormous power under conditions of war. We Trotskyists had more confidence in the vitality of Soviet economy than anyone else, including the conservative and cowardly bureaucracy, but all our calculations were far surpassed.

The results of the Soviet-Nazi war must have had profound effects on the Russian masses. We are shut off from every scrap of authentic information on this score. But how can anyone doubt that their self-confidence has been raised and that the returning soldiers will demand something from their victories bought at such a heavy price?

What will they do when the bureaucracy offers them nothing but a still more odious oppression and an even sharper division between the privileged caste and the mass of the people? We had better not assume prematurely that the Russian workers have said their last word. We had better wait and see what is going to happen before we even think of playing with the idea of changing or modifying our policy which, of all schools of thought on the Russian question, is the only one that turned out to be based on the realities of the situation; the only policy that stood up under the test of such a devastating war that, as Churchill rightly said, no other regime in history could have survived it. (More to follow.)

October, 1944

LETTER 104-B

SANDSTONE, OCTOBER 1, 1944

I finished Volume 6 of Grote and *Pictures in the Hallway*. This is the second volume of O'Casey's autobiography and nothing much has happened yet. These writers seem to take a lot of words to tell about themselves.

*

Continuing: Our "Russian" policy, however, is only one section of a complete program based on a fundamental class concept and a world view. Our active political slogans of the day must always be consistent with our general program and express *that phase of it* which has the greatest urgency at the moment. It is important always to keep in mind this subordinate relationship of active slogans to the program as a whole and not to identify the one with the other. Serious politics is impossible without a firm program of Marxist internationalism; those who dispense with this chart produce nothing, as we have seen, but speculation, guesswork and irresponsible experimentation.

We do not change our program. No amount of criticism and impatience can modify our "conservatism" in this respect. But to stand firmly by the program, naturally, does not authorize us to repeat the same active political slogans all the time with the same degree of emphasis. That would reduce the art of politics to memory work and, as the Old Man once remarked, make every sectarian a master politician. The art of politics consists in knowing what to do next; that is, how to *apply* the program of Marxism to the specific situation of the day.

We do not change any of our slogans insofar as they represent, each in its own way, the various sections of our complete program. But if we are alive to the complexities and quick changes in the world political situation as well as that at home, we must always be ready to change the *emphasis* with which we advance one or more slogans while holding others more or less in reserve as the situation may require.

We think Aunt's letter must be considered from this point of view. When the Nazi military machine threatened the destruction of the Soviet Union every communist had to put the slogan of the defense of the Soviet Union in first place. Those who denied this defense were then no longer comrades having a different opinion on a theoretical question, as Morrison still wants to treat them, as if nothing had happened, but people on the other side of the barricade with whom comradely arguments were out of season.

But this fight for the defense of the Soviet Union against Nazi militarism has been decisively won. The problem will most probably arise again, with another power in place of the Nazis, but that will take some time. The political reality of the present day is: The military, economic and moral collapse of the Hitler "new order in Europe" which some people, even in our own ranks, took far too seriously; the military occupation of the continent by Anglo-American and Soviet troops; the indicated beginning of a workers' revolutionary movement and the conspiracy of the imperialists to crush it with the active aid of the Stalinists. Our active slogans, the slogans which we put in first place and *emphasize* in all our agitation, must correspond with this political reality.

In our opinion there can be no question of abandoning

the slogan of the defense of the Soviet Union; in principle it retains all its validity and will most likely acquire burning urgency again at a later stage of events. But to continue to shout this slogan in the present situation would be the greatest political ineptitude, putting us out of tune with events.

All our *emphasis* now must be placed on the *defense of the European Revolution* against the conspirators. Our program gives us all the guidance we need, first to evaluate the problem theoretically, and on that basis to deduce the appropriate active political slogans of the day. (I will send some notes on this in my next letter.)

LETTER 105

SANDSTONE, OCTOBER 3, 1944

Is the CRDC planning a going-out fund for the comrades who go out October 20? Is a "Christmas Fund" being planned on the model established by the ILD in our day?

*

Continuing: As far as we can judge from recent issues of *The Militant*, the editors have been aiming to shift their emphasis to the new situation in Europe along the lines indicated in my last letter. But, as we have remarked some weeks ago, we think they got ahead of themselves in applying this treatment to the battle of Warsaw, the scene then—and still—of a major test of strength between the Soviet troops and the Nazi military machine. We don't like haste, impatience and jumpiness. Leave that to the literary politicians; we have no need of it.

Let us, rather, be a little slow, if necessary, but sure, in a complex European situation which is not going to be definitively resolved in a day or a year or, perhaps, for many years.

And, above all, don't be ambiguous. Don't try to answer in advance every "riddle" which the literary politicians may propound. We have the impression that *The Militant* is publishing too many formal statements "by the Editors" which are, in effect, programmatic declarations on new turns in the military situation, the contents of which are not fully known and are far from clear.

Nobody can justly blame us if we proceed slowly and cautiously in expressing ourselves categorically on far-off events taking place behind a thick curtain of censorship. I mean to say, no serious people will blame us. But on the other hand, it is hard to think of anything that can do more to undermine our authority in the eyes of serious people than the practice of going off half-cocked.

I don't know to what extent the supplementary resolution deals with the potentialities of the American labor movement in its analysis of the European situation. I should add also the British labor movement. This is most important, for the labor movement in the home countries of the victorious imperialists may well turn out to be the factor which undermines their grandiose schemes of a Roman peace to last, as Hitler dreamed of his own "New Order," for "a thousand years."

We should be careful not to project the European revolution as an apocalyptic event that will be over and done with in short order. We must see it rather as a drawn-out affair, uneven in its development, whose final outcome, however, can only be the victory of the workers. Despite any defeats and setbacks the workers may encounter—and we have no doubt there will be many of them—we still will have no reason to believe in the viability of capitalism or the possibility of creating a new slave society more productive than capitalism as the historical alternative to socialism.

All the bourgeois thinkers are convinced that great revolutionary upheavals are on the European agenda, but they imagine that military force, plus the help of Stalin, will suffice to deal with them. They cannot, however, rejuvenate the ruined economy of Europe. On the contrary, every plan they devise is more reactionary than the preceding one and, consequently, more revolutionary in its implications. They cannot restore Britain's ruined foreign trade, and they cannot by one quarter satisfy the Moloch demands of America for markets and fields of investment. The perspective is revolutionary in the victor countries as well as in the vanquished. (More.)

LETTER 106

SANDSTONE, OCTOBER 5, 1944

I am interrupting the notes I have been sending you about Stalinism and will resume in my next letter. Here I wish to send you some impressions "In Defense of Daniel J. Tobin." Please file them in my "Notebook" folder.

*

Is there no limit to the skulduggery of the Republicans in an election year? Now, don't play innocent and pretend you don't know what I mean. I am referring to the hue and cry they are raising because a couple of naval officers got tapped on their noggins at the grand conference, dinner and free-for-all which Daniel J. Tobin threw for President Roosevelt at the Statler Hotel in Washington last week. Roosevelt did the speaking, Tobin was in the chair, and the goon squads put the knuckles to the foolish people in the corridors who didn't have sense enough to put on Roosevelt buttons when Tobin gave the word.

All the beefs they are making in the newspapers and the demands for a Congressional investigation are nothing but dirty politics. I got the dope straight from one of the attending business agents who was so enthused by Roosevelt's speech and everything that he voluntarily pledged a donation to the Democratic campaign fund of one-half the *per diem* and traveling expenses allowed him for the trip. The other boys did the same, without any pressure from Tobin. All he said was, "Boys, I think it would be a good idea for you to kick in something."

Our President (of the United States, I mean) gave as slick a speech in favor of the working people as a business agent could ever wish to hear. In organizing the affair, our President (of the Teamsters International) put in the hardest job of work he has done since he quit driving a team of spavined nags in Boston fifty years ago, come spring. And I am authorized to state as a fact that all the business agents, including the eighteen from Minneapolis, came to the meeting absolutely clean. All their blackjacks and brass knuckles were checked and accounted for with the clerk of the hotel.

It was a great shindig, if you want to know the truth about it, and one long to be remembered by all the business agents, international representatives, muscle men and personal representatives of Tobin who came to Washington for the occasion from far and near. Why, there were even two members of the union present who are not and never have been on the payroll of the International Brotherhood of Teamsters. These were the two fellows in charge of the beer truck who stayed over between loads to hear the President's speech.

It's a shame to see the dirty Republicans trying to smear and discredit this crowning achievement of President Tobin's career and turn it against a good friend of labor like President Roosevelt. They have absolutely no call to complain about those two sailors getting slugged, because these sailors themselves admit that, when asked in a nice way, what horse they were backing in the presidential race, answered:

"It's none of your damned business." They said this right after President Tobin had stated that everybody should go down the line 100 percent for Roosevelt. What else can you do with wise guys like that but belt them around a bit?

The knockers are even going so far as to whisper around that Daniel J. Tobin himself was personally involved in the brawl. That can't be true. Harold H. Seavey, secretary-treasurer, Teamsters' Joint Council, Minneapolis, told the *Minneapolis Star Journal* that, in his opinion, the smear campaign "is not in keeping with the best naval tradition." Pee-wee Seavey may be right as far as he goes, but he doesn't go far enough. The insinuation that Daniel J. Tobin does his own fighting is "not in keeping with the tradition" of the Teamsters International. What are the goon squads for?

＊

I am very glad indeed to hear that Carl is getting married, and wish I could attend the wedding. Ask little Mick to go as my representative and kiss the bride for me. Also, ask Carl to write and tell me all about it.

LETTER 107

SANDSTONE, OCTOBER 6, 1944

I have been granted permission to write four letters per week. This is the extra one. I am very anxious to get more information about Carl's wedding. I am enthused about it and feel in my bones that he has made a good decision. I want to hear all about Angelica.

Continuing from October 3: Our tendency is the only one in the labor movement that analyzes the role of Stalinism in the capitalist countries correctly, that is, *an agency of capitalist imperialism* in the labor movement seeking to buy concessions for the nationalist bureaucracy of the USSR at the expense of the world proletariat and the colonial people. In this they are like any other group of privileged bureaucrats and aristocrats of labor who ally themselves with the exploiters against the deprived and oppressed masses—only magnified a thousand times. This is the little secret which explains the phenomenon which mystifies and baffles the professional "democrats"—the "hearty," if temporary, accord between the Stalinist bureaucracy and the Anglo-American imperialists.

Those who do not understand that Stalinism, as represented by the bureaucracy in the Soviet Union as well as by its foreign agencies, is a tendency, a section, of the *world labor movement* cannot begin to understand it or the reason it wields such great influence, and consequently cannot fight it effectively. On the contrary, the opportunists of all shades, all those who look for some way of compromise with capitalism, are at bottom no different from the Stalinists and sooner or later cooperate with them in one form or another when the vital interests of the capitalist order imperiously require it.

It is the degree of acuteness of the class struggle, not the "ideology" of the different varieties of imperialist agencies in the labor movement, that decides whether they quarrel among themselves or work together against the revolutionary masses. Witness the anarchists and socialists of Spain, the French People's Front, the socialist-Stalinist cooperation in Italy. Here at home we have already seen the Hillman-Browder amity in the PAC, the no-strike pledge bloc at the auto convention, and the Stalinist-Tobin combination against us.

When the masses really take the road of resolute struggle in their own interests they are compelled to turn against Stalinism because they come up against its malign policy at every step. They can wage this struggle only under our leadership, and no other. We, however, can lead this struggle only if we insist upon irreconcilable programmatic clarity on the question of the Soviet Union, and hence of Stalinism; sternly reject any kind of unity with other groups who bring confusion into this question; and tolerate no taint of conciliationism in this respect.

We firmly believe that the cadres of the Fourth International which are again emerging in Europe can grow and prosper, and come to the leadership of the revolutionary struggle of the workers against imperialism and its Stalinist agents, only insofar as they follow this line. We believe that the tendency in our own ranks in the U.S. toward conciliation with the petty-bourgeois opposition, represented by the present opposition to the party leadership, is an anti-Trotskyist tendency.

LETTER 108

SANDSTONE, OCTOBER 8, 1944

The most important reason of all to add another day to the convention time is to allow time for a real consideration and democratic election of the NC. I will write a special letter about this later. In publishing the material of the plenum I hope you don't overlook Cassidy's original list of amendments which were in reality a counterresolution.

*

The incident of the New York membership meeting (where several comrades were censured for conducting political discussions with WP members without the knowledge of the party) appears to have touched off a debate in which some fundamental questions, on which the party has more than once spoken decisively, are again called up for review. That is strange, for even at a distance, without knowing the details of the affair, it is difficult for one to misunderstand the simple issue involved.

The New York Organization wants to control and direct all the political activity of its members, and took this method of asserting its will in this respect. A Leninist can only applaud this attitude. Of course, one may hold the opinion, since it is our traditional practice to go very slow with organizational measures, that a pedagogical explanation of this elementary principle, without a formal censure, would have been sufficient. If the protests were limited to this secondary, organizational side of the affair, redress of the grievance could undoubtedly be obtained. A big discussion over such a small matter would not be worthwhile.

The article of Comrade Morrison, however, raises larger issues. This was the case also, as I am informed, in the discussion at the New York membership meeting. These issues require discussion and clarification.

In appealing to the party against the procedure of Local New York, Morrison resorts to arguments which are far-reaching in their implications. A discussion of these arguments is decidedly in order and necessary since, whether so intended or not, they represent an assault against the traditions of Bolshevism all along the line in the name of—the traditions of Bolshevism.

This anomaly can be explained on only one of two hypotheses. Either Morrison has neglected to inform himself of the traditional practices of Bolshevik organization; or he is again indulging his well-known penchant for underestimating the intelligence of other people—this time of people who know something about the tradition which he invokes, the tradition of Bolshevism. Morrison's arguments have a tradition, but it is not the tradition of Bolshevism.

What does Morrison mean when he refers to the history of Bolshevism? Doesn't he know that it is our own history?

What have we been doing for the past sixteen years but writing the continuing history of Bolshevism in life? Bolshevism is not a mummy preserved in a Russian museum, but a living movement which long ago crossed the borders of the Soviet Union and became worldwide in its scope.

The Russian part of the history of Bolshevism was never definitively written; and although its main outlines are well known, there is a sad lack of documentation in the English language available to the modern student. Our part of this history, however—the history of the Fourth International in general and of our party in particular—has been written and documented.

The history of our party is a chapter of the history of living Bolshevism. And not the poorest chapter either, for it was written in sixteen years of reaction, defeats and uphill struggle all the way from the beginning up to the present day. (More.)

LETTER 109

SANDSTONE, OCTOBER 9, 1944

I read *Citizen Tom Paine* by Howard Fast. The factual material about this great figure was most interesting to me. But I am always irked when writers try to psychoanalyze men of action. They don't understand them and only end by giving unintended psychologic portraits of themselves.

❋

Continuing: We have waged an unceasing and irreconcilable theoretical and political fight against the Stalinist degeneration. But not only that. Our record is also a record of struggle against all other anti-Marxist tendencies as well. Our fight against sectarianism was conducted on classic lines.

Our fight on all fronts—theoretical, political and organizational—against the petty-bourgeois revisionists recapitulated the whole historical struggle of Bolshevism and Menshevism. In building our party we employed, from the beginning, the organizational methods of Lenin, and successfully fought off every attempt—and there were many—to replace them by anarcho-Menshevik substitutes.

The older members of our party know its history as a part of the authentic history of Bolshevism. They do not need to be told that Morrison's arguments are not drawn from this arsenal. The younger party members who want to know what the traditional practices of Bolshevism are have not far to seek. They need only study the history of their own party. There is no lack of material.

The contentions of Morrison can find no support in this history, but on the contrary are directed against it. In a published letter, written while at work on the pamphlet which forms the first section of *The Struggle for a Proletarian Party*, I remarked that the pamphlet was not designed to influence the course of the inner-party struggle then drawing to its end, but was, rather, being "written for the future." The arguments of Morrison transform this "future" into the present. The answer to these arguments, written in advance, appears in the polemics directed against the organizational conceptions of the petty-bourgeois opposition.

When it comes to organization we follow Lenin, and nobody is going to talk us out of it. Lenin always paid far more attention to the "organization question," was far stricter, firmer, more definite about it, precisely because he really aimed to build a party to lead a revolution. The Mensheviks only dabbled with the idea, but Lenin was in earnest; he had it in his blood.

This difference—and what a difference!—manifested itself even before any political differences were formulated. So it has always been. "Hard" and "soft" approaches to the

organization question have marked every conflict of the two
opposing tendencies from the very first preliminary skir-
mishes at the Russian party congress of 1903 up to the present time. The documents of our party history testify to the
role this question played in the last great party fight against
the petty-bourgeois faction of Burnham and Shachtman.

It is a historical fact that the 1903 split between the Bolsheviks and the Mensheviks—a premature split, to be sure—
took place over the formulation of the first paragraph of the
party constitution defining party membership. Even there,
says Trotsky in his autobiography, "the two divergent tendencies were unmistakable. Lenin wanted clear-cut, perfectly
definite relationships (More.)

LETTER 110

SANDSTONE, OCTOBER 10, 1944

What do you think of the idea of a new edition of *Whither England?* to be printed in England, with a few thousand
unbound sheets to be shipped to Pioneer? Please get facts
and figures on this.

Continuing the quotation where I broke off in my last letter: within the party. Martov tended toward diffuse forms."
The debate which has arisen over the affair of the New York
membership meeting in the year 1944 sounds like an echo
of these words.

Insisting on "perfectly definite relationships within the
party," Bolshevism—all the outraged howling of its opponents to the contrary notwithstanding—has nevertheless
always been, and is now, completely free from any trace
of dogmatic rigidity, fixity or finality in its organizational
forms and procedures. Our organizational methods are designed to serve political ends, are always subordinated to

them, and are readily amended, changed or even turned upside down to suit them.

Democratic centralism, for example, is not a dogma to be understood statically as a formula containing the unchanging quantities of 50 percent democracy and 50 percent centralism. Democratic centralism is a dialectical concept in which the emphasis is continually being shifted in consonance with the changing needs of the party in its process of development.

A period of virtually unrestricted internal democracy, which is normally the rule during the discussion of disputed questions under legal conditions, can be replaced by a regime of military centralism for party action under conditions of external persecution and danger, and vice versa; and all conceivable gradations between these two extremes can be resorted to without doing violence to the principle of democratic centralism.

What is essential is that the right *emphasis* be placed at the right *time*. Bolshevism, far from any dogmatic rigidity ascribed to it by superficial critics, is distinguished by the great flexibility of its organizational forms and methods. This does not signify, however, that there are no definite rules, no basic principles. These principles, in fact, are unchanging in their *essence* no matter how flexibly the party may see fit to apply them in different situations.

Two of these basic principles, which are recognized by every Bolshevik but which appear to need reassertion in the light of the dispute over the New York incident, may be set down as follows:

1) The party is conceived as a combat organization destined to lead a revolution. It is not a freethinkers' discussion club, not a mere forum for self-expression and self-improvement, imposing no personal obligations on its members. The party is not an anarchist madhouse where everyone does as he pleases, but an army which faces the outside world as a unit.

2) Following from this, it is an unchanging party *law* that the party has the right to control and direct the political activity of each and every member; to be informed about and to regulate and supervise the relations, if any, of each and every member with political opponents of the party; and to demand of each and every member disciplined compliance with party decisions and instructions, and 100 percent—not 99 percent—*loyalty to the party.*

Anyone who disputes these principles does not talk our language. (I will have to continue this paragraph in my next letter.)

LETTER 111

SANDSTONE, OCTOBER 12, 1944

I received Moish's memo. We think the most important thing now is to develop the pedagogical discussion and to cut down the organizational base of the opposition. Chicago is the most important point. We are very much against any rotten compromise there.

Continuing the paragraph where I broke off: Anyone who disputes these principles must seek support for his arguments from some other source than the history of our party. He will not find it there.

Here are some notes on "The Danger of Stalinism—and Other Dangers." Morrison discerns evidence of "Stalinism" in the procedure of the New York organization and other incidents, and is greatly disturbed by symptoms of "degeneration" which he sees, or thinks he sees, on every side. He says: "Since the terrible Stalinist degeneration, every serious person in the Marxist movement fears and thinks of possible degeneration." Again: "Let not one single Stalinist germ penetrate into our ranks." And so on and so forth.

Such warnings have a familiar ring. We have heard them many times before. But up till now our party has successfully resisted all dangers of Stalinist degeneration, with or without benefit from the numerous warnings, while their authors, unfortunately, were not always equally successful in resisting other forms of degeneration no better than the Stalinist variety. The history of our party contains some instructive lessons on this point also.

The danger of degeneration in a revolutionary party comes from the pressure of its environment. The founding cadres of our party came exclusively from the Communist Party; and for the first five years of our existence we maintained the position of a faction, seeking to reform the parent organization and disclaiming any desire to form an independent party. Our most immediate environment, therefore, was the Communist Party in which the process of Stalinist degeneration was in full swing.

Moreover, the successes of the Soviet industrialization at that time—the period of the first Five Year Plan—contrasted to the destructive crisis in the capitalist world, were lending great prestige to the Stalinists. The CP was rapidly expanding in membership and influence; its domination of the progressive labor movement and of the radical intellectual circles was complete.

The pressure upon our small dissident group was very strong at that time. It is a historical fact worth noting that the great majority of the original cadres of the Left Opposition throughout the world succumbed to this pressure. "Capitulation" to the Stalinist regime decimated the ranks of the Opposition like a plague in one country after another.

How did the young Trotskyist organization in America fare under these hard conditions? Nothing of the kind happened here. A few casual individuals of no special influence who had joined us on "democratic" grounds—perhaps half a dozen all told—gave up the fight and went back to the

Stalinist camp as capitulators; "democracy" alone is not an adequate platform for a serious and protracted political fight. But not a single leader, not a single American Trotskyist of influence nationally or locally, *then* or *ever* made peace with Stalinism.

*

I will continue with more notes on the same subject in my letter.

LETTER 112

SANDSTONE, OCTOBER 15, 1944

We went on "the payroll" today. The convicts say the ten dollars which the government gives to the discharged prisoner is ten cents per day wages for the last hundred days. Strictly figuring, we still have to serve 99 days and a "git." The last day you git up and git out.

Continuing from No. 111: From this fact, which speaks louder than anybody's words, one is entitled to infer that the American section of the International Left Opposition, the predecessor of the Fourth International, was pretty well inoculated against the Stalinist degeneration from the start. And that inference would be 100 percent correct. We educated our cadres (and ourselves) to fight the theoretical and political positions of Stalinism, not only its organizational methods and techniques.

Yes, it may be said once again, you thoroughly exposed Stalinism and taught the advanced workers to despise it. But in waging this fight you yourselves adopted the "methods" of Stalinism. Of course, of course. We know all about that. We have heard all about that before. And we answered then, as we answer now: Stalinism is not a system of "methods," as its superficial critics imagine, but a *political tendency* with a definite social basis—the social basis of a privileged bureaucracy in the Soviet Union and its hired agents throughout the world.

The "methods" are the result, not the cause. These methods—bureaucratic violence, lying, falsifying, double-dealing, betraying—are needed by a bureaucracy serving special interests in forcing through a policy which violates the doctrines and traditions of Bolshevism.

But what need have we of these methods? What special interests do we serve which conflict with the interests of the rank and file of the party and the working class? What false policy do we have to impose on them by violence and fraud? Burnham and Shachtman are still trying to find a plausible answer to these questions. Morrison will have no better success.

It is not much of an answer to say that this or that individual is by nature a Stalinist who perversely employs its methods in a small party dedicated to the struggle against Stalinism. Why has the party, which is anti-Stalinist to the core, tolerated such individuals and even placed them in central positions of leadership? Better yet, why have such Stalinists by nature, if they have any sense at all and if they are not simply Stalinist agents in our ranks—why have they wasted their time in a small persecuted party whose internal democracy has always been a model for the whole world.

Why haven't they gone back to the Stalinist party where they would feel more at home? Such questions have never seriously arisen for the simple reason that Stalinist influence in our party has existed only in the imagination of people who have exaggerated its dangers and overlooked other and far greater ones to which they themselves were yielding.

The danger of degeneration in a revolutionary party comes from the pressure of its environment. The environment in which our party has operated, especially since our

definitive break with the Comintern in 1933, is the bourgeois society in the strongest and richest of all bourgeois
countries. (More.)

LETTER 113

SANDSTONE, OCTOBER 16, 1944

We think it would be a good idea to acquaint the party
members with the discussion we have conducted in the leadership over the role of Stalinism, developments in the USSR
and the defense slogan. This should first go into the *Internal Bulletin.* Let the membership see and participate in the
adaptation of basic principles to new conditions.

＊

Continuing from my last letter: This pressure has been
real, not imaginary; it has claimed not a few victims in the
past; and today, with the reaction engendered by the war, it
presses against us more heavily than ever. If one is seriously
looking for signs of "degeneration" he should turn his attention in the direction of the real danger. He should quit
babbling about Stalinism for a while and become more sensitive to evidences of weak-willed yielding to the powerful
influences of the class enemy.

Stalinism itself, properly understood, is not at all an independent force, but one of the forms of adaptation to the
material and moral terror of the bourgeoisie; and, thereby, it
is one of its agencies in the labor movement. There are other
forms of adaptation and capitulation. We have had enough
experience with them already to be able to identify them at
first sight. *In their finished form* they all seek to oppose a
petty-bourgeois program to the program of Bolshevism, but
they almost invariably *begin* by revolting against its irrecon-

cilable spirit and its organizational methods. Such tendencies, wherever they appear in the party, reveal the *real* danger of degeneration as unfailingly as the holes where water seeps through show the weak spots in a dike.

Since the earliest days of our movement in the United States nobody has gone over to Stalinism. But deserters to the camp of "democratic" capitalism have been rather numerous. What is to be guarded against, on the basis of this experience, is any tendency of conciliationism toward these deserters in any stage of their degeneration. Such conciliationist tendencies are the real, not imaginary, "danger of degeneration" in our ranks.

*

Here are some notes on "The Trotskyist Party and Other Parties—the History of the Question": Morrison rejects the idea that the party has the right and duty to be informed about, and to regulate and control, any and all relations which party members may have with political opponents. This idea, concretely demonstrated by the ruling in the case of the four New York comrades, impresses him as "having a resemblance to Stalinist procedure." When the party leadership insists on strict rules in this regard, it indicates, to Morrison, only that "the leadership thinks it is impermissible to discuss questions with members of the WP"; that they lack pride and confidence in their ideas.

In contrast to the party leadership's attitude toward opponent organizations, Morrison proceeds to lay down some rules of his own. Relating what his own practices have been, he recommends them to the party members as a guide. Morrison sees nothing abnormal in a member of our organization shopping around at the meetings and affairs of other political organizations, fraternizing with their members and discussing political questions with them, formally or informally, on his own responsibility. Whether such activity should be reported to the party or not—that, says Morrison, is up to the individual member to decide. On this point, he again refers to Lenin and the Bolsheviks.

It would have been better to leave Lenin out of it. Morrison's view of this matter is not new, to be sure, but it has no right to represent itself as a Leninist conception of normal relations between rival political organizations and their members. This question also has a history, which apparently has made no impression on Morrison. (More.)

LETTER 114

SANDSTONE, OCTOBER 17, 1944

We are disturbed by Aunt's complaints about Grandizo [Munis]. She should be given full satisfaction on this matter without delay. I had previously made a note to ask him to write more for the magazine, especially about Spain.

*

Continuing: The formulas he offers would take us back to the primitive conceptions of party organization which dominated American labor radicalism before the First World War; that is, before the movement grew up and learned the meaning of a program and a party. It was precisely what we learned from Lenin that enabled us to discard these outmoded and entirely inadequate conceptions of a full quarter of a century ago. And in this, as in so many other fields, experience corroborated Lenin's theory and, in turn, supplied its own instructive lessons along the same line. Morrison's formulas contradict the theory and disregard the experience.

Before the First World War the dominating sentiment among the various social protest organizations and groups, despite all their differences and quarrels, was that of fraternity—the feeling of oneness, the opinion that all the groups were part of one and the same *movement,* and that all would, sooner or later, "get together." As a rule, a definite distinction was made between the terms "organization" and "the movement."

One's own particular organization, be it the Socialist Party, the IWW, any one of the numerous anarchist groups, local forums, or even a club of Single Taxers or an independent socialist educational society—was thought of as a *part;* the "movement" was the *whole.* It was common practice for the "radicals" of different affiliations to patronize each other's meetings and affairs, to participate in common forums, reading clubs and purely social organizations. In Kansas City and San Francisco, to my knowledge, "Radical Clubs" were deliberately organized to promote fraternization at monthly dinners. Radicals of all tendencies mingled socially and intermarried without thought of personal incompatibility arising from a conflict of ideas.

Nor did the separate organizations draw sharp lines in their admittance of members. With the exception of DeLeon's Socialist Labor Party, which stood aloof and was with some justice regarded as intolerant and sectarian, they were all rather catholic in their composition. Reformists and revolutionists, "ballot boxers" and "direct actionists," belonged to one and the same Socialist Party. Christian socialists and professional "God-killers," prohibitionists and partisans of the open saloon, kept them company. The propaganda branches of the syndicalist IWW extended their hospitality alike to socialists and anarchists. Anarchism was thought by many to be more radical, more revolutionary, than socialism; and anyone who was against "authority" was free to call himself an anarchist. Free-lance radicals, whose name was legion, were regarded as part of "the movement" on even terms with all the others.

In Europe, the prewar Social-Democracy was an "all-inclusive party." Unity was fetishized; the left wing shrank from the thought of split. Luxemburg and Liebknecht were party comrades with Kautsky, Noske and Scheidemann. In Russia, Lenin resolutely carried through the split, but Trotsky insisted on the unification of the Bolsheviks and Mensheviks.

The state of affairs in American labor radicalism prior to the First World War is related here without intention either to praise or to blame. It was due to the circumstances of the time; the organizations, in their membership composition and in their relations with each other, could not rise above the level of their own understanding. This was the period of the infancy of the American revolutionary movement. Neither theory nor experience had yet taught us any better. The differences between the theories and tendencies, and their respective organizations, had not been fully thought out. None of the tendencies had yet been put to great historic tests. (More.)

LETTER 115

SANDSTONE, OCTOBER 19, 1944

Continuing from No. 114: The lines between them were not drawn finally and irreconcilably. "Unity" sentiments were strong in all groups. Organizational looseness was the rule, and there was a widespread feeling that someday, somehow, all would "get together."

Great events shattered this idyll. The [First World] War and then the Russian Revolution put all theories and tendencies to the test and drew them out to their ultimate conclusions. Reformist socialism was revealed as class treachery. Anarchism and syndicalism, with their "denial" of the state, revealed their theoretical inadequacy, their bankruptcy, despite their grandiloquent revolutionary pretensions. Revolutionary Marxism—Bolshevism—alone stood up under the test of war and revolution. The Russian Bolsheviks taught us this in word and deed. We American militants learned from them, for the first time, the full meaning of the program, and simultaneously, the significance, the role, of the vanguard party.

The revolutionary workers of the whole world went to the same school. A worldwide realignment of forces began to take place under the impact of the war and the revolution. Lines were sharply drawn. Sentimental unification gave way to ruthless splits, and the splits became definitive, irreconcilable. The revolutionary militants, instructed by the war and the revolution, learned to counterpose the Marxist program to all other programs. Instructed by the precise teachings of Lenin, they learned the necessity of organizing their own party, separate and apart from all others.

Once these ABC lessons were assimilated—and, I repeat, we learned them twenty-five years ago—the revolutionary vanguard broke decisively with the old tradition of mishmash parties and loose coalitions, with free-lance radicalism and bohemian irresponsibility. In place of all that, the organizational principles laid down by Lenin were adopted: unity on the basis of a principled program; all devotion, all loyalty, to one party and only one party; strict responsibility and accountability of every member to the party; professional leadership; democratic centralism.

The pioneer American communists and we, their heirs and continuators, have worked on these lines consistently and unswervingly since 1919. If our party stands today on far higher ground than that occupied by the amorphous rebel workers' movement prior to the First World War— and that is indubitably the case—it is not due solely to the superiority of our program, but also to the consistent application in practice of the principles and methods of Bolshevik organization. The experience of a quarter of a century has convinced us over and over again that this is the right way, the only way, to build a revolutionary party.

It is absurd to think that we can unwind the film of this experience and go back to where we started. But if Morrison's criticisms and formulas mean anything seriously, that is what they mean. We cannot entertain any such propositions for a moment.

In politics nothing is more stupid, more infantile than to retrace ground that has already been covered, to go back and start all over again as if nothing had happened and nothing has been learned. Serious revolutionists must learn from every experience and apply what they have learned in new experiences. We insist on that. The new generation must not begin from the beginning. The fruit of the experience of the past, all that has been acquired and learned by others, is their heritage.

They *begin* with that. Translated into terms of the "organizational question," this means that they begin, not from the prehistoric confusion of prewar days—where Morrison's conceptions would take them—but from the most recent experiences in which our organizational principles and methods were tested in life: the great struggle against the petty-bourgeois opposition in 1939–40. (More.)

LETTER 116

SANDSTONE, OCTOBER 22, 1944

I didn't have room for the final paragraph in my last letter. Here it is:

All the forty years experience of Bolshevism—in organization as well as in theory and politics—was recapitulated in that historic struggle. The new party recruits can learn about Bolshevism and Menshevism on the organization question by a study of the documents of this fight. It is not without interest to note that the party leadership, in the dispute over the incident of the New York membership meeting, shows its unqualified hostility to any sign of looseness or irresponsibility—to say nothing of disloyalty—in relations with the Menshevik traitor clique of Shachtman and Co.; while Morrison, in his plea for unsupervised fraternization, manifests a more conciliatory attitude. On both sides, here as always, the organizational method serves the political line.

✳

We parted from our three dear comrades [released after serving a shorter sentence] Friday with mixed emotions on both sides. Prison either draws men together more firmly or pulls them apart irreparably. We are bound to the three who left us with the undying love of brothers. We were glad to see them go out into the air of freedom, but sorry to lose their companionship. They were glad to go, but sorry to leave us behind.

✳

We do not understand the expression "Stalin's Red Army" in the article on Bulgaria, October 14. Is this a journalistic locution or a political designation? If it is meant as a political term, then in our opinion it is one-sided and therefore incorrect.

✳

If the New York comrades decide to get my dictionary stand before I return, tell them I prefer the standing size.

What is the basis of all this talk about "democratic slogans" in the criticism of the NC resolution? Are we represented as being opposed to such slogans? That seems to us to put the issue falsely.

The Count did not show up here. If you see him, tell him the "clearance papers" which I gave him in San Francisco have about expired, but if he brings me another pipe I will renew them.

*

I wish you would send me the table of contents of each of the *Internal Bulletins* with a brief synopsis of each article. Perhaps Joe can help you on this, if necessary.

I think we will be ready to settle matters with the Germans soon after our return.

*

In our opinion the most important reason for stretching the convention out for another day is to give adequate time for a *free* and *well-deliberated* selection by the delegates of the new National Committee. This is one of the strongest guarantees of the democracy of the party. Our party has always been more democratic, ten times more democratic, in this respect than any other party. But there is room for improvement, and we should consciously seek out the necessary methods.

We never went in for any of the rigging, wangling, vote-trading and leadership-pressure devices by which, in practically all other parties (strike out the word "practically") the convention delegates are usually defrauded of a large part of their democratic freedom of choice. If one has a self-sufficient revolutionary party in mind, all such methods are self-defeating. A revolutionary party needs a leadership that really represents the party, that is really one with the party.

Without this democratic corrective, freely brought into play at every convention, centralization and discipline inevitably become caricatures and forms of abuse which injure the organization every time they are exercised. A revolutionary leadership must feel free at all times to act boldly and confidently in the name of the party. For that, it needs to be sure that there is no flaw in its mandate. (More.)

LETTER 117

SANDSTONE, OCTOBER 23, 1944

Continuing: No rules exist to guide us in the technical execution of this difficult and delicate task to the best advantage of the party. The democratic selection of the primary and secondary leaders is a sufficiently important question— nobody knows how much damage can be done by bungling it—but, as far as I know, nobody has ever written anything about it. Nobody has taught us anything. We are obliged to think and experiment for ourselves.

The democratic impulses of the rank and file incline them to react unfavorably to "slates," as they feel, not without reason, that they narrow down for all practical purposes the freedom of choice. The Social-Democratic politicians, who are as undemocratic a collection of rascals as one can ever expect to meet, have always exploited this sentiment by announcing their firm, democratic opposition to slates. Of course, there was a little catch to their virtuous slogan of "no slates." They meant no openly avowed slates which would possibly be open to discussion and amendment. Instead of that, the noble Social-Democrats rig up secret slates by means of horse trades and petty bribes to ensure their control. A good 50 percent of Social-Democratic convention "politics" is always devoted to this kind of business.

From the first days of American communism, which also

coincided with the first appearance on the scene of a new type of leaders with a new conception of "politics," we tried to break through the "no-slate" fraud and devise a more honest system by which the leaders would take open responsibility for their proposals and give reasons for their preferences in the makeup of the leading committee. It became rather common practice for the leading committees, in national as well as local conventions in the communist movement, to propose a slate of candidates for the new committee to be elected. We carried the practice with us in the independent movement of Trotskyism. (During factional struggles the slate-making arrangements were carried on in the separate caucuses of the factions.) This method was, without doubt, far superior to the "no-slate" tricks of our socialist predecessors, being more honest, and in the essence of the matter, even more democratic.

But this system also was not free from negative aspects, and even dangers. I perceived some of them long ago, have thought much about the matter, and from time to time have tried to devise corrective experiments. What impressed me most of all was the quite obvious fact that while the presentation of a slate of candidates by the leadership is the most "efficient" way to get through the business of the election of the NC—usually the last point on the agenda, carried through in a great hurry—it concentrates too much power in the leadership just at that very point—the convention— where the democratic corrective of rank-and-file control should be asserted most strongly.

It is not the election of the central, most prominent and influential leaders themselves. That problem solves itself almost automatically in the interplay of party work and internal strife. The problem arises over the selection of the secondary leaders, the new committee members, the potential leaders of the future. As a rule this part of the slate if presented by the most authoritative central leaders, is accepted, whether

enthusiastically or not, by the convention; many delegates
are reluctant to oppose them. (More.)

LETTER 118

SANDSTONE, OCTOBER 24, 1944

Continuing from No. 117: It is senseless, of course, to
speak of a revolutionary combat party without recognizing
the necessity of a centralized, fully empowered leadership.
But this states only one half of the problem. Leninist centralism is *democratic* centralism, a profoundly dialectical
concept. The other half of the Leninist formula recognizes
no less the necessity of subordinating the leadership, really
as well as formally, to the party; keeping it under the control
of the party. The party constitution does everything that
can be done in a formal sense to provide for the interaction
of centralism and democracy.

The structure of the party is strictly hierarchical. Higher
committees command the lower. Full authority over all is
vested in the National Committee. But the NC, like all other
committees, is required to render accounts and surrender
its mandate at stated intervals to the party convention to
which it is subordinated. This is the formal, constitutional
guarantee both for centralization and the ultimate control
of the leadership.

But it is also necessary to think about the spirit as well
as the letter of the party constitution. A farsighted leadership should concern itself with the elusive, intangible factors
which can play such a great role in determining the actual
relationship between the NC and the ranks.

Some of these factors arise from the composition of the
NC and the division of functions within it. Nominally, this
body consists of twenty-five members, and they all have

equal rights. In addition there are fifteen alternates. But the majority come to the center only for meetings of the plenum which are not held very often. Between plenums the power is delegated to the Political Committee. From this it is quite clear that one section of the National Committee is in a position to exert far more influence on the day-to-day work and interpretation of party policy than the other.

Again, some are older, more experienced and more prominent than others, and consequently wield greater authority in the committee as well as in the party as a whole. On the other side, the committee members from the districts and the younger members of the committee generally, who are active in local work, are closer to the rank and file than the central leaders of the party are, and represent them more directly and intimately. This gives them a special function in the NC of extraordinary importance.

Their presence represents a form of continuing rank-and-file control and supervision over the central leaders. They can fulfill this function, however, only insofar as they are people of independent influence and popularity in their own localities; only insofar as they are freely elected on their own merits, not handpicked.

To be sure, the central leaders cannot be indifferent to the selection of the secondary leadership. In this, as in everything else, leaders must lead. In a certain sense, the central party leaders "select" their collaborators and eventual successors. The question is, how to go about it? It is often easy for politically experienced leaders to convince themselves that they are better judges of the qualifications and potentialities of certain candidates than the rank-and-file delegates. And, as a rule, it is not too difficult to force their selections through by means of the "slate." This may appear to be the most "efficient" way. But in my opinion, there is a better way. (More.)

LETTER 119

SANDSTONE, OCTOBER 26, 1944

We received the memo on Chicago with great satisfaction—as a report of progress on a problem that is yet far from solution. When I said we were opposed to any "rotten compromise," I meant to say that we are against any compromise whatever with the intellectualist carbuncle on the party's neck; and we are highly gratified to hear that Moish has begun the campaign in this spirit.

This is not the first time that discussion fanatics have shown a disposition to call the discussion off just at the point where it really begins, i.e., where the issues are posed in their fundamental meaning. Behind this "harmony" maneuver is the wish, whether consciously formulated or not, to evade a party decision on their criticisms by the convention in order to be free to reopen them the next day as if nothing had happened.

Well, *this time* we are also in favor of continuing the discussion after the convention, because we want to carry this discussion with the Morrison-Cassidy tendency, once it has been fairly started, clear through to the end, to a definitive decision by the party on each and every point and on the tendency as a whole—it is *one* tendency; the "differences" between them are incidental, the points of agreement are fundamental. And we think the forthcoming convention will only be able, for obvious reasons, to *mark a stage* in the education of the party through the discussion, to make *a good beginning* in the mobilization of party public opinion.

But we insist that the convention mark this stage, make this beginning. The Chicago critics of the leadership, for example, must be asked to bring all their beefs with them *to the convention*, and present them there. We, on our part, must discuss *the Chicago branch* at the convention; not only to refute their criticisms, but to take the offensive against them along the lines of Moish's memo in order to inoculate the new recruits against this disease, and to prepare the way to move in on Chicago for the next stage of our fight against the disease on its home grounds—under the leadership of a politically qualified representative of the NC.

We cannot accept any support for the NC resolution on the ground that it "incorporates" Cassidy's amendments and is therefore acceptable. As far as I know, the amendments we accepted to the original draft of the plenum resolution conceded absolutely nothing in principle either to Cassidy or Morrison. This will be clear to anyone who has read the original "amendments" proposed to the plenum by Cassidy. (By the way, has this document been published in the *Internal Bulletin*? It should be.)

These original amendments were, in the essence of the matter, a counterthesis. So also must be construed his post-plenum "criticism." I have not read this precious document, and don't need to. The mere fact that it was written, and publication demanded, *after* the plenum must identify it in the eyes of anyone who does not play with ideas and political resolutions as a counterthesis.

In our opinion the NC should draw up and submit short motions, for votes at the end of the branch discussions and at the convention, to *endorse* the NC political resolution and *reject* the Cassidy "criticism" and any other documents in the same spirit which may be submitted. They may be willing to have an ambiguous, inconclusive expression of party opinion at the end of the discussion, but we must try to *bar* it.

*

The continuation of my remarks on the NC elections must go over. I am putting down for the first time in written form the thoughts of many years on this question.

LETTER 120

SANDSTONE, OCTOBER 29, 1944

I was glad to get Murry's report of the Los Angeles discussion. Now I would like to get similar reports of the discussion in other locals. From Seattle; tell Larry I would like to get also a general report on the Seattle branch and the Turner family—especially about the better two-thirds.

And, while I am on this subject, please send me a round-up report of Mick's activities since she came back to town. I am thinking of her this glorious Indian summer Sunday morning, and wondering what her accent will sound like the first time she returns from our house and tells her mother excitedly: *"Ich lerne Deutsch!"* (This is the influence of the book I just laid down—Schiller's *Wilhelm Tell*.)

Finished the seventh volume of Grote and started on the eighth. If they keep me here long enough I will at least learn something about the history of Greece. Alas, the time is drawing too short to permit me and my friend, who is traveling in the opposite direction, to meet at the historical point we planned. He is reading from the American Civil War backward and I am reading forward from the Heroic Age of Greece. We planned to meet at the Renaissance, but it now seems that we will be more than a century and a half apart when we leave here. Will we again have time to study?

Wouldn't it be best to start the Expansion Fund campaign now, if it is expected to be finished by Jan. 23? Perhaps the quotas could be assigned, pledges taken and—at least in New York—the collections started. The press publicity could wait till the formal action of the convention.

The discussion about the prospects of bourgeois democracy in Europe provides an excellent occasion to teach the new party members an elementary lesson in Marxism. Those who speak of "bourgeois democracy coming to the fore"—as you quote Cassidy as saying in *Internal Bulletin No. 5*—seem to cry aloud for someone to explain, in the analysis of a concrete social phenomenon, what the Marxist historical *method* means:

1) The historical conditions which determined the *origin* of bourgeois democracy.

2) The history of its development, flowering, crisis and decline, and the basic economic factors which determined that process in all its stages.

3) The accelerated ruination of European economy by the war and the utter impossibility of restoring it to health on a national-capitalist basis.

Against all that, there is, to be sure, a countervailing factor to which some people attach a suprahistorical importance, to wit: the *promise* of Roosevelt and Churchill to restore democracy to Europe in all its pristine glory. But unfortunately, this promise cannot be harmonized with the announced plan to dismember Germany and expand American foreign trade— a joint plan which is far more eloquent and sincere than the aforesaid promise precisely because it is determined by the economic necessities of American imperialism.

I believe the majority of the new recruits can be made to understand this simple lesson in the course of the present discussion. That alone will give them a better real understanding of Marxism than the critics of the NC resolution are displaying.

By the way, I spoke my piece about "iconoclasts" in "The Dog Days of the Left Opposition"; by name on page 93. Morrison wants to take us back to the dog days and make the condition permanent. But such a condition could not be permanent in any case. The workers would not stay in such an organization, and the "iconoclasts" would talk each other to death. Then someone would have to begin all over again, and he could not begin otherwise than by reinstating the "authorities" which the iconoclasts had so light-mindedly overthrown.

LETTER 121

SANDSTONE, OCTOBER 30, 1944

To continue where I left off on the NC question:

Wisdom lies in "selecting" people who have popularity and influence in their own right, and whose promotion coincides with the wishes of the party members who know them best. That means to select people who are advancing under their own power.

I came to this conclusion a long time ago, and as far as I have been able to influence the course of things it has been the party method of selecting the NC. Extensive and varied experience, with every imaginable kind of experiment, has convinced me that this method, even at the cost of incidental mistakes, works out best in the long run.

The central leaders of the party, who work from day to day without close contact with the internal life of the branches, need such a constitution of the NC if they are to lead the party confidently; lead it with the assurance that they know the moods and sentiments of the ranks and are in step with them. When doubt arises, or when some new important step is under consideration, it is only necessary to consult the out-of-town members of the NC by mail, or to call a plenum, in order to get a reliable sounding of the party. Approval of a given course by the plenum is a pretty certain forecast of similar action by the party.

Conversely, when the plenum finds it necessary to overrule the Political Committee—and this has happened more than once, notably in 1938–39—it is a sign that the Political Committee is out of line with the party and requires a change in its composition. The 1938–39 National Committee rebuked the PC several times and finally reorganized it, and later tests showed that the full plenum most accurately reflected the sentiment of the party.

A serious and conscientious party leadership should deliberately aim at a National Committee so composed as to be, in effect, a microcosm of the party. When the full plenum of such a National Committee meets between conventions, to all intents and purposes *the party is there in the room*. That is far more useful to responsible political leaders than a roomful of handpicked supporters without independent influence and authority. Bureaucrats who have special interests of their own to defend against the rank and file need to surround themselves with dependent henchmen; but revolutionary political leaders need support of an entirely different kind, the support of people who really represent the rank and file of the party.

There is another, and even more important, reason why the rank-and-file convention delegates should take over the election of the National Committee and be free from undue pressure and influence on the part of the national political leadership in exercising this function. The free selection of the full membership of the National Committee is perhaps the most decisive way to strengthen and reinforce genuine party democracy. It puts the political leaders under the direct supervision and control of a second line of leaders who are in intimate daily contact with the local and district organizations and, in fact, represent them in the plenum.

This control doesn't have to be exercised every day to be effective. The fact that it is there, and can be demonstrated when necessary, is what counts. Strange to relate, the professional democrats have never once in the history of our party bothered their heads about the method of selecting the National Committee from the standpoint of reinforcing party democracy. This, in my opinion, is because they tend to think of democracy almost exclusively in terms of unlimited and unrestricted self-expression and forget that control of the central leadership, which in day-to-day practices is limited to a very small group, by a larger group standing closer to the rank and file, is the most important mechanism to assure the democratic half of the Leninist formula: democratic centralism. (More.)

LETTER 122

SANDSTONE, OCTOBER 31, 1944

The report of the New York membership meeting is very interesting. We should like to get detailed reports of all these discussions. I will wait for Moish's memo before commenting.

＊

To continue: Throwing the floor open for nominations on the last day of the convention is not the only alternative to a slate presented by the outgoing NC. That only throws the delegate body into disorganized confusion and facilitates the manipulation of the election by means of secret slates and horse trades, the favorite method of Social-Democratic pseudo-democrats.

There is no infallible formula, but the results of our experiments over a period of many years argue most convincingly in favor of a slate prepared by a *nominating commission*. Of course, there are nominating commissions and nominating commissions. But the best, that is, the most democratic, is not the nominating commission appointed by the outgoing NC, nor the one elected at random from the floor of the convention. The most efficient, for the purposes set forth above, is the nominating commission selected by the branch or district delegations on a roughly proportional basis—each delegation selecting its own representatives—and then ratified by the convention. The nominating commission, thus conceived, is a body actually representing the rank-and-file delegations from the districts.

It would be grossly improper for individual central leaders to intrude themselves upon the commission and seek to dominate its proceedings. That would amount to a circumvention of the democratic process aimed at in the proposal. It is the part of wisdom for the central leaders to leave the nominating commission to its own devices, respecting the essence of party democracy as well as the form.

The nominating commission should be selected on the first day of the convention; it should begin its sessions at once and meet at least once a day thereafter to consider the various nominations until a slate is decided upon for presentation to the convention when the election of the NC comes up on the agenda.

In my opinion, the first step of the commission at the 1944 convention should be to discard formally the ruling which paralyzed the work of the nominating commission at the 1942 convention—the utterly stupid and reactionary principle that every member of the outgoing NC was, as a matter of course, to be reelected unless good cause was shown to *remove* him. That turns things upside down. Nobody can be "frozen" in any position in a revolutionary party. He must stand for election at each convention, and the election must be free and open.

Room must be left for competition and rivalry and differences of opinion to operate without artificial restraints. Members of the outgoing NC should be placed in exactly the same status as new aspirants—as *candidates* for election. The nominating commission should adopt a rule to this effect at its first session.

The most practical next step is to take a preliminary poll to ascertain how many candidates are generally favored for election as *national* leaders who are not counted as representatives of any special district of the party. This will clear the road for the apportionment of the remaining places on the slate for local and district representatives. Here, again, there should be no "freezing" of old representation and no automatic closing of the door to new candidates from districts previously not represented.

The object should be to provide the fairest possible representation of the districts in the new NC; but the principle of proportional representation should be modified by other considerations: the relative importance of the district; the quality of the candidates; the special role played by certain candidates, etc. (More.)

November, 1944

SANDSTONE, NOVEMBER 2, 1944

Continuing: The commission should announce the time and place of its daily sessions, and invite any delegate who wishes to argue for or against any candidate to appear and take the floor. The slate finally decided upon, either by agreement or majority vote, should be presented to the convention as the *nominations* of the commission. That leaves the floor open for other nominations and free discussion before the ballot is taken.

Naturally, one would have to have some good arguments for another candidate to hope to amend the slate of the nominating commission. But if he thinks he has a strong case, there is no reason why he shouldn't make the attempt. Adequate time and patience must be accorded for the presentation of any such proposed amendments. The heavens will not fall if a slate is amended once in a while.

One word more. The convention should not shunt the election of the new NC off till the last hurried half-hour of the convention, when impatience of departing delegations would tend to discourage full discussion and ample consideration of the various nominations. The best procedure would be to fix a definite hour and day to take up the election of the NC whether the rest of the agenda is finished or not at that time. This decision should be made demonstratively in order to call sharp attention to the vital importance of full and careful deliberation in selecting the party leadership. And even more important, the convention will thus give itself time to do the job right.

All of these measures will not guarantee the election of an ideal National Committee. But they should help to provide us with the best committee that a free party can select from the material at hand by the method of party democracy. If the returning delegates go home with the feeling that this has been accomplished, the new NC will be able to begin its work with a strong authority. On the other hand, the leadership, precisely because of the care and deliberation taken in the selection of the personnel of the NC, will feel itself to be more than ever under the watchful supervision and control of the party.

*

Memo for Sylvia: Please gather up for me all the literature of our movement you can get hold of—papers, pamphlets, *Internal Bulletins* and books—in French, German and Spanish. I will be able to read all three languages when I come back. What I want most of all is the collected letters of Marx and Engels in *German*. Perhaps Usick can help you on this as well as on the other stuff. Somewhere in my stuff at home I had a magazine-shaped French edition of the theses of the *Second* Congress of the Comintern. Did you find it, or had I given it to Usick?

Also: Please get a catalogue of Blue Ribbon Books and several other reprint editions. Also: Get all my letters from the party files as far back as they go and index them by year, place sent and person to whom sent. I expect to be able to dig a lot of material for articles from these letters.

The book *In Defense of Marxism* didn't show up here. If this book has been approved, please ask Pioneer to ship another copy right away. I want to read the sections on dialectics again; this is my favorite study these days.

Bill Haywood gave a good account of prison life in his book. Perhaps that chapter, or parts of it, could be reprinted in *The Militant*.

Back to Sylvia: Try to get Kropotkin's *Appeal to the Young*, a small pamphlet once published by Kerr and Co. Also: All anarchist literature of any type you can get. I expect to write something about this and want a complete collection of material. Also: the writings of Thomas Paine. The record office here requires my Selective Service card. If you can't find it, ask the Board for a duplicate.

LETTER 124

SANDSTONE, NOVEMBER 5, 1944

We read the story about the European conference with reservations and misgivings. Is it possible that the PC authorized the publication of this story? The Italian experience should have taught us to proceed very cautiously and be sure of our facts before publicizing reports from Europe. Our press should not publish one word from Europe unless it has been scrutinized and approved by the PC.

The following questions come to mind about the report in the November 4 *Militant*:

1) It is stated that a five-party conference was held last *February*. Your Paris correspondent in the October *FI*, writing in *September*, reports activities of the French Trotskyists but makes no mention of the conference.

2) The French POI and PCI are referred to equally as "sections" of the FI. This is not correct. The French section of the FI was the POI. The PCI was the name of the expelled Molinierist group.

3) Reference is made to seventy issues of *La Vérité* pub-

lished since 1940 but no mention is made of the official paper which we know was published and which, if I remember correctly, had a different name.

4) It is stated that the official organ of the united French section is called *La Vérité* and that the name of the united section is PCI. That does not sound like a unification.

5) It is stated that a European Secretariat and European Executive Committee were set up, but no reference is made to the necessarily provisional character of such a proceeding pending the sanction of the IEC set up by the World Conference of 1940. This is more a Molinierist than a Trotskyist way of proceeding. It produced nothing but harm in France in the past and can only produce worse harm if transferred to the international field.

If there is anything I detest more than careless journalism in political matters it is undisciplined, shotgun organizational methods. Because of our experience and the knowledge dearly bought by this experience, we must oppose these methods as aggressively and as unrelentingly as we oppose any tampering with the program.

Our urgent advice is to *say no more* about the European conference until reliable information, which can be checked and verified, is received. From the way the international situation is opening up you should soon be in a position to get reliable reports from numerous sources. Meantime, look before you leap.

We are glad to note that Moish is not mincing words in dealing with what my pal here calls "the microbe hunters." We must distinguish between the new rank-and-file members who are coming forward seeking education and those who are slipping backward and trying to drag the party backward with them. We must be patiently pedagogical with the former. They are far more important than the latter because they want to learn. We must do everything we can to help them. The "microbe hunters" would corrupt the party. We must prevent them. And if some of them, who were mistaken for leaders, get hurt in the process, we can't stop to worry about that.

I have often had occasion to notice that the most violent and unreasoning critics of others, the most ruthless "iconoclasts," soon "holler *gewalt*" when their own sensitive skins are pierced by the point of a pin. We must explain to them once again that their "right to criticize" is only one-third of party democracy. The second third is the right to answer their criticisms. And the third third is the right of the party to judge both the accuser and the accused.

* * *

Please be sure to let the party members have my letter on the NC [election] question. As we see it, this is now the most important aspect of real party democracy.

LETTER 125

SANDSTONE, NOVEMBER 6, 1944

You can tell the friends who inquire about my health that I am all right. I continue to stick strictly to my diet of boiled eggs and milk three times a day, seven days a week, and will stick to it until January 22. Then, I think, I will be entitled to a little variety and I am beginning to look forward to the special menus previously sent to you.

I don't sleep well. That, however, is nothing new. I haven't slept well since I came here and am getting used to it as one gets used to everything in time. By and large, my health is good enough; far better than I ever expected it to be under these circumstances. As the convicts say, there is nothing the matter with me that the key to the front gate won't cure.

I am disappointed to hear that you are having trouble with

your teeth. I understood that you were having them taken care of last spring. By all means get it done and over with. Have you attended to the supplementary heat question at home as I previously instructed you? This is important to me. The cold Minnesota winds are beginning to blow here, and I like to think of you warm and snug at home. My greatest joy in life is for you to have everything just the way you want it; the way it ought to be, and will be if I can make it so.

*

I am most anxious that Moish personally sponsor and explain my letter on the NC question to the convention from the point of view of strengthening party democracy. Democracy means something far more than the privilege of listening to articulate critics, although the professional democrats seem to think that is the beginning and end of it. Democracy means the right of the rank and file to *decide*. Whoever helps them to decide most intelligently is the best party democrat.

From this point of view the educational plan has a right to be considered a profoundly democratic proposal, for it aims to equip the party membership with a more systematic knowledge of Marxism which will enable them to judge political disputes more critically, more independently. My letter on the selection of the NC is a democratic proposal because it urges the rank-and-file delegates to look more closely into the question; to determine its composition more deliberately; to take more time at the convention and inquire more closely into the qualifications of each and every candidate.

In my opinion the composition of the NC needs a thorough shaking up and overhauling. I am not speaking for or against any candidate. I only propose that the convention delegates familiarize themselves more intimately with the records and the qualifications of the candidates and act more knowingly when they exercise the greatest democratic right of all—the right to elect the leadership freely, in an atmosphere free from pressure or any kind of deceit or manipulation.

The present NC was elected four years ago; four and one-half years ago, to be more exact. They were formally reelected two years ago in a proceeding that left much to be desired from the standpoint of discriminating, deliberate judgment in each individual case. That is, they were reelected *en bloc* under the formula put over on the nominating commission by Cassidy. That, in my opinion, was an encroachment on party democracy, insofar as it automatically blocked off any real competition or contest. Let us have a real election this time.

LETTER 126

SANDSTONE, NOVEMBER 7, 1944

This is the twenty-seventh anniversary of the day the Russian Bolsheviks took hold of the world and changed it, and in doing so, changed and reshaped our lives too. I am grateful today to the Russian Bolsheviks, and I am convinced to the bottom of my soul that it is better to be here with them, to feel that here I am one with them, than to be anywhere else under any conditions and be against them.

＊

It pays to live right, and good things come to the godly. Today the bulletin board carries the official announcement that "for the period December 15 to December 31 the rules forbidding the receipt of packages by prisoners may, in the discretion of the Warden, be modified to permit each prisoner in good standing to receive from any of his authorized correspondents *one* package of reasonable size, and weighing not more than two pounds, consisting of any of the following articles: Candy, shelled nuts, glacé or conserved fruits, and books."

I know what I want, and it is not two pounds of books or nuts. It is a two-pound box of Barricini's mixed chocolates. I will remind you of this about a month from now. It is a long time since I looked forward with real interest to candy for Christmas.

I have been studying Christian Science! That is, I have been reading a French edition of *The Herald of Christian Science*. I read the whole magazine through, from cover to cover, including the advertisements, and came to the following conclusion: The French language, including the irregular and "defective" verbs, is more scientific than *La Science Chrétienne*.

*

I had made some notes for a final chapter on the WP to follow what I wrote about the history of the relations and attitude of the Marxist party to other organizations. Finally, I decided to let that go until the second stage of the discussion when, I thought, Morrison would be obliged to develop more openly the conciliationist attitude implied in his first letters on the New York branch incident.

Now I learn from the quotation cited by Stein in his speech that Morrison didn't wait long to show how badly he misunderstands this question. We thought Stein answered him quite correctly and, incidentally, put his finger on the source of weakness and inadequacy in all of Morrison's political thinking—his static, formally logical approach to phenomena that are ever moving, ever changing. I used to think that his sneers about dialectics were merely the expression of theoretical indifference. That would be bad enough in a leader, but his contributions to the present discussion show very clearly that he simply does not know how to think dialectically. That is fatal for a political leader.

In my chapter on Muste, his training in the preacher profession was pointed to as an apparently insuperable obstacle to one's development into a revolutionary politician. Must I now add that the legal profession is not much better? I am afraid so. The formal logic of the law and the way of thinking which goes with it are helpless in the face of living, and therefore changing, realities in the political struggle.

The discussion is just getting started! Every time these people open their mouths they provide the theme for an article expounding some elementary idea which they challenge. Morrison was more right than he knew when he said, in his criticism of the educational plan, that comrades learn most by discussion. They will learn a great deal about Bolshevism from our critical discussion of his perverted version of it.

LETTER 127

SANDSTONE, NOVEMBER 9, 1944

Here are some proposals regarding the convention.

1) Be sure to have the plenum in New York at least for a full day before the convention and have all proposals, resolutions, etc., come from the plenum.

2) Insist that the convention take a position on all the *concrete* questions raised in the discussion.

3) The NC should present a short resolution or motion embodying two points: a) *endorsing* the political resolution of the NC; b) *rejecting* the amendments and criticisms of Cassidy and others insofar as they conflict with the line of the NC resolution. Do not permit any fictitious "unanimity" to negate the conclusions of the discussion.

4) *Implement* the decision of the convention majority by a special motion with the following points:

a) The political resolutions of the NC, having been adopted

by the convention by a vote of . . . to . . . , after free democratic discussion in the party ranks, the press and all public
activities of the party must strictly conform to the convention decisions.

b) The discussion may, in the discretion of the NC, be
continued in the *Internal Bulletin*.

5) Publish the convention resolutions in the *FI* rather than
in *The Militant*. Since the latter is becoming more and more
a mass paper, it will perhaps be best to print there only a
general story of the convention with digests of the resolutions. (Perhaps this will also help the *FI* editors to catch up
on their publication schedule.)

6) Publish also the rejected amendments and criticisms
with an editorial note giving the convention vote as in the
case of the adopted resolutions.

7) Be sure to emphasize over and over again the plan of
the Expansion Program to make *The Militant* an eight-page,
more popular and cheaper paper ($1 a year).

8) *Organize* the participation of the leading people in the
discussion by assigning single points in the main reports to
be elaborated and supplemented in the discussion. The various members of the NC, other than the reporters, should
be prepared in advance to develop certain points. This is by
far the best way to get the most out of a number of shorter
speeches.

9) Don't let the convention discussion get sidetracked
on some secondary question. As soon as anything like this
gets started—and it always gets started—some one of the
assigned NC speakers should take the floor and steer the
discussion back into the main channel of the important
questions.

10) Put up a convention blackboard or bulletin board
where the names of candidates for the NC will be posted
as soon as received by the nominating commission. This is
a good means of familiarizing the delegates from the start

with the names of the candidates and stimulating them to a greater interest in the elections.

*

I see by the *Times Magazine* (November 5) that Charles Rumford Walker is secretary of "Yale University Committee on Post-War Planning and Reconstruction." I remember Walker as a Trotskyist sympathizer who was once very much worried about the danger of "Stalinist degeneration" in our party. One has only to read his pathetic article in the *Times* to convince himself that there are other forms and kinds of degeneration. Walker is one of the many who fell victim to the other kind.

LETTER 128

SANDSTONE, NOVEMBER 12, 1944

We will be "doing hard time" this week, bogged down here while the convention is going on. This is the first party convention I have missed in twenty-two years! The only other one I missed since 1919 was the 1922 underground convention at Bridgman. I was in Moscow at the Fourth Congress then. I wish some arrangements could be made to send me daily factual reports. I know it is quite an imposition to ask this when you will all be so busy at the convention. Perhaps you can get Joe to help you.

I noticed that in one of your letters Murry referred to "patience." Patience means: to see a discussion unfolding that is rich in possibilities for the clarification of communist ideas and the education of the party in these ideas; to have a thick pamphlet in your system on the subjects under discussion; and to reconcile yourself to the writing of telescoped notes on one sheet of paper. That is what patience means.

If anyone asks you what my letter on the NC election means, tell them it means just exactly what it says. *I want more democracy in the party!* Democracy means that the leaders, not only collectively but also individually, must be called to account before the party; that the party must pass judgment on their conduct, their activity and their abilities as well as on their political ideas. But not only that. Party democracy also means that the party must pass judgment also on the critics of the leadership. *Everybody* is responsible to the party. And what is the party? The convention is the party. Everything and everybody must be prepared to render account to the convention.

And this only sums up and crowns the principle that all party members, at all times, are responsible to the party. Nobody, *nobody*, stands above the party. It seems to us that this is the crucial point of the dispute over the unauthorized conferences with the Shachtmanites. Morrison, commenting on Stein's article on this question, says, "We all stand for the same thing." Not on your tintype! In another place he says his objective "has been achieved to the extent of 90 percent." He is deluding himself. We will not accept his conceptions of organizational responsibility to the extent of even 10 percent.

It appears to us that, in blowing up the New York incident out of all proportions and then claiming that "his objective has been achieved," as well as in the formulas he advances in *Internal Bulletin No. 7*—Morrison has other "objectives" in mind than the minor incidents under dispute. Is he, perhaps—again indulging his weakness for underestimating the intelligence of other people—assuming as "achieved" a construction which will free him and other thinkers from any real party control and party discipline in the future, in more important matters, and assuming at the same time that no one will notice it? If so, he and any others who entertain such ideas are due for a rude awakening.

It is important now to observe each and every leader, local and national, in this discussion. In my opinion, Morrison's articles are an insult to the party. Any leader who does not angrily react to these insults is lacking in respect for himself and for the party. Such people will be weak reeds to lean on in a crisis.

LETTER 129

SANDSTONE, NOVEMBER 13, 1944

We are waiting with interest to receive Aunt's comments on the letters sent from here. Till then we will not try to surmise where her disagreement arises. When Don comes ask him to give you a roundup report for me. I also want reports from Grant, Burch, Murry and Bill.

If anyone, including Gerland, wants to know my opinion, you can say I think it would be better to dispense with the *hauteur* and instead show precisely wherein any of the political resolutions of the NC for the past four years have been "disproved by events." Nobody has been able to show that yet, as far as I know. What have been "disproved by events" up till now are the criticisms of these resolutions. I would like to receive the Chicago article. Also the points of the articles of Jack and of Oscar and Al.

The reference in my letter No. 128 to *Internal Bulletin No. 7* should be corrected to read "No. 6." I just noticed this error in checking your letter No. 119.

We didn't think it worth while to comment on the proposal to give critical support to the SP. It seems to us that the elections themselves have given the best possible answer to this lifeless attempt at an application of a Leninist tactic when the conditions which gave point to the tactic in previous instances are entirely lacking. Nothing is more hopeless than to approach with formal logical rules political situations which are constantly changing.

The SP is *still* changing, and not for the better either. Even in 1940, when we discussed the election campaign with the Old Man, he said, "The SP is not a party. It is a misunderstanding," or words to that effect. Even then, when the SP had a presumably anti-war position, he dismissed it out of hand and said we should predict that Thomas would support the war.

He thought the CP was a real party with a serious base in the labor movement. But his main reason for proposing that we give the CP critical support in the election was its negative attitude to the war at that time. This gave us, he thought, a point of approach to those Communist Party members who were sincerely opposed to the war. Such a tactic, he thought, might help us to break perhaps "a few hundred" of them away when the inevitable change of Stalinist policy came.

He was very much in earnest about it; wanted very much for us to try it. Despite that, when he found us in disagreement, he said to me: "All right, if you are opposed to it, I will not start a discussion about the question." You see (his name was not Cassidy or Morrison), he did not demand a discussion in the party every time he had a disagreement.

The present flare-up in the party is simply the expression of the fact that the sharp turn which the party has taken toward more effective mass work has thrown a few self-centered people off balance. *The Militant* has become a real popular workers' paper; new people are coming toward us, not by scores any longer but by thousands. This is shown beyond dispute by the successes of the sub campaign, the defense work, the call-backs and the trade-union developments.

The new people who are coming forward are more important than those who are falling behind. The discussion is justified by the extent to which it is utilized to educate the new people.

LETTER 130

SANDSTONE, NOVEMBER 14, 1944

I finished Volume 8 of Grote and started on 9.

With only sixty-nine days and a "git" left to do, my thoughts turn again very often to food and drink. I find myself tarrying over the wine advertisements in the papers, especially those picturing combinations of wine and food. When I saw an appetizing picture of a roasted chicken on a table with a bottle of wine beside it, I thought: If they will give me the chicken I will meet them halfway and take the wine too.

Ask George if he will take us someday to that Chinese place where he and Evelyn took their in-laws. I want to see how a sophisticated man of the world orders "the works" in a place like that. Incidentally, I will be more receptive to Chinese food than I used to be. Could George teach me to order? In the grand manner? I think I might be able to learn. In the past I never paid much attention to restaurant techniques, but I always made out all right with bartenders.

*

I think often of the Old Man these days, with an ever greater appreciation of what he was and what he did for us and for all mankind, under conditions of work and daily existence which were far from ideal. My experience here, far removed from the center of activities, unable to participate directly in party affairs and reduced to the narrow means of trying to influence the course of developments exclusively through abbreviated correspondence, has given me a better understanding of the Old Man's work in exile; a new, poignant sympathy for his brave, persistent efforts over so many difficult years.

He who was so sure-handed, so capable of doing things

personally and doing them right, had to depend entirely on others far away; and not on people ideally selected, but on such human material as he could find at hand. How often did he have to restrain himself, to curb his anger? How often did he have to resort to diplomacy, to phrase his criticisms euphemistically for fear of offending some thin-skinned and self-centered person who might spoil everything because of pique or wounded vanity? And how often, in spite of all his patient efforts, did he have to see this happen in the most critical situations? How much energy did he burn up in futile rage on such occasions? How often did he have to say to himself: "If I were not bound hand and foot I could prevent this"?

He had to create an international organization under such conditions during the whole eleven years of his last exile; twelve years, counting the time at Alma Ata. I feel deeply thankful to be able to assure myself that he had very little of such *unnecessary* trouble with me. When I someday write my memories of Sandstone days and nights my thoughts here of the Old Man will constitute a chapter.

❋

How is the song-book project coming along? Tell Sylvia not to trust entirely to the current edition of the IWW song book. There have been many editions, and some of the best songs have been omitted from the later editions. If she can't get the old editions, they can probably be located at the Crerar library in Chicago.

❋

Here is a proposal for another important project: a new anthology of revolutionary poetry. Begin *now* to accumulate the material by starting a "Poets' Corner" in *The Militant*. Here are the best sources to begin with: Sinclair's *Cry for Justice*; Graham's *Anthology of Revolutionary Poetry* (an anarchist publication); Chaplin's *Prison Poems;* files of old revolutionary papers—the *International Socialist Review,* the *Labor Defender* and the *Masses* and *Liberator* especially; William Ellery Leonard's works. The "Poets' Corner" will make a good addition to the paper.

Poetry is out of style with the sophisticates, but the people have always loved it and always will. We aim to publish a paper for the people.

LETTER 131

SANDSTONE, NOVEMBER 16, 1944

I will need the following material: the files of Calverton's *Modern Monthly* and *Modern Quarterly;* files of *Revolutionary Age* and *Workers' Age;* files of *Labor Action* and *New International* (Shachtman version); anything of Hook's on philosophy in the *Southern Quarterly* and philosophical reviews. Books: the Modern Library Giant edition of *John Dewey's Philosophy;* Durant's new book, *Caesar and Christ; The Loom of Language;* all of Kropotkin's and Berkman's writings that can be found anywhere. (Try the anarchist groups); files of that anarcho-Menshevik magazine which was printed in New York during the period 1936–37, I forget the name of it. Anything procurable of Kautsky and Bernstein (German or English).

*

What became of the project to publish some informative articles about wartime political and religious prisoners? It would be a worthwhile task for someone to dig up the facts and figures on the situation in World War I in comparison to the present one. Some interesting contrasts will be apparent. In the last war there were hundreds of labor and socialist war prisoners; this time our party alone is represented. There were many representatives last time of "recognized" religious bodies in prison for pacifist convictions; today the Jehovah's Witnesses take their places.

I believe investigation will also show that the number of conscientious objectors on non-religious grounds is far less today. The "JWs" are scornful of the war position of the "Socialists" in the present war, contrasted to the record twenty-six years ago. "The Socialist Party sold out this time," they say. They are very friendly to us because we are a "different" kind of "socialist."

*

I am still waiting to hear what Edith and Mike [Bartell] think of my two books; whether they throw a different light on the troublesome "organization question." I think nostalgically of California; we are past due for another sojourn there. It would be good to make the 1940 trip again: to California by way of Mexico City and Acapulco. Try thinking of Acapulco whenever the steam goes down in the radiators. Perhaps the thought will keep you warm. We are waiting for Don's report.

I notice that the *Times Book Review* is now featuring reviews by college professors. That, to me, is a sign that the readers are sick of the literary hacks who all say the same thing. Unfortunately, the college hacks are no better, no more original, no more honest. There is going to be a terrific revulsion of the young generation against all the writers who have so shamefully betrayed them. It warms the heart to see our activists' reports of new subscribers who speak of *The Militant* as "that paper that tells the truth."

*

We thought the old Haymarket drawing lighted up the page of the paper this week. Why can't we experiment with illustrated current articles? Drawings are so much better as a rule than photographs; the artist's eye sees more than the camera. The cartoons keep up their high standard; even seem to improve. But the "Stalinist Press at Work" drawing has just about played itself out, and we will be glad when the pamphlet campaign is finished, if only because we won't have to look at the same illustration every week. We were also glad to get rid of the monotonously repeated illustration of the *History* even if it meant the end of all advertising for this badly treated book.

✻

Did you ever hear the spiritual: "There's goin' to be a great gittin'-up morning"? That will be January 23, 1945.

LETTER 132

SANDSTONE, NOVEMBER 19, 1944

Defense of Marxism arrived and I have already read it through again. While my mind was still fresh from Trotsky's writing, soaked in his *method,* I forced myself to read the two appendices: Burnham's "Science and Style" and his farewell letter to his abandoned "Workers' Party." What a contrast! And what a convincing empirical demonstration— this contrast—of the bankruptcy of empiricism!

I could appreciate the philosophical parts of the book far better this time, since I now have a far surer grasp on the whole question of philosophy. I still have much to read and learn to supplement and round out my knowledge, but I already know the essence of the question and know its decisive importance for a revolutionary politician. I hope to devote my main energies in the next period to learning more on this subject and helping others to learn. Bourgeois philosophy, in all its variations, is as crooked, as falsified by class bias and class interest, as bourgeois economics.

The deer season is open here in the northwest, and the papers are full of the stories of the hunts and the fun the hunters are having. But that is not a patch on the fun I am going to have when I load up my shotgun and go hunting for the fakers who have infested the fringes of the revolutionary workers' movement and even penetrated into its ranks.

*

We signed our release papers yesterday. It really begins to look as though they are fixing to let us out of here. They say that all convicts begin to do hard time when they are "getting short," that is, close to the end of their time. I have seen many painful evidences of this. So far, however, the sickness has not struck us very hard. The main reason, I suppose, is that every day is a full day of study and achievement in preparation for the future. When "time" is crowded this way it doesn't have much chance to drag.

We have learned much here that will be useful for others who follow in our footsteps. But the most important thing of all we will have to say to the young militants who have to do time in the future is that they should immerse themselves in intellectual work. The concrete walls and the steel bars are real. But, after all, they are only one kind of prison. There are also the prisons of ignorance and prejudice, of selfishness and of thought limited to the present day. If one sets himself to the task of breaking out of these prisons; if he feels that with every day's work and study he has made a little headway; then the time passes and the concrete walls don't crowd in so closely.

It helps also, I believe, if one has previously been blessed with a sound philosophy of personal living; has had sense enough to take his fun where he could find it in this world of the present and not postponed it to the problematical future. My mother taught me to love the good things of life and to grasp them on the wing. And since we didn't have too many of them, considering the hard poverty of our family, she helped us, through her shrewd pedagogical devices, to squeeze the most out of those which came our way—first by anticipation, then by realization, and finally by reminiscence.

Thus our Christmas was drawn out from the first snowfall until the spring thaw; and by then we were getting set for the Fourth of July with plenty of firecrackers. Our Fourth of July is not far away.

LETTER 133

SANDSTONE, NOVEMBER 20, 1944

Please send the $15 now to Evie [DeBoer] and tell her to make sure her husband doesn't drink it up or spend it on egg sandwiches.

*

Ask the CRDC to find out definitely about Skogie's [Carl Skoglund] bond and make sure that [Roger] Baldwin makes all the arrangements so that he will not be detained. Follow up on this and let me know when everything is arranged, and definitely how it is arranged so that we will have no uncertainties about the matter.

*

Here is a little poem which Goethe wrote for little Mick. Tell her I want her to learn it by heart and believe it.

Willst du immer weiter schweifen?
Sieh, das Gute liegt so nah.

Lerne nur das Glück ergreifen,
Denn das Glück ist immer da.

＊

I need: Kautsky's *Ethics and the Materialistic Conception of History* (Kerr & Co.). Also get Kerr's catalogue; I want to check and see if I have everything of theirs I will need in my work. Query them also about bound volumes of the *International Socialist Review*. I will badly need a complete set of these if they are at all obtainable. If they can't be had from Kerr, ask the bookstore to shop around. It is clear, I presume, that all the books I am asking for now are for use after our return. No more are needed here.

Ask our philosophers to prepare for me a reading list in philosophy. If Hegel's works or essential parts of them (or other necessary philosophical writing, for that matter) are not to be had in English, then German, French or Spanish editions will do.

＊

Here is another way of organizing study classes which I left out of the plan. This was an oversight, as the scheme may well be timely right now in places like Los Angeles or elsewhere where several branches are too far apart for common classes.

This is the "circuit system" of study classes which I inaugurated in the old Communist Party back in 1924 when I was national educational director. I personally taught on one circuit centering in Chicago. The idea is to prepare a set of lectures on a given subject and give each one in different cities on succeeding nights. For example: I gave the first lecture in my course in Chicago on Monday night; Gary, Tuesday; Milwaukee, Wednesday; Kenosha, Thursday; and Waukegan, Friday. Then, the following Monday, I gave the second lecture in Chicago and repeated it on schedule in the other cities.

It is a very good system; it worked out well and was greatly appreciated by the comrades. At the same time it is very efficient from the standpoint of the instructor. *One* job of preparation enables him to take care of five classes every week; or more, or less, according to the circumstances.

＊

I greatly regret that I couldn't hear the discussion at the convention on the educational plan, and take part in it. The "organizational" side—that is, the practical planning to reach ends with the means at hand—is very important in this question also. Isn't it strange that the "intellectuals" never thought of that?

LETTER 134

SANDSTONE, NOVEMBER 21, 1944

The Militant, due Saturday, hasn't arrived yet. We are hoping it will come in today. We got used to this paper and miss it. (Later: The paper arrived Tuesday night.)

Have adequate numbers of all the *Internal Bulletins* been sent to the foreign parties? This is very important, in more ways than one.

＊

We should stimulate and encourage the development of a genuine student group in the party. I mean students of Marxism and the labor movement who have the will to begin a serious work of study, not ex-students—of whom we have already seen too many—who imagine that they already knew all that is to be known when they left the university.

The educational department should concern itself with devices and methods to aid and inspire our students. Here is one proposal: Appoint a commission to prepare a bibliography of communism, socialism, anarchism and syndicalism. Start with a preliminary list of books, pamphlets and publications. Then invite the students to participate in the work of rounding out the bibliography; send them to the libraries and ask them to submit concise informative digests of every important item they run across and tell where it is to be found.

The goal should be the compilation of a definitive bibliography listing each significant article, telling what are its main points and in what library or libraries it may be found. I understand the Crerar library in Chicago and the library of the University of Wisconsin contain rich material. Put some students to work listing and classifying it. Other veins will be turned up if enough prospectors go to work. I believe this project will arouse real enthusiasm among our student-minded youth.

Let the educational department take a leaf from the colleges and assign theses for the serious students to prepare. An informal student body could be assembled on a national scale under the friendly supervision of the educational director. All that is necessary is to send a circular to the branches announcing the project and asking prospective students to send in their names to receive specific assignments according to their special interests. Assign theses to be written on such subjects as the origin and development of the Knights of Labor; the Haymarket Martyrs—who they were, their work and ideas; Engels' critique of the early American socialist movement; Gompers and the AFL; Debs and The American Railway Union; the old *Appeal to Reason;* the IWW; the right and left wings in the Socialist Party up to the First World War; the beginnings of American communism.

The field is virtually limitless. The *better* theses could be published in a special bulletin of the educational department and submitted to discussion and criticism there. The *best* theses might be published in our press. Let our eager youth be set to work on this project. Something good may come of it. In any event, it should stimulate interest in serious study of the rich history of our movement and its progenitors. To the above list of suggested subjects should be added DeLeon and the SLP. He was a great figure.

LETTER 135

SANDSTONE, NOVEMBER 23, 1944

Here are some more books I wish Sylvia to get for me. There will be many others needed in the work I contemplate. Fowler's *Modern Usage;* Rosmer's book on the labor movement and the war (French); *English Synonyms, Antonyms and Prepositions* by James C. Fernald (Funk and Wagnalls).

*

I see by the *Times* that Hutchins Hapgood is dead. He was well known in the old days when anarchist-liberalism was thought to be very radical. His books, *An Anarchist Woman* and *The Spirit of Labor,* give a picture of the anarchist trend in the labor movement of prewar times. *The Spirit of Labor* is a novel based on the life of Anton Johannsen. I knew him well in the defense movement for Schmidt and Kaplan, the McNamaras and Tom Mooney. Both these books should be in the New York party library. Students will find them very useful in delving into the traditional background of the modern movement.

The development of the library should also be brought under the hegemony of consciousness and plan. A commission should be set up. We should deliberately aim at the goal of a complete library of books necessary for functionaries and students, draw up the list and move progressively toward acquiring it. As we visualize the future, we will soon need a librarian.

*

Who reads copy on *The Militant?* A commission should be appointed to wage war on sloppy writing from a literary point of view. The first and most urgent necessity is a campaign against long sentences running together, one after another. This is the surest way to kill a reader's interest and make him stop in the middle of the first part of an article. Long sentences have to be broken up and balanced against short ones. (Usick should have a special session with Bell on this important defect in his writing.)

*

What did the post-convention plenum decide to do about Chicago?

*

Have arrangements yet been made with the [British] RCP to send bundles of their paper to our branches? We might get a little revenue for them this way—the branches should pay for their bundles—and also deepen the interest of our members in international affairs. Did the RCP make any progress in drawing the unaffiliated Trotskyist elements into the unified party? Have any decisive moves been made toward fusion with the left wing of the ILP? In my opinion the RCP needs a broad program of unification. The best and cheapest way to test out the assimilability of all the elements is through common work in one organization.

＊

I see by the *Times Book Review* that a book of Roosevelt's speeches entitled *Rendezvous with Destiny* is edited by J.B.S. Hardman. This advertisement struck me as a timely footnote to my remarks about him in my *History*. By the way, have the English comrades shown any interest in this book? It should be more useful to them than to our own party, as they still have to go through many of the stages of party development recounted there. Have copies of the book been sent to England? How many?

＊

Did you run across the notes of my speech at the fifteenth anniversary celebration? I should like to reconstruct that speech for inclusion in the *Twenty Years—1923–1943* collection of speeches and articles. I guess we will have to get that book out of the way first, to clear the way for other writing.

LETTER 136

SANDSTONE, NOVEMBER 26, 1944

We are blanketed in snow this Sunday morning and more is coming down. The Minnesota snow, long overdue, held off till the close of the deer season yesterday, to give the deer a better chance against the hunters.

I feel sorry for kids who never have any snow. That is one of the drawbacks of California. The radio is beginning to give a heavy play to the song about a "White Christmas." I left New York last year with that song in my ears. To hear it again reminds me that the time to return is approaching. It is nice to think of good things which are "not far away." I like that song because it reminds me of the Christmases of my boyhood which were all good, and mostly white. I am waiting, however, to hear Bing Crosby sing it. I don't care for this upstart, Sinatra.

＊

I am following with earnest sympathy the brave struggle of little "Nubbins" Hoffman, the three-year-old Cheyenne boy, to hold out till "Christmas" against a supposedly incurable ailment. The latest report we have is that he has been taken to Denver and that the doctor says he is "responding to treatment" and that the odds are swinging in his favor. I have strong hopes that he will make it. Medical science is mighty and beneficent, and so is the idea of "Christmas"— which means "the good time coming."

People cannot live without perspectives, without hopes for the future. Those who hope to organize a great movement of the masses must never forget this, never fail to inspire them with confidence that the future will be better than the present if they only strive to make it so.

The greatest power of Marxism derives from the fact that it gives a rational basis to the impulse of the masses to make a better world; a scientific assurance that the irresistible laws of social evolution are working on their side; that the idea of socialism, of the good society of the free and equal, is not a utopian fantasy but the projection of future reality. When this idea takes hold of the people it will truly be the greatest power in the world.

It seems to me somewhat undignified, somewhat lacking in the sense of proportion, for one who has grasped this idea to be deterred or turned aside by such trifles as concern for one's personal fate. *No importa*, as they say in Spanish—"it does not matter." What matters, as the Old Man expressed it, is "the consciousness that one participates in the building of a better future, that one carries on his shoulders a particle of the fate of mankind, and that one's life will not have been lived in vain."

I was very glad to see that Murry built his twenty-seventh anniversary speech around this conception of the party and the reciprocal relations between the party and its individual members. Much of the propaganda of the past has been too matter-of-fact; the conception of the role of the party too limited; the self-assumed obligations of the individual too paltry, too narrowly calculated. The world will be changed by people who believe in the boundless power of the ideas of the party and who set no limits to the demands which the party may make upon them.

*

I intended to write about the convention today. But the foregoing remarks are, so to speak, comments on the convention.

LETTER 137

SANDSTONE, NOVEMBER 27, 1944

The worst fault of the thinkers' faction is that they don't think. This is demonstrated once again by the party convention. I am not referring here to the votes—although they are not without meaning for those who are capable of learning—but to the fact of the convention itself, its success as a demonstration of party viability, optimism and energy, and the formal seal it was able to place on solid achievements of the past year.

The general success of the convention should not have surprised anyone who is able to observe what is taking place before his eyes and to reflect on what he observes. Conventions rarely introduce anything new; they cannot rise above the party as it is and as it has been in the preceding period. The *role* of the convention, if one takes time to think about it, is simply to formalize decisions which have already been prepared and to project such new activities as have been made possible by previous work.

If the thinkers had devoted one-tenth as much time to thinking as they devoted to talking and writing about the leader cult and the lack of party democracy, they would have been able to foresee that the convention itself, a concentrated expression of all that has been done and learned in sixteen years of struggle, was bound to impress the party members as a crushing empirical refutation of their thesis.

What kind of Stalinist bureaucratism is it when a new recruit, who knows from his trade-union experience—his daily life!—what Stalinist methods are, takes the floor and says: "I don't see anything like that in this party, either here or in Los Angeles"? And what kind of a "leader cult" is the party dedicated to when the convention, held after a year's absence of the *second-line* leaders, and four years after the death of the *first-line* leader, acclaims the *third-line* leaders for their direction of the party during the year of its greatest progress?

In fact, the convention and the year's experience which it summarized and represented was a great triumph for the conception of a party based on great principles, whose cadres have been educated and selected in the struggle for these principles, not arbitrarily but by the struggle itself; a party whose members are bound together and inspired by common ideas which are not the personal property of an individual leader like his personal qualities, which he cannot transmit to others, but common property which can be *acquired* by those who are willing to study, and *transmitted* by them to others who are willing to learn.

The party which has celebrated this triumphant convention under such adverse conditions, and after such heavy blows had been dealt to its leading staff nationally and internationally, has a full right to speak of the *education* of its cadres; and it was nothing more than the logical outcome of all preceding developments that put a systematic plan for the higher organization of party educational work at the center of the convention's agenda.

Those who foolishly put themselves crossways with the forward trend of the convention had better begin to think seriously about these things. We, the party—said the convention—don't want your prejudices, and we are impatient with your twaddle.

LETTER 138

SANDSTONE, NOVEMBER 28, 1944

Continuing: Logically, such a decisive vote as that recorded by the convention, after an unrestricted preparatory discussion in the party, should impel the opposition to reconsider their position and make an effort to learn something from their experience. Unfortunately, logic makes but slow headway in establishing its hegemony over certain types of human minds where prejudice fights on its home grounds. Past experience tends to discount any optimistic hopes that may be entertained in this respect. I can't remember ever knowing a professional democrat who paid respectful attention to the cardinal principle of democracy, i.e., the subordination of the minority to the majority. They demand "democracy" but they are firmly convinced that *demos* is a fool.

It would not be realistic to consider the disputes as settled, as far as the illogical "democrats" are concerned, by the simple fact that the party membership has given its decision. It is to be expected, rather, that an attempt will now be made to transfer the debate to the international field where, as a result of present world conditions, the free exchange of information encounters many difficulties. We should take these difficulties into consideration and do our best to overcome them without losing time that can never be made up.

Concentrated attention should be devoted to the problem of supplying every possible section of the Fourth International with all available material bearing on the disputes. The work of transmitting full sets of the *Internal Bulletins* to the foreign parties should be *organized* and periodically checked until every possibility is exhausted. This, in our opinion, is the most important follow-up on the convention and the discussion which preceded it.

Next, we deem it essential, as we have previously remarked, to publish the convention resolutions in the magazine; and to publish with them the rejected amendments of Logan and the rejected criticisms of Cassidy—giving the vote in each case. And a *report* of the convention should be published in the magazine giving an explanation, from the point of view of the majority, of the reasons for the convention's decisions. It goes without saying that the report should be fairly and objectively written, in a style and tone befitting the dignity of our theoretical journal.

There must be no mistake, however, and no misunderstanding as to the character the press must assume in the ensuing period. The press must be edited in strict accord with the decisions of the party convention; not only in the letter, but in the spirit too. Our party democracy must express itself in majority rule without any ambiguity whatever. This must be automatically guaranteed by the decisions made in the assignments to the posts of *executive* editors for each organ. Naturally, representatives of the minority must be given full opportunity to participate in the editorial work both of the paper and the magazine. But the executive editor charged with the duty of guarding the line of the convention must, in each case, be a man who understands the line and believes in it. The decisions should be made now.

LETTER 139

SANDSTONE, NOVEMBER 30, 1944

We have read reports of the contents of the November *FI* in two issues of *The Militant* but our copies have not yet arrived. It is wrong to advertise the magazine before it comes off the press. This must cause disappointment to many people who look vainly for it in every mail. Or perhaps there is some delay in mailing our copies. Ask Sylvia to check this once again. We received Tuesday's *Times* Wednesday night.

✱

In negotiating for the new edition of *Whither England?* take note that the edition originally published in England under the title *Where Is Britain Going?* is a very bad translation which distorts the meaning of some important passages. The International Publishers edition under the title *Whither England?* is much better. The text of the original British edition should not be used in any case.

✱

Looking forward to the Sedoff memorial, perhaps we should plan a new edition of the pamphlet if the old one is out of stock. I think I will write a memory of Sedoff this time. I have something to say about him that hasn't been said before.

✱

Please get for me a copy of the pamphlet about Tito by Howard Fast which you mentioned in a letter many months ago. I am going to study the publishing business—*somebody* has to study it—and the style of this pamphlet on the technical side, which you mentioned, may suggest some ideas.

❋

I will need these books for my philosophical studies: Plato; Spinoza; Descartes (in French or English); Hume; Kant (in English or German); *The Holy Family, Feuerbach* and *The Poverty of Philosophy* (in English or German); Hegel (in English or German); Heine: *History of German Philosophy;* Charles Pierce: *Chance, Love and Logic;* Tarski: *An Introduction to Logic;* Morris R. Cohen and Ernest Nagel: *Logic and Scientific Method;* Locke and Berkeley.

❋

Notes for future reference: Aristotle on Habit. "Control Sickness" of early American Communist movement (in re: English overemphasis on this point). Winwood Reade: *The Martyrdom of Man.* Study ancient history not as an "escape" from contemporary politics but in order to return to it more effectively and with better perspective.

In checking my accumulated notes today I found the following item: "New organizers and NC alternates. Mike Bartell as candidate." Was the NC reading my thoughts?

❋

The listing of the Flint branch at the top of the call-back scoreboard seems like a bad joke. Perhaps next time we should devise a better system. Branches from which little or nothing is expected should not even be listed. The scoreboard should tell the true story of branch accomplishments.

Places like Flint and Philadelphia must be rehabilitated by forced measures from the outside. If the organization fund permits, we should work out a system of transplanting young couples to concentrate on contact and house-to-house work to build up a subscription and contact list to put a new foundation under the branches. The political education of Boston has been too long neglected. We *must* send a good organizer there.

December, 1944

SANDSTONE, DECEMBER 3, 1944

I'll be seeing you *next month!* It sounds nearer when you put it that way. Besides it is literally true. We are "getting short" and I think some of the boys are beginning to do hard time. All convicts do that when they begin to count the days—"Fifty-five and a git," "fifty-four and a git," etc. Today it stands at fifty-one and a git. The "git" is what I am waiting for.

Your idea of meeting me at Minneapolis and stopping over there for two days would be fine for me, but I am afraid the long train ride and the frigid Minnesota weather might not be good for you. You can think about that side of it. Meantime you can ask the CRDC to apply, perhaps through Roger [Baldwin], to the Washington authorities for me to stop over at Minneapolis for two days to meet you and attend to some personal affairs before proceeding to New York. It is necessary to get this special permission; otherwise, under the regulations, I will be obliged to proceed directly to my "destination" which cannot be any place but New York.

Our friends can arrange anything they see fit after our arrival in New York. The only thing that must not be interfered with is my Christmas tree and chicken stew (with dumplings) and Mick. I want you to pick out a ring for her, as I promised. And tell her not to forget a calabash pipe and a pair of opera slippers for me—to keep at her house so I can smoke and rest in comfort when I come to see her.

I finished Volume 9 of Grote and started on 11. (Volume 10 is missing from the set here.)

The notes of the speech I inquired about are those used at the *fifteenth anniversary* plenum banquet, not the farewell speech; the speech about "the plow and the stars."

＊

If Mike is going to Chicago, he should have a clear understanding of his political task there. From this point of view you should let him read all the remarks I made about Chicago in recent months. My remarks about activism, however, should not be taken one-sidedly. Activism alone cannot cure a politically sick branch, because new members become infected or drop away. But activism correlated with a correct political line and good pedagogical methods by the leadership can work wonders. The new workers recruited then become additional weight in the scale against the bohemian tendency.

This was decisive in the ultimate solution of the stalemate of our "dog days." It was the "turn to mass work," started in 1933, which in the end sealed the doom of the petty-bourgeois opposition in 1940. The new people recruited and the cadres selected in the process of developing the mass work of the party shifted the weight steadily against the "internal" specialists of whom Abern was the archetype. By 1939–40 we had a different and better composition of the party membership to appeal to. This was decisive.

The easy victory of the National Committee in the recent discussion was assured from the start precisely because the work of proletarianization and activization in general had been carried on in earnest since the split. I neglected to bring out this important point in past writings. Another subject for the future.

LETTER 141

SANDSTONE, DECEMBER 4, 1944

The November magazine has not arrived yet.

Our publishing activity should be made the subject of consideration and discussion in the PC with the object of fixing its place in the overall plan of party work and introducing the planning principle into the publishing work itself. From a routine agency of distribution it must be transformed into a publishing institution in the full sense of the word, developing its own methods of promotion and becoming expert in all the methods, devices and economies of the trade.

I propose a five-year publishing plan, with a list of classical works to be published as scheduled at intervals over this period and published on time. Space can be left open in the schedule for the publication of contemporary writings. The fundamental aim of the plan should be to fill out the gaps in the present list of Marxist classics available in English, and automatically assure the prompt publication of any new literary material which may be produced and approved by the party.

There is no lack of material pressing now either for first publication in English, or republication of out-of-print classics. It must be borne in mind that we are now the *sole* agency interested in providing the necessary texts for the Marxist education of the new generation. And we have no time to waste, for this generation is already knocking at the door.

The publishing program is no small part of the historical responsibility devolving upon us. To discharge it worthily we must understand that it is not a technical departmental problem but a major political task of the party leadership. There must be a *revolutionary transforma-*

tion of the *conception* of the publishing department, and following from that the reorganization of its work on a higher basis.

The *volume* of books produced must be determined solely by (1) the amount of capital we can reasonably count on, and (2) the number of new books our branches can be organized to distribute in a year. No other limitations can be allowed for in the plan; technical problems and difficulties must be solved by the publishing company just as any other similar concern does.

The party leadership has the duty and responsibility only to say what is possible and necessary, to provide the means—money and distributing agents—and then assign the staff to carry out the practical work of the plan. In my opinion our present forces can assimilate and distribute a minimum of three books a year, and means can be found for the initial expenses to publish them.

A commission should be appointed to study both the editorial and practical side of the question and prepare the five-year plan and schedule. Perhaps the educational department can double in this field. A maximum of three months should be allowed for the preparation of the definitive report of the commission and the final adoption of the plan.

Here are a few suggestions to consider: the *complete* Marx-Engels correspondence; all of Trotsky's writings since 1917 not published in book form, or now out of print; any basic writing of Marx and Engels not hitherto published in English or now out of print; try to buy *plates* of *Revolution Betrayed, My Life* and such socialist novels as *The Iron Heel, The Jungle* and *Pelle the Conqueror*.

Visualize a complete socialist library for the new generation and plan to fill it, book by book, in the order of importance.

LETTER 142

SANDSTONE, DECEMBER 5, 1944

In planning the future development of the publishing house we must conceive of it as a great institution which must serve the needs of an expanding movement whose members and sympathizers will, in their great majority, consist of a new generation without any previous political schooling. It must undertake to serve all their needs, as far as literature is concerned; and to do this, it must unfold in full scope and with professional efficiency three departments of activity: (1) its own original publications; (2) reprints of other publishers' out-of-print items; (3) the distribution of important books of other publishers.

One of the most important immediate tasks is to devote concentrated study and investigation to the problem of cutting down the initial capital outlay required to publish *the first edition* of each book so that more volumes can be issued annually with the funds at our disposal. Two possibilities must be investigated and considered along this line.

1) Ascertain the cost of publishing from plates instead of from type. At first glance this may appear as an added expense, since the plates cost money. But since we can't expect at present to sell more than a thousand or so copies of any book the first year, it might work out that the added cost of the plates for the *first edition* of, say, 1,500 copies would still leave us with a much smaller outlay than is required for an edition of 5,000 printed from type.

With the plates on hand we could then run off another edition of 1,000 or so when needed. Meantime, the capital now frozen in slow-moving stocks of books would be released to finance new publications. It would be far better and more economical, it seems to me, to have the bulk of our capital stock represented by plates than by books. This proposition should be investigated in connection with the next book scheduled for publication.

It will be a real important achievement for us if we can reduce the initial expense, and thus facilitate the earlier publication of another volume. To be sure, we will have to dig up more money later on to put a second edition through the press. But later on we will have more money because we will have a bigger movement to get it from. Our program of expansion in all fields must proceed in every case from our confidence that the movement is really going to expand and "catch up with and outstrip" all our most ambitious plans.

2) We must now again investigate to the bottom and consider the feasibility of getting our own linotype to be operated by comrades. The last experience with the print-shop was a rather unhappy one. But this should not scare us away from even the thought of another attempt, better planned, on a more modest scale. This time we should limit ourselves to the project of setting type and making up the forms *only for our books and pamphlets*, having the press work done outside, and leaving the *publications* out of the scheme altogether. The idea is worth investigating.

If it will enable us to produce books cheaper, we should undertake it. Perhaps a couple of reliable comrades, possibly girl comrades, may be inspired by the idea of going to linotype school and making a definite place for themselves as party printers. That would be a worthy ambition and a great service to the party.

Professional techniques must be worked out. Book designing, etc., studied with the object of working out our own distinctive, uniform format, not inferior to those of the Modern Library, Random House and Everyman's Library. Conservative, solid, cheap.

LETTER 143

SANDSTONE, DECEMBER 7, 1944

The objections we hear to our practice of praising our party, its institutions and—once in a while—its individual members, is at bottom an expression of the capitulatory skepticism of the petty bourgeois; his deep-seated lack of confidence in the proletariat, in the party, and in himself. All petty-bourgeois parties, groups and tendencies, no matter how much they may quarrel among themselves, make it an article of their creed that "no one party" can be trusted with the leadership of the workers' movement.

The main lesson they deduce from the Russian Revolution is that the "monopoly" of leadership by the Bolsheviks was the source of all evils. To be sure, they feel in their hearts that the Revolution itself was a "mistake," but their criticism of the "one-party" leadership is a more timid, more roundabout way of expressing the same sentiment. It is a way of saying, "It must not happen again."

To the frankly expressed ambition and determination of the Trotskyists to lead the movement for the reconstruction of the International, all the centrists of the London Bureau counterposed the idea of a coalition of groups and tendencies, none of which would have "hegemony." Against our idea of the Marxist party leading the proletarian revolution and the workers' state they visualized this grandiose social transformation, insofar as they visualized it at all, as being smoothly effected by the amicable cooperation of a coalition of parties.

Norman Thomas, in a press interview after the recent election, expressed the belief—and hope—that a "new party" of the workers would arise. By that he meant to say that he had no confidence in his own party except, as he added, as "an educational force." Any Shachtmanite you meet on the street, assuming that you do not search for the philosopher's stone by shopping around at their meetings, will tell you that his hopes for the future are centered in some kind of a unification from which a new party will arise. That is his way of saying that he does not assign any great historic role to his own party. The so-called modesty of all petty-bourgeois politicians and commentators simply corresponds to their own pessimism, to the low valuation which they place on their own ideas, their own organization, and their own future prospects.

They cannot understand how others can feel and act differently and still be "normal," just as the petty shopkeeper or the small landowner buried in the idiocy of rural life imagines that his prejudices, his morality and his narrow acquisitive traits, along with his rule-of-thumb ignorance which he calls "common sense," represent universal and unchanging human nature. We who believe in the world-conquering power of our ideas, and consequently in our party and in ourselves, seem "queer" to them. They break out into a rash at every demonstration of our self-assurance; they think it is conceit, a trait which, they have been taught to believe, should be decorously screened, not openly flaunted.

I am inclined to think that we made an impermissible concession to this petty-bourgeois prejudice in the recent discussion, to the extent that we did not frankly characterize it and counterpose our ideas to it.

LETTER 144

SANDSTONE, DECEMBER 10, 1944

I finished the eleventh volume of Grote and started on the twelfth and last. I am now in the midst of Alexander's campaigns. Do you know how Alexander untied the famous

Gordian knot? He cut it with a sword. Sometimes that is the best way.

I read a book called *Liquor, the Servant of Man* by a doctor and a chemist. After an extensive scientific investigation and study they come to the conclusion that the anti-liquor propaganda is based on prejudice and that liquor is good for what ails you. My Uncle Jim on my father's side—I had two uncle Jims—came to the same conclusion over fifty years ago solely on the basis of empirical tests of his own. He was a sort of unconscious pragmatist. I don't claim to have any independent opinions on the question, but I don't see anything wrong in deferring to the judgment of the experts. Who am I to fight the scientists—especially when they decide in my favor.

The scientific authors of this book state that liquor—used in wise moderation, of course—has an especially beneficent effect on people of advancing years, aiding both their digestion and their disposition and promoting a philosophical view of life. Now, isn't it a happy coincidence that I am not as young as I used to be, that my digestion needs special consideration and that I have just discovered the "dear delight" of philosophy? All I need now is a number of appropriate coming-out presents—and I don't mean the armchair you wrote about or things of that sort.

I think you had better let the armchair wait till I return. After sitting on a severely straight iron chair for thirteen months I will want to be sure to select a chair which fits my bones. In this case, also, the experimental method will be the best. We will have plenty of time on our vacation and we can shop around at secondhand stores till we find one that fits.

Another coming-out present I am greatly interested in is pajamas. When I get out of this place I am going to quit the uncivilized habit of sleeping in my underwear. I read all the pajamas ads attentively and make a problem of the selection of patterns and colors. I also worry about you getting the wrong size, which for me is 38—not 42! Any pattern will do as long as it is not conservative, and any color will do as long as it is bright. The same prescription goes for neckties. I want to clear the distance from no necktie at all to a flowery-patterned one at a single bound.

I am also daily studying the ads for soft mattresses and pillows, marveling at the poetic gifts of the authors and artists who describe these prosaic utilities so simply and yet so powerfully, and make a simple ad stir the imagination like the green hills of faraway. Or could it be that my imagination raises the ads to the ideal standard they should attain? I have always known that the audience makes the orator, and that the most appreciative audience is the one that hears the orator articulate its own thoughts, hopes and aspirations. The same may be true of advertisements.

LETTER 145

SANDSTONE, DECEMBER 11, 1944

My No. 143 started out as an introductory paragraph to some concluding remarks on our publishing department, but my pen ran away with me. What I really meant to say at the end was that the unconscious concession to the philistine criticisms seems to express itself in a hesitancy to devote the necessary "promotion" to our institutions and their work. This seems to apply especially to Pioneer Publishers which has such a great role to play and must "tell the world" about it. An army that is on the march and sure of its destination has to beat its own drums.

When the next book comes off the press it should be made the occasion for a planned promotional campaign which will compensate for past deficiencies in this respect. We should deliberately aim to arouse party pride in the past achievements and future prospects of Pioneer; build up a devotion to this institution as a constituent element of party patriotism. Neither promotional nor any other serious campaigns can be carried out without plans and imagination brought to bear on an assured purpose. The next campaign should be a buildup for Pioneer as well as for the new book. It's our institution, isn't it? Then why shouldn't we build it up?

I would like to see the campaign planned in advance and developed in stages as every good campaign should be. The following suggestions might be incorporated.

1) Start a column of "Pioneer Notes" in the paper and see that a news reference is made to the new book often enough to arouse expectation for its appearance.

2) Assign the writing of the reviews prior to the publication date and have them ready to appear simultaneously with the appearance of the book. The first *leading* reviews in both the magazine and the paper should be seriously prepared theoretical and political evaluations of the book by leading members of the PC. These should be followed up systematically by shorter reviews and comments on separate aspects of the volume, then by news reports on the progress of the sales, the comments of rank-and-file members, etc.

3) The ads for the book should be planned imaginatively and varied from issue to issue as every other enterprising publishing house does. The constant repetition of the same ad until everybody is sick of looking at it shows an attitude of routine and indifference which must be completely discarded in the publishing department as in every other branch of party work. It does not fit in with our ambitious program of expansion in the next period.

4) The appearance of the new book should be saluted by a good article on the history and achievements of Pioneer Publishers, illustrated perhaps by a "montage" picture of all the books and pamphlets published since the beginning. The

date of the founding of Pioneer can be established from the files of *The Militant*. I wrote an article promoting our first Program of Expansion (I think in 1931 or 1932) in which the plan to start our own publishing house was announced.

Quotations could be made from this article and the atmosphere of those heroic days recreated. Pioneer must be depicted as part of our great tradition. The new people need this.

LETTER 146

SANDSTONE, DECEMBER 12, 1944

We must devote some thought to the function which *The Militant* has to fill in the next period and then deliberately plan to shape its character accordingly. (The magazine is a separate question, or at any rate a distinctly special and peculiar part of the general question of the press in the visualized immediate future.) Editorial and financial policy both must fit the new requirements. We should not improvise aimlessly and stumble on changes and innovations, but rather plan them. At least, we should try to see clearly what is needed, what is wanted in general, and then seek, to a certain extent by trial and error, for the necessary improvements and changes to serve the general aim and plan.

The Militant originated as a cadre organ in the narrower sense of the word, and was directed almost exclusively to the Communists, and even among them to the more advanced, more conscious elements. Later, by stages, the appeal of the paper was broadened. As we went through the experiences of the fusion with the AWP and the entry into the Socialist Party, the paper reflected the new tasks and addressed itself to a somewhat wider, more variegated audience. At times *The Militant* attempted to express the "turn to mass work," which began in 1933, as a transformation already achieved instead of merely projected and barely started, and spoke primarily for an audience which was not yet ready to listen.

The readers of the paper were mainly limited all the time to vanguard elements whose first interest was the ideological struggles of the more conscious political tendencies. These struggles were also the main preoccupation of the party members, despite our resolute ambition, and even impatience to "turn to mass work" in earnest. On the one hand, the masses were not yet ready to hear us. On the other hand, we had first to fit the party for revolutionary mass work. This took much time and effort. The struggles to carry out the "turn" in the case of the fusion and the entry were in large measure struggles within our own ranks. Despite that, we made substantial headway in each case.

It was no small achievement, viewed in retrospect, to defeat the sectarian dogmas so completely that they could not arise to plague us again. But after these great ideological conquests, accompanied all the time by modest improvements in our mass work, we still had to defeat the petty-bourgeois opposition and *proletarianize the party composition* before we, on our part, could carry out the turn to mass work in deed as well as in word. A change in the mood of *the masses* was also needed to enable our party to find a completely new and different milieu for its main activities. This change was made for us by objective circumstances and is now clearly observable, at least in its preliminary manifestations.

Fortunately, the beginning of a new mass radicalism did not find us unprepared. The outstanding feature of the past year's work of the party has been the sustained, although not always planned and organized, effort to adapt the party and its press to the new milieu. The first successes can rightly be considered as a mere down-payment for the great work of internal preparation carried out beforehand, in time.

Nothing could be more anachronistic than a revival of

sentimental toleration toward the petty-bourgeois opposition of 1939–40. It is perfectly obvious that the achievements of the past year were made possible, in the first place, by the victorious fight against the petty-bourgeois tendency and the consequent transformation of the party composition; which, in turn, made possible the serious beginning of the transformation of all the party work, methods and outlook.

LETTER 147

SANDSTONE, DECEMBER 14, 1944

The experiences of the past year have shown quite clearly that the party has entered a new stage of its development. The more accurately we judge just what this new stage consists of, the more consciously and the more precisely will we be able to adapt the press to the new tasks and opportunities which flow from it. Most of us have seen and felt the necessity of new ways of working and new methods of propaganda. But most of the changes and improvements we have introduced have been improvisations, made under the pressure of the new situation.

In my opinion all these improvisations, or nearly all of them, have pointed in the right direction. But it is not sufficient for us to continue to feel our way along the new path. It is time to generalize our conception of the new situation and the new opportunities, problems and tasks which it creates. We should survey the road ahead, draw general conclusions, and then take the necessary practical steps to bring the work of every department into line with a general scheme.

As far as we can judge from the outline of the domestic political resolution, it gave a good answer to the pressing questions confronting the *class*. That, of course, is the foundation for all plans of party work. However, such a general political resolution does not answer but only poses the next question: What *can* and what *must* the *party do* to implement its political resolution most efficiently?

The program of expansion is a partial answer which should keep us in step with developments while we are studying the problem more attentively, more searchingly, and more precisely. In the light of such a study the program of expansion itself will be seen for what it really is—a bold improvisation, partly consciously and partly instinctively elaborated, to meet pressing new problems which permit no delay.

It would be a great gain if the next period of the work of the NC should produce a general analysis of the new stage of the development of the party, and flowing from that, specific detailed and motivated resolutions to govern the work of each *department* of party activity. That would be to answer the question "what to do next" in a Trotskyist, that is, thoroughgoing manner. If we proceed in this conscious, deliberate way we can reduce the overhead charges of experimentation to a minimum.

That is not a small consideration, for wasted opportunities on the one side and wasted energies from too ambitious plans on the other can never be reclaimed. More important even than that, nothing can do more to strengthen and fortify the already splendid morale of the party ranks than the assurance that we have thought about our problems in all their aspects; that we know what we are doing and propose to do, and how, and why.

Everything we do must be done with the party and through the party. Political speculation without a party, or a definite program to create one, is as barren as military strategy without an army.

We can give the right answers to the questions mentioned above only insofar as we correctly answer the *prior* question: What kind of a party have we now? Therefore, proceeding from the political analysis, national and international, made by the convention, we should devote our thought to the evolutionary process by which American communism, as represented now solely and exclusively by our party, has developed from its inception in the left wing of the old Socialist Party up to the present. What are the permanent conquests of the past experiences, and what is the line of further, continuing development?

LETTER 148

SANDSTONE, DECEMBER 15, 1944

The Minnesota sun is very bright this frosty Sunday morning. This is always the one hour of the week when I think most of home. If anyone were to ask me what freedom means, I could tell him. Freedom means home on Sunday morning. This is also the hour when little Mick, who is ever present in my thoughts, seems closest to me, most vividly present. I see her happy smile dancing on the sunbeams which stream through the bars and make a checkerboard pattern on my bed.

*

I see by the press dispatches that our little pal, "Nubbins" Hoffman, is "getting along nicely"; the doctor who performed the lifesaving operation expresses the confidence that the "incurable" disease which threatened to cheat "Nubbins" out of his "Christmas" has been conquered. Medical science is the benign science, benign and stern; the science which puts nature under discipline and forbids her to destroy people blindly. What a great flowering this science will have under socialism!

I have seen a triumph of medical science which was also a triumph of human solidarity here at Sandstone. When

I went up to the hospital at "sick call" one day to have my sore toes dressed I immediately sensed that something was missing, something was wrong. There were no nurses in evidence, the door of the doctor's office was locked and the other convicts on sick call were standing in the corridor in oppressive silence.

The reason soon became manifest. Through the glass door of the record office, and beyond that through the glass door of the operating room, we could see the masked doctors and nurses moving back and forth around the operating table. Not a sound reached us through the double door. Now a doctor, now a nurse moved in and out of view, only their heads or rather their drawn faces showing, like figures on a silent movie screen.

The word was passed along the "line" in hushed whispers: A colored man was dying. A desperate emergency operation was failing; the poor black convict's life was slipping out of the doctors' hands like a greased thread. But we could see that the doctors were still working, still trying, and one could sense the unspoken thought of all the men on the line; their concern, their sympathy, and in spite of everything, their hope, for their comrade on the operating table.

After what seemed an endless time, the prison pharmacist who was assisting in the operation came out through the double door into the corridor. His face was the picture of exhaustion, of defeat and despair. There would be no sick call, he said; the doctors would not be free for some time. The case of the colored man was apparently hopeless, but the doctors were going to make one final desperate effort. They were sewing up the abdominal wound on the slender, practically nonexistent chance that by blood transfusions they could keep the man alive and then build up his strength for the shock of another stage of the complicated and drawn-out operation.

Then came a new difficulty. The sick man's blood was

hard to "type." The blood of the first colored fellow convicts who volunteered was unsuitable. But the sick Negro got the blood he needed just the same. The white convicts rose up *en masse* to volunteer for transfusions. I think every man in our dormitory offered to give his blood. The sick man hung between life and death for weeks; but this life-giving fluid of the white convicts, steadily transfused into his body, eventually gave him the strength for a second and successful operation.

I saw him line up with the rest of us for the yard count yesterday, this Negro with the blood of white men coursing through his veins, and I thought: The whites, over the centuries, have taken a lot of blood from the blacks; it is no more than right that one of them should get a little of it back.

LETTER 149

SANDSTONE, DECEMBER 18, 1944

Grant's memo contained some very interesting factual material and for that reason was especially welcomed here.

We are still waiting for a report on the work of the nominating commission. What went on there? Who was nominated? How did the commission go about its work? What contests took place in the commission? How many and who were almost elected but not quite? Didn't Buffalo put up a fight for representation after the showing they have made? What was the general impression of the proposals I made? Was the convention as a whole satisfied with the work of the commission? Did they feel at the end that they have an NC of their own free selection?

If my remarks are sent abroad, a postscript should be added to the effect that they are designed for the method of selecting the NC in our party as it is today, at the given stage of its development, and are not meant as a universal formula. Every party must work out its methods on the basis of its own experiences.

From the brief remarks made by George in the limited time he visited with me alone I got the impression that the spirit of *conciliationism*, which is another name for theoretical indifference and political slovenliness, is manifested to a certain extent also on the international field. Thanks to the action of the convention we can now proceed confidently to lead the international fight against this disintegrating tendency under the most favorable conditions; that is, *as a party*.

Our *press* must be put in order, to carry out its function in this respect. Our press is and can be no longer neutral on any question decided by the convention, but must appear as an aggressive partisan of all these decisions in the international discussion. In deciding the question of the allocation of personnel to the press as in every other question, the first concern of the NC should be to assure the faithful execution of the convention decisions. That is the quintessence of genuine party democracy. *We* discuss in order to *decide*.

The international situation should now become the subject of thoroughgoing consideration; we must examine and analyze it from all sides, come to an agreement in the party leadership, and then plan and organize the campaign to discharge our obligations to the international movement and its program. Being thoroughgoing party democrats and not mere devotees of the cult of self-expression, we must draw the rank and file into conscious, informed participation. Being political fighters and not mere ideological speculators, we must fight not as individuals but as an organized party.

In our opinion the necessary next step is a planned and organized international discussion. As in the party during the pre-convention period, "organizational measures," "discipline," all formalities, should be laid aside, suspended, while all attention of the international movement is concentrated on *discussion* and *clarification*. We must ward off the inevitable attempts to muddle up the situation by complaints of "American imperialism" just as we dealt with the red herring of "bureaucratism" in the recent party discussion. We don't *decide* or *demand* anything. We simply put forward the opinions *of our party*, modestly, pedagogically and firmly.

LETTER 150

SANDSTONE, DECEMBER 19, 1944

As the day of our release draws near I find with deep satisfaction that the projects which I was sent here to work on are being brought to a successful completion in synchronism with the completion of our sentences. Today I finished the twelfth and last volume of Grote's *History of Greece*. Thursday I will finish Lenin's *Materialism and Empirio-Criticism*. In two more weeks, doing a regular stint every day, I will finish *John Dewey's Philosophy* and a very light, popularly written book by Durant called *The Story of Philosophy*.

This is enough of history and philosophy for one year, and I will not begin the study of any books on these subjects, or any other subject. During the next five weeks I will concentrate all my time on reading French, German and Spanish. These tasks, as far as a reading knowledge goes, are already conquered. Five more weeks of intensive reading should greatly improve my vocabulary and increase my facility to the point where the study of any subject in any of these three languages will present no difficulties.

It is always a great satisfaction to one who likes order and system in thought and work to make a plan, to organize one's work on the basis of the plan, and then to carry it through to a successful conclusion. I had secretly hoped, although I did not plan and promise myself, to be able also to study the Greek dramatists and some Roman history. But the inflexibility of mathematical law barred the way. Even in prison there are only twenty-four hours in the day.

I have also put in order and consider finished the limited work which conditions here permitted me to do for the party. My remaining notes, classified under the headings, "School," "Press," "Literary Secretariat" and "Miscellaneous," will be sent to you in abbreviated form in subsequent letters. There will be time later to elaborate them and put them into life, insofar as they are found acceptable to the NC. I still have to learn to discipline myself to simply writing down the notes in my letters without space-taking, motivating introductions. But time limitations from now on, pressing more urgently every week, will compel me to fit my writing to a narrow frame. I must reconcile myself to the inexorable fact that there isn't much more time. January 23 seems to keep nudging my elbow and saying: "You must make it short now, your time is up!"

＊

I received the Christmas box of chocolates, but I couldn't wait for Christmas to start sampling them and sharing them with others. I will not thank Evelyn now. But in the not distant future I will plan, organize and execute in a thoroughgoing Trotskyist manner an action which will express my gratitude and appreciation more suitably than mere words. How can that be done better than by personally concocting and serving her a cocktail that fits her personality: an Old Fashioned, based on *l'eau de vie*, and spiced with angostura bitters and lemon peel and sweetened with sugar.

Grant's report of festive occasions planned to celebrate our return appeals powerfully to the imagination. I dread the thought of formal affairs with attendant speeches and other duties, but I will be a good customer for any kind of a shindig where one can have some fun.

LETTER 151

The new stage in the development of the party is strikingly expressed both internally and externally. In both fields a transformation of quantity into quality—a veritable revolution—has taken place. It is not the same party that it used to be, either in regard to its internal life and composition or in the nature of its external activity. These changes should be studied attentively from each side as well as in their interrelation. Here I wish only to deal with our external work, with particular reference to the press. (Later on I hope to add something to the discussion of our public propaganda work in general, and also in its various particular departments. A big field, one that has never been properly surveyed and charted, is open here.)

What kind of a paper will best serve the needs of the new party *in the next period* which lies immediately before us? We used to think, or rather take for granted, that as we broke out of the narrow propaganda circle and began to get a hearing from the workers, we should aim at changing the weekly into a daily. That was the motivation for the launching of the twice-a-week experiment and the later proposal, put on the shelf by the outbreak of the internal struggle of 1939, to proceed to a three-a-week issue.

It was also assumed that, as the paper became a "mass" paper, it would be obliged to adapt itself to the political understanding of the average, if not to the lowest common denominator, among its new readers; leaving the more complicated political and theoretical explanations to the monthly magazine. On closer analysis, with the question no longer speculative but concrete and immediate, both these ideas require radical revision.

With our present resources and manpower, and those which can reasonably be counted on in the next period of expansion, a *daily* paper would devour such huge sums as to starve the other departments of our work and defeat our plans for a symmetrical development of the movement. The task of *distributing* a daily would consume so much of the energies of our limited forces as to sacrifice volume of circulation for frequency of issue. The experience with the twice-a-week paper taught us a preliminary lesson in this respect; the circulation *per issue* actually declined despite the added efforts exerted by the party members.

But what we have to *do next* is to reach more and more *new* people, catch their attention at the moment when they are just awakening from political indifference, and try to reach them with our message *regularly*. A big national weekly is ideally suited to this task. And this is a project within our means and potential resources, financial and physical. The whole situation cries out for concentration on the task of developing *The Militant* into an eight-page national paper, published at the cheapest price possible so as to facilitate not merely the expansion but the *multiplication* of its present circulation; a weekly which is not just another radical paper but *the* national paper, dominating the radical labor field.

This is our central task. It is within our means and resources. And its successful execution will help, *not hinder*, the symmetrical development of all other departments of party work—organization, publishing house and educational system.

Why must the new *Militant* be eight pages and why must we cut the subscription rate to $1 per year? The necessity for these steps—they are not optional but necessary—flows from an analysis of the many-sided purposes which the paper must serve in the given situation on the one side, and the resources which we can reasonably depend on, on the other.

LETTER 152

SANDSTONE, DECEMBER 24, 1944

The bad news about Mick, which I received only last night, darkens the Christmas weekend for me as if the sun had been knocked out of the sky. Things are made worse by the knowledge that there will not be another mail delivery here until Monday night. I will be doing hard time till then. My emotions are divided between impatient resentment because you did not think to send me daily telegrams about Mick's condition and dread that a telegram now would mean bad news. All my "good" thoughts seem to be personified in the baby.

＊

I received the quotation Usick sent from Wolfe about pity as the "learned" emotion, the emotion which is fed by an accumulation of experience in memory. I think prison above all is the place where one can learn such things, learn and feel them. We are only partly here, and for a short time. We are still bound in memory to the normal life outside, and we anticipate the future. Besides that, thanks to our education and our philosophy, we have only to open the pages of a book as simply as one turns the key in a lock in order to leave this barren place, to walk beside the heroes who have shown how to storm heaven, and to listen to the philosophers who have tried to understand both earth and heaven.

But, nevertheless, here in prison one must see every day the lost men, the men who never had a chance; men who have been in and out of prison nearly all their lives; men who have never learned to read and thereby to project themselves into another world; men who know nothing and, God help them, will never know anything but prison. *There* is something to knock the smart-aleckness out of a man and teach him humility and compassion. There is pity.

Yes, pity is the "learned" emotion, but one does not learn it from books. Life is the instructor here, more specifically that part of life which inflicts pain and sorrow. I see proofs of this every day in the tender sympathy and concern which bind the prison-broken old convicts together as in an unspoken brotherhood. Politeness, respect for the wishes and feelings of others—everything that goes by the slick word "courtesy"—is very often only a thin veneer of the most "educated," book-learned people. Here at Sandstone I have seen the real article, pure and simple and sincere. In all my life I have never seen anything more beautiful than the compassion of lost men for each other.

We will soon be leaving here. But I believe that hereafter I will always remain, to a certain extent, a prisoner, a comrade of prisoners. I will never be able to see or hear about a prison without thinking of the men inside its walls. Everytime I read a reference to a prison in my historical studies I feel a stab of pity for the men who suffered there. I shall not forget what I have seen and learned here. Someday, I hope, I will write about it; some words with blood in them in behalf of all men in prison.

We will leave friends behind us here, and many who crossed paths with us here will be our friends, and friends of what we stand for, for the rest of their lives. A man left here not long ago who had been in one prison after another most of his life. He said to me the morning he was leaving: "I just wanted to tell you that I'll never forget how good you treated me here. You certainly meet some good people in prison. If they were all like you Trotskyites it wouldn't be so hard to do time."

I never did anything for him except to joke with him in a friendly way and "trust" him with an occasional package of cigarettes until he could bum enough matches to pay me back at the rate of a penny a box. But a convict is grateful if you simply respect him as a man.

LETTER 153

SANDSTONE, DECEMBER 25, 1944

We unexpectedly got a special mail delivery last night, so I heard the good news about the improvement of Sweetums. It was the best possible Christmas present under the circumstances. As further proof that everything is in order now, the sun, who was ashamed to show his face yesterday, is out today bright and shining. It turned out to be a good White Christmas after all.

*

More on the press: The decision to reduce the subscription price to $1 per year was an important and necessary step at the present time. The objection that this is "too cheap" would be well grounded only if it could be shown that we can't *afford* to cut the price. But according to our figures which we have checked and cross-checked very carefully, our present resources permit us to make this drastic reduction without disorganizing our budget. If we have erred in our calculations, experience will soon teach us and we can make the necessary correction. In any case the experiment will be a useful experience.

The principle that readers must *pay* for the paper is a sound one; people are inclined to put a higher value on things they pay for, even if it is a very small amount, than on throwaway sheets which they get for nothing. I believe all experienced organizers recognize that throwaway leaflets are the most expensive and least productive of all propaganda methods. That, however, does not prevent some people, who have not yet formed the habit of thinking and weighing experience, from periodically making excited proposals for free leaflet distribution as a panacea. But, nevertheless, experience has also shown that it is *the principle of paying*, not the *amount* paid, that is most important. The two should not be confused and lumped together.

It is not our task to vindicate a commercial principle but to assure the widest possible distribution of our paper to people who value it enough to read it. As said, that is best guaranteed if they pay something for it. But then comes a second proposition to whose validity all contemporary publishing experience testifies. That is, that once the principle of payment is firmly established, the paper must be sold at a cheap price in order to attain a wide circulation; the cheaper, the better. This is the publishing principle of the great metropolitan dailies as well as the national weeklies of wide circulation such as *Collier's* and the *Saturday Evening Post*.

Such publications do not give away a single copy—at least the Audit Bureau of Circulation does not recognize free copies as actual circulation—but their *price per volume* is far cheaper than the $1-a-year *Militant*. The *New York Times*, for example, gives a fifty-page paper for three cents. That, by volume, is at the rate of about sixteen pages for a penny. The $1-a-year *Militant* figures out at the rate of *four* pages for a penny. Yet nobody thinks of the *Times* as a "cheap" paper. The $1-a-year *Militant* will not be thought "too cheap" either.

The question is solely: How cheap can we *afford* to make the subscription price in order to facilitate the widest possible distribution? The answer depends on how much *subsidy* we can count on allocating to this department of our work. The *Times* circulation is subsidized by advertising revenue.

We must do the same thing, on a more modest scale, from voluntary contributions. At present, this subsidy permits us to sell the paper for $1 per year. If later we can make it cheaper yet, we will do so. We want *circulation*!

LETTER 154

SANDSTONE, DECEMBER 26, 1944

There will be some delay on my request for a stopover at Minneapolis. As soon as I get an answer I will let you know.

Included among the things I would like to "get" which I will never get for myself are a couple of good pipes and a wallet. I haven't had a *good* pipe since we started the Left Opposition. It is a very long time also since I carried a wallet. But if I am going to have a lot of money when I get out I might as well have a good leather wallet to carry it in— until it is spent. I am firmly determined not to waste this money on necessities or to invest it in real estate.

I am waiting for tonight's mail for another report on Mick.

*

A postscript should be added to my notes on the price of *The Militant*. It is not necessary to cut the *retail* price of *single copies*. The newsstands don't like to handle a weekly paper selling for less than five cents. Once before we cut the price to three cents. The only result was to reduce the revenue without increasing the sales. It seems that people who know the paper and want it enough to hunt it up on a newsstand and pay for it are just as willing to pay five cents, the traditional retail price of radical papers. The situation is different when a larger amount of money for a subscription is involved. The difference between fifty cents and a dollar, or between one and two dollars is noticed by most people.

I have always believed that one of the big secrets of the great circulation of the old *Appeal to Reason* was the cheap subscription rate—twenty-five cents per year. Wayland and Warren were of the same opinion. That was why, when rising costs made the twenty-five cents per year subscription rate untenable, they adjusted the budget by cutting the length of the subscription rather than by increasing the price of the prepaid sub card. I well remember when the new rate of twenty-five cents for *forty weeks* went into effect. Fifty cents today is about the equivalent of a quarter at that time.

I anticipate a great increase of fifty-cent, six-month subs when the new rate goes into effect. The difference in price does not mean so much and is not necessary for old *Militant* patriots and radicals who want to keep track of us. But for new people who are just beginning to be interested—and these are precisely the ones we are most anxious to reach—the cheaper price can easily be decisive in three cases out of four.

I am especially interested in the report George gave us about the new subscriptions secured from new readers, especially in New York. This experience may show us one of the most important avenues to that expansion which is our *idée fixe* for the next period. The great circulation of the *Appeal to Reason* was maintained by the "Appeal Army" of individual "sub hustlers" to which new members were constantly recruited. Wayland and Warren's instrument for recruiting and keeping this army together was the "Appeal Army" column in the paper. There the humble workers in the field received personal recognition and appreciation.

People like to have acknowledgment of their efforts. And I think there is no acknowledgment more universally agreeable than seeing one's "name in the paper," as a report of work performed. My father was a member of Wayland's

"Appeal Army." Many a time one could read in the column such an item as this: "Four more subs from John Cannon of Rosedale, Kansas, last week. This is the kind of work that counts for Socialism."

My father was a popular man, with many friends who didn't spare praises. But I believe the little notices of his work which appeared from time to time in the "Appeal Army" column gave him more satisfaction than anything else, because that was recognition of the *value of his work*.

LETTER 155

SANDSTONE, DECEMBER 28, 1944

We need and must have an eight-page paper now, not because there is any magic in the figure eight and not because this is the right size for a paper under all circumstances, but because it can be best adapted to the specific tasks which our press must serve at the present time, and is within our prospective means.

The decisions we make on such questions as the size and frequency of issue of a paper, as on all other so-called practical questions, should be as carefully reasoned as our political decisions. This is one of the surest signs of the introduction of professionalism, i.e., consciousness into our work. *The Militant* is a tool which in the past served primarily, almost exclusively, the task which the circumstances of the time obliged us to concentrate on: the recruitment and education of a cadre of the most advanced political elements. It is quite obvious that the whole objective situation is changing now, and therewith the position of our party within it.

The tasks and the opportunities of the party are changing. The press must be regulated accordingly. We all recognize this. But we can waste a lot of energy and neglect many opportunities if we see the new problems only "in general" and make a haphazard adjustment of the press to them. We should examine the new problem closely and try to make as *precise* an adjustment of the press as possible.

Viewing *The Militant* as a tool, I should like to refine the definition by saying that, in the next period, it must serve us as a *combination* tool which can be used on several different jobs. I believe this qualification is very important.

The paper, for the first time, is getting a good reception from masses of workers without previous political education or interest. The majority of its readers at the present moment are new people, and it is to be expected that this majority will become larger. *The Militant* must serve this new audience, adapt itself to the stage of their political development, under penalty of losing their interest.

This dictates a new journalistic technique. Our language and our arguments must be simplified and made more accessible to the new type of reader. This does not mean to vulgarize, to talk down in *Labor Action* fashion, but to study and learn the art of popularizing our propaganda. It is an art and it can be learned and practiced without revising or watering down a single basic principle. The problem is one of *presentation*, with the new readers in mind. They are only, for the most part, newly interested, only partly interested, and the paper must be lightened up and brightened up in order to hold their interest and lead them into deeper studies. The paper has improved enormously along this line during the past year, but we must keep the direction clear and go farther.

I have no doubt that a "Gallup poll" would show conclusively that the cartoons and drawings and the new feature columns account to a great degree for the increased popularity of the paper. With the increased space which the eight-pager will provide we must try deliberately to make further advances along this line. More cartoons and drawings; more light features, especially *short* features; more effort to give *information* not found elsewhere; more studied effort to convey our ideas in small doses, subtly and sometimes indirectly, for the average worker doesn't like to be pounded over the head with direct arguments in every article and every headline.

LETTER 156

SANDSTONE, DECEMBER 31, 1944

Perhaps your report on the nominating commission went astray. I seem to be missing letters No. 136 and No. 137. Contrary to your impression, I rely on your reports more than on any others when you relate facts you know about. All I wanted about the nominating commission was a factual report, not an interpretation.

*

On the press: For the benefit of the new reader we must tell the history of the movement over and over again, dramatizing the great events and personalities of the past, in order to build up one of the most powerful supporting ideas any movement can have—the idea of *tradition*.

Man does not live by argument alone. He needs a variety of interest; color; entertainment; information; drama; recollection of things past, especially where these recollections bring human personalities into view. The more and better the paper is dressed up with these variations on the theme of communism the better will the paper be liked, and the more surely will the first interest of the new readers be drawn into firm convictions and grateful devotion to the paper which has opened for them a window on a new rich world.

The eight-page paper will give us more room, but it

should not be used merely to add sixteen more columns of the same. The aim should be primarily to add greater variety. We should experiment with sketches and stories about *people*. That is mainly what the "Diary of a Steel Worker" consists of, and that is why it is so popular. Not everybody understands it, but people like to read about people.

We here have discussed the idea of reprinting in serial form the socialist and labor novels of the past. We will have room for it, and I believe the plates or serial rights could be secured for very small amounts. We thought the new generation would be interested in *The Jungle, The Iron Heel, Pelle the Conqueror,* Gorky's *Mother, Comrade Yetta,* etc. In fact we know it. An earlier generation of social rebels were profoundly moved and influenced by these stories. Their children and grandchildren are no different.

The dominant notes of the eight-page paper must be *simplification* and *agitation,* i.e., concentrated hammering on a very few basic slogans of the day. These are the indispensable characteristics of a popular paper. But—and here is the catch, here is the main reason we need a bigger paper—our *Militant* cannot be *merely* a popular paper even if every line of its contents is irreproachably correct as far as it goes.

The Militant must strive to be a *combination* paper; a paper which interests and serves the needs of the new reader who picks it up for the first time, the reader who is beginning to think of himself as a Trotskyist without yet thinking about the party, and the educated party militant—all at the same time. If we get this conception clearly in our heads we will be able to avoid some of the most costly errors of the past and close big gaps through which many thousands of potential socialists slipped away from the movement in the past.

We can only afford to publish one paper. And we must address ourselves to the politically educated as well as to the uninitiated. And we must also remember that between the best posted party member of years of study and experience and the new reader there are numerous strata in different degrees of development. And we must publish a paper for all of them. Most important of all, we must bear in mind that the new reader does not remain a new reader all his life. The average intelligent worker quickly absorbs the few simple ideas which attracted him to the paper in the first place. Then he begins to feel the need of more substantial food.

January, 1945

Happy New Year!

This finishes my remarks on the press. Tomorrow I will send the first of five letters on the "Literary Secretariat." Perhaps you had better wait till you get them all before copying them. We are in the same jail as last New Year's. Everything is the same, but the *perspective* is different!

✳

Continuing: An agitational paper which does not lead him from the first reader to the second, and then still higher, in time becomes monotonous. He doesn't feel the need of mere "agitation" so strongly on matters on which he is already convinced; and may even get tired of it and fall back into passivity and indifference unless he is led, step by step, into the deeper questions of Marxism with the ever new and ever changing variety of interests aroused by their presentation and discussion.

Precisely here was the Achilles' heel of the old *Appeal to Reason*. Its unrivaled agitation on a few simple points, and its sensational exposures, made the *Appeal* very attractive to thousands of new readers who were making the first break in their allegiance to the bourgeois parties. But the *Appeal* left them, so to speak, on the first step of the ladder, never raised them higher. The readers, after a spell of enthusiasm, got tired of the singsong which they already knew by heart and fell away. At a certain stage of its development, the *Appeal* was confronted with the life-and-death problem of getting new thousands of readers to take the place of other thousands who were falling away.

I know all this very well because I was one of them. It was my good fortune to discover the IWW and the new problems of theory and tactics raised by it, and to get an introduction into Marxist economics at the old Socialist Educational Society in Kansas City, just at the time I was beginning to feel that the *Appeal to Reason* had nothing more to teach me.

My case was rather typical. Most of the militants I knew in those days had gone through the *Appeal to Reason* school. But the point is, they had gone *through* it. I finally stopped reading the *Appeal* altogether. Occasionally, when I picked it up later, it lacked the old interest for me. The *Appeal* was too simple, too exclusively agitational, to hold the continuing interest of a developing militant and aid his further education.

Of course, this example may appear to be exaggerated, insofar as it expresses the conditions of the time and the general ideological poverty of the old movement. But it is worth mentioning in any case, if only as a "horrible example." We are a head taller than the movement from which we grew, but that puts upon us the obligation to use our head. We must try to do everything understandingly, consciously. Applied to *The Militant*, this means among other things, that we should deliberately plan it as a variegated combination paper which has something in it of special interest to all of its readers in all stages of their development; which conducts the new reader by stages from agitation on the burning issues of the day into all the more profound questions of the class and the party, and continues to interest him after he has assimilated them.

The capitalist press solves the problem of attracting and holding readers of different social strata and different interests in its own way. Their prescription is simple: They provide a great variety of departments and features ranging from comic strips and crossword puzzles to market reports and the society column. Something for everybody. They even have editorials and some people read them.

In our own way, and for our own purposes, and with our own resources, we should follow this pattern. But for that we need eight pages.

LETTER 158

SANDSTONE, JANUARY 2, 1945

I am greatly disappointed to learn that you did not get the heater. I don't care so much about the other things, but I can't be comfortable here unless I know that you are snug and warm at home. My letter about the heater was addressed to Moish. Did you show it to him? The best way to get along with me is to take care of my Rosie.

＊

At the October plenum a year ago Joe advanced the idea of a secretariat for literary work. This idea, new to me at that time, has been considered and discussed here, and I am now ready to offer a motivated proposal to adopt the idea in expanded form and to outline a tentative program of work for the Literary Secretariat. It is our opinion that the party can now afford, has the necessary forces, and requires the introduction of the principles of organization and planning in the field of literary production, with a new special emphasis on specialization and division of labor.

Such a decision, if the Secretariat properly carries out the mission indicated, would represent another conscious, positive move to organize the party, another victory over planlessness and amateurism which bear down on the party with the dead weight of tradition. The Secretariat should be composed, at the start, of the three comrades previously indicated, and should be provided, from the start, with the necessary technical assistance to facilitate efficient work.

The members of the Secretariat must, of necessity, be exempted from other executive and administrative duties. On the other hand they could be expected to serve, and no doubt with greater efficiency and productiveness, on *staffs* of the press and the school system and as *members* of the political bodies of the party.

1. *Function.* It will be the task of the Secretariat to organize and lead the offensive struggle of the party against the ideological opponents of orthodox Marxism on every field; show and prove the utter worthlessness of each and every revisionist, non-Marxist and anti-Marxist social philosophy; study and prepare material expounding and answering all questions of Marxism in popular form for the education of the new generation; serve the press, school and publishing house with articles, lectures, pamphlets and books on fundamental questions.

2. *Relation to Party Organs.* The Literary Secretariat is to be conceived of not as an institution or even as a new party organ, but rather as an informal body, an auxiliary instrument of the NC, the editorial board and the educational department. It should be a *part* of the school system, charged with the duty of preparing lectures which later can be published as textbooks throughout the national school system. It can be the organizing center from which will radiate other "collectives" of students and investigators of

certain topics requiring specialized knowledge and concentrated attention.

3. *Methods of Work.* The Secretariat should undertake to turn out literary productions by the method of cooperative labor which is a higher and more efficient stage than handicraft production in this field also, especially as regards the *preparation* of material. As a matter of fact, the application of the principles of *organization* will very probably yield richer fruits in this field than in any other for the simple reason that it has been employed there less than anywhere.

Naturally, each individual will do the actual writing and be fully responsible for the final draft of each production bearing his name. But the principle of organized cooperative labor can operate to powerful effect in surveying and discussing the literary project to be undertaken; in assembling material and outlining the form; and in criticizing and editing the final draft. Every document issuing from the Literary Secretariat—every article, lecture, pamphlet and book—must go through a triple screen of criticism and checking for facts, style, and theoretical and political accuracy. (More.)

LETTER 159

SANDSTONE, JANUARY 4, 1945

The proposal about the introduction to *Five Years of the Comintern* is acceptable. Let the "Lit Sec" make notes and block out a rough outline. This introduction can be the first product of our factory. Let's make it good!

＊

To continue: If the plan is accepted the Secretariat could begin to function right away, at least to the extent of making the technical arrangements and beginning to assemble material which will later be turned into finished products. A list of projects should be tentatively agreed upon, aiming far ahead. A *five-year plan* should be drawn up and folders prepared for filing of preliminary thoughts and data on the various subjects to be dealt with.

Every discussion and every special study engaged in by any of the participants should be made to yield some notes in the form of raw material for later use on one of the projected subjects. Preliminary outlines of various documents can be drawn up now. The necessary books, publications and other working material should be assembled. Some preliminary research on specific subjects scheduled for early treatment can be done or assigned to others who want to help. Quotes and references can be gathered and filed away under appropriate headings.

4. *Materials Needed:* We will need a good central office; a completely equipped workshop and library. To set this workshop up and to be able to get all books and other materials promptly when we want them, including all essential publications, the Secretariat will need a special fund. The best way, in my opinion, would be for the PC to authorize us to promote such a fund without intruding on the party's sources, so that we will not have to go to the party general fund every time we need to make an expenditure. From the start we should have the following:

a) A *complete* library of the literature of Marxism. Those classics not available in English must be found in other languages. This library of Marxism must include not only books, but also bound volumes of essential publications, such as *Neue Zeit,* if obtainable in any language.

b) A complete library of revisionism. We must have at hand everything significant written by the revisionists beginning with Bernstein so that we can teach the new generation, especially the students in our school, what revisionism is—from the original sources.

c) All material critical of Lenin written by Luxemburg, Trotsky and Martov. One of the tasks of the Secretariat will be to teach the history of Bolshevism, Menshevism and conciliationism from original sources.

d) A library of anti-Marxism written from the bourgeois viewpoint.

e) A library of anarchist and syndicalist literature.

f) A working library of philosophy; the most essential books of the foremost representatives of all schools.

g) A library of American socialist and labor history. (There isn't much, but we need it as raw material and factual data from which to prepare something better, much better.)

h) All published material available in any language on the "theory" of the Russian "bureaucratic class." The prewar Russian Makhaisky, Bruno R., Berkman and Goldman, Ciliga and other pioneers of the Burnham-Shachtman discovery.

i) All available published material on utopian socialism in all versions.

j) All material on the Dewey-Hutchins controversy on pedagogy. Get Professor Edman's article "Which Road for Education" in *Sunday Times Magazine* (June or July, 1944).

k) The important recent books on U.S. foreign policy, such as Lippman's *U.S. War Aims*, Sumner Welles' book, etc. (More.)

LETTER 160

SANDSTONE, JANUARY 7, 1945

The "many requests," to which you continually refer, were meant primarily as requisitions for tools and materials for my projected work: notes for my future reference, to avoid burdening my memory with these trifles. They were included in my letters to you only because I have no other means of communication.

*

To continue: Assemble the following in separate folders: (a) All I have written (articles, parts of articles, resolutions, letters) on the question of building a professional party staff. (b) My published speeches from 1940 on. (c) All my correspondence from the old party files.

5. *Tentative Projects.* It is to be assumed that the members of the Secretariat will each do a regular stint of current writing for the press and lecturing in the school. In addition, the following projects, most of which have been considered and discussed and partly outlined here, are suggested, for which preliminary notes should be made and filed.

a) *American Labor Leaders.* A book in thirteen chapters (or lectures) on American socialist and labor history, written in informal, popular style and hooked onto biographical sketches and appraisals of the outstanding personalities who represented and symbolized the various tendencies and stages of development. This book, like all our publications, should be written not for the academic world but for the new generation of proletarian militants; to let them know who we are and where we came from.

Chapters:

1. *The Beginners.* The labor movement and its role from the first days of the Republic through the civil war.

2. *Terence V. Powderly*—The Grand Master Workman of the Knights of Labor.

3. *Parsons.* The Haymarket Martyrs and the Eight-hour Movement.

4. *Gompers.* Trade Unionism, Pure and Simple.

5. *Debs.* The Socialist Agitator.

6. *DeLeon.* The Socialist Theoretician.

7. *Hillquit and Berger.* Reformist Socialism in America.

8. *Haywood and St. John.* The Story of the IWW.

9. *John L. Lewis.* The United Mine Workers and the Early CIO.

10. *Hillman and Dubinsky.* The Tragedy of the Jewish Labor Movement. (The Truth about *Tailors' Progress.*)

11. *William Z. Foster.* The Blight of Stalinism.

12. *Thomas and Reuther.* The Fill-in Men. The CIO in Transition.

13. *Labor Leaders to Come.* A Preview of the Revolutionary Labor Movement.

b) *America's Road to Socialism.* Expanding and bringing up-to-date the notes of my Los Angeles lectures (1937). A popular exposition of the whole range of Marxism. Analysis and refutation of all opposing tendencies. A historical review of social development. The ineluctable situation of capitalism. The inevitability of the social revolution. An outline of the socialist society. The limitless vistas of man's future.

c) *History of the Comintern.* This is quite a big project, but we alone are equipped to do it. Nobody else can or will do it. If the Secretariat lays out a long-term schedule we can do this job too.

d) *Volume II of the History of American Trotskyism.* A new series of twelve lectures dealing with party history from the launching of the SWP until the imprisonment of the eighteen, including the year 1944.

e) *A Treatise on the United Front.* A thoroughgoing exposition and clarification of this question based on a historical review.

f) *Trotsky as Party Organizer.* The organizational principles and methods by which he built the Fourth International. Either a collection of his articles and letters edited and with an introduction by me, or a small book by me with rich use of quotations to illustrate the principles and methods in concrete situations. (More.)

LETTER 161

SANDSTONE, JANUARY 8, 1945

I still have no answer on the request for a stopover at Minneapolis. As soon as I get the answer I will let you know. Please send copies of the Lit Sec proposals to Murry and Larry when you get the last installment tomorrow. I would like to hear their opinions. The document is not "official"; is meant only for interested friends.

＊

g) *A Treatise on Ethics and Communism.* Perhaps a series of lectures to be published afterward. As far as I know, Marx and Engels did not treat this question. They were too much occupied with the first task: demolishing the conception of the utopians that "socialism is a moral ideal." Lenin was too much occupied with the revolution. Kautsky wrote a pamphlet. Besides that, we have Trotsky's *Their Morals and Ours.*

I believe there is much more to be said; and I also believe that this subject has a great interest for the new generation, especially that phase of it which concerns the morals of the socialist society, the *changeability* of human nature, and communism as a moral *way of life* in the struggle. I think we can add something and fill a gap left in revolutionary propaganda in the past.

I know the philistines are very squeamish on this point and resent it very much when we talk about "morality" in forthright terms. But I believe there is a strain of rascality in every petty-bourgeois moralist, even the "honest" ones like Macdonald, and that I can prove it. I also believe our movement is greatly strengthened by *moral* assurance.

h) *The Principles of Revolutionary Propaganda.* The secret is to *aim at the young* who are inspired by appeals to the best in men, by great goals transcending the petty interests and concerns of the moment. See Aristotle on the Characteristics of Youth and Age. See Kropotkin's *Appeal to the Young.* Youth is in the mind; see Homer: "Green old age," spoken of the veteran Nestor who fought beside the young men at Troy.

Elucidate the principles of pedagogy. Explain the inspiration of example. Why the party, as an army, needs a martial spirit. The significance of "tone," which is not at all a question of manners but of discrimination between friends and enemies. Trotsky's comment on the SAP leaders' reference to Blum as "Comrade Blum." A whole *political line* is contained in that one expression.

Reduce to principles and written formulas, which can be studied and learned by others, the basic methods by which the morale of the movement is built. Show why some speakers are successful with the people, and others are not. Show why scientifically grounded faith in the future has such a powerful appeal. (I always "knew" all of this more or less, and acted on it; but I didn't know why until I began to study and deliberate over the question. I believe an explanation of the basic rules for effective propaganda would be useful.)

i) *The Rogues' Gallery of Academic Tinhorns.* Gather material for the exposure of such shysters as Hook and Hacker who promised to teach the youth and then betrayed them. By "material" I mean their writings. Track them down in the *Modern Monthly* and *Modern Quarterly, Nation, New Republic,* etc. Get Hacker's review of Browder's book (1936 or 1937) in the *Nation.*

j) *"Violence Will Wither Away."* A treatise showing that this is the ultimate meaning of the Marxian formula "the withering away of the state." See the note on the prize-fight incident in *The Iron Heel.* See Natalia's use of this expression in the magazine article. Show what freedom in its full implication really means. Show the great world-shaking significance of The Declaration of the Rights of Man and of the Citizen.

Show how the class society does not represent "human nature" but prevents its development and free expression. Show the falsity and the folly of permitting apologists of democratic capitalism to masquerade as champions of the rights of man. It is necessary to emphasize in our propaganda the dignity and worth of the individual, and that it will find its full recognition only through the revolution. (More.)

LETTER 162

SANDSTONE, JANUARY 9, 1945

I found the missing letters No. 136 and No. 137. I haven't heard from you now, however, for eight days. The last letter received here was No. 145 dated December 29. I am trying to take it for granted that you are all right, otherwise Walta would notify me.

✳

Last installment on the Lit Sec:

k) *Socialism and Democracy.*

l) *Lenin's Concept of Professional Revolutionists.* How is this idea to be applied in a country like the United States?

m) *The Leader Cult:* Its Social Basis and Its Political Role. A historical examination of this question: the ancient despots and Caesars, the Pope, the absolute monarchies, the fascists, the Stalinists. The Brandler-Lovestone theory of the Comintern, and the Fourth International.

✳

This is all I have to say for the present in answer to the proposition Joe made at the October plenum. There is only one catch to it that I can see. If Usick agrees with the proposition, he will have to forgo that position as district organizer in North Dakota. Somebody else will have to organize the kulaks there.

✻

Please drop a note to Evie right away and say for me: "Med's mother has some things for me. Please pick them up and hold them for me till I see you on January 24. I want to take them with me to New York. I hear Harry is doing hard time. Tell him to walk slow and drink plenty of water."

✻

I was pleased to get the photo of my pal Stevie. He is a handsome boy, and he comes by it honestly.

There are many things in our letters which I should answer, but I am getting badly crowded for space to pack in the rest of my notes.

I have some things to say to you too, but I doubt whether I will write them. I seem to be very strongly inhibited against saying the most intimate personal things, those words in which the soul speaks in full sincerity, in letters which must pass through censorship and be read by others.

That alone is the explanation why my letters for the whole past year may appear so impersonal, so businesslike in content. As such they could not express my full thoughts and sentiments, nor even the most profoundly felt ones. I believe you will understand me if I simply say that on my part nothing is changed and that if I were in a position to express myself freely, in letters to be read by you alone, I would not write otherwise than I have written before under such conditions.

I have had my heart set above all on meeting you in Minneapolis so that we could have a couple of days and the train ride to New York alone and together. If that concession is denied us the next best thing, I think, would be for you to reserve a place at a New York hotel so that we can be completely alone and together for a few days before people and duty swallow us up again.

The dominant feature of prison life from beginning to end is the *complete* lack of privacy. The popular impression of the prisoner being "alone in his cell" is the most ironic misunderstanding imaginable. I have lived in one room with fifty-odd other men for a whole year without one moment's privacy night or day.

The brief period when I was in a cell was better, since it was more suitable for study, but it was not more *private*. In that respect, the cell is perhaps worse than the dormitory, inasmuch as there is the simulacrum, not the reality, of privacy. One cannot see out the little window in the door but others can see in.

LETTER 163

SANDSTONE, JANUARY 11, 1945

I am somewhat disturbed by the reference in *FI* convention report to a "National Training School" to be "organized next summer." I hope the conception of the Training School is not, as seems to be implied, that of a shotgun summer course. Our program for the Training School must be far more ambitious. It must contemplate not less than six months of concentrated study for each class from the very beginning. Candidates for the School must be taken from the ranks of *present party functionaries;* and all of them, with very few exceptions, must be put through the School in their turn. Only later, with expanded membership and resources, can the student body be broadened.

We should begin with a class of six. We must resolutely

decide to take that many functionaries out of active party work for the time specified. It might be best to try to select six who are about equal in book education and experience so that they can study the same courses together most profitably. The problem is not to find candidates but to find people to take their places for six months. But such problems are always bigger in imagination than in reality.

We must simply take hold of six more promising comrades and thrust them into responsibility. They will learn by doing while those whom they fill in for are learning by study. At the end of six months we will have a double gain and the selection of the second class of six will be easier.

The problem of teachers is no problem at all; our students will not be college boys for whom the teacher has to do most of the work. Our students will do their own work. They need teachers mainly to tell them what to study, and in what order and to show them how. Lectures should be only a *feature* of the instruction in certain subjects. The *fundamental method* of the school should be the *study* of original sources by the students organized under the seminar system.

If we start modestly with a class of six students, the financial problem will not be as difficult as it may seem. It will cost a lot of money; we must not deceive ourselves on this score. But on the other side, the Training School, once it gets fairly started in actual operation, will arouse an absolutely unheard of response from the party members and sympathizers. New donations in sizable amounts will come forward from sources now unknown. Every ambitious young militant will be inspired to increased activity and self-study with the School as a realizable goal. The School will not be a financial burden to the party.

I heard that G. [Munis] objected to the plan to pay the expenses of the students on the ground that this will promote subservience to the bureaucracy (leadership). Such possibilities cannot be denied. Every paid leadership is a bureaucracy in one sense of the word. In every measure of centralism there is a danger of the development of bureaucratism in the invidious sense of the word. The concentration of finances in the hands of the leadership, and therewith the power to grant or withhold appointments to paid positions (including paid scholarships), contains the danger of corruption at each end—bureaucratic abuse and subservience. The history of the Stalinist degeneration of the Comintern outside Russia is convincing evidence that even revolutionary militants are not permanently immune to this danger.

But what is the alternative to centralization, including its financial appurtenances?—that is the question. In the field of party organization in general the alternative is that primitive amateurism in the field of leadership which characterized the pre-Communist radical movement in the U.S. That is a program for futility. Amateur leaders only play at revolution. Professional leaders work at it. (More.)

LETTER 164

SANDSTONE, JANUARY 14, 1945

I just got a twenty-four-hour stopover at Minneapolis and will expect to meet you there. Take the Pennsylvania so you won't have to change depots at Chicago. Henry will take care of our reservations to New York. Wire Elaine to reserve a room at the *Andrews Hotel*. Please bring my shaving outfit and toothbrush. I will be leaving here "clean."

*

More on the School: The fact that professional leadership sometimes works out badly; that under certain conditions it has been seen to degenerate and be put to the service of ends opposite to those it was originally designed to serve—this is something to keep constantly in mind. It is a warning to keep all the democratic correctives of centralism in working order and not let them get rusty from disuse; to devise new methods of making the democratic correctives more actual, more effective.

This was the thought which motivated my proposals on the election of the NC at the recent party convention. But to guard against the degeneration of centralization is one thing. To discard centralism altogether, or one of its most essential features, the professional staff, would mean in effect to renounce the idea of a combat party. And that in turn would mean to reduce the program of proletarian revolution to a dilettante play with ideas.

The professional staff must be an educated staff, or at any rate, in process of acquiring the necessary education. Militant workers do not come to the party already thus equipped. And if they have to work every day in the factory and carry a load of practical party work in addition, their educational advancement must necessarily be slow and difficult. We must try to speed up and facilitate this process because we rely mainly on workers for the future leadership of the party.

I will not accept the idea that the intellectual leadership belongs of necessity to those who have been taught at college at the expense of mamma and papa. Neither do I think it right to leave the talented workers to their own devices, to the hard and bitter task of educating themselves in their limited spare time, for fear of corrupting them by full-time periods of study at party expense. That means, in effect, to close the doors of the higher circles of the leadership to the worker militants. That, in my opinion, would be the greatest error of all; precisely the error that has taken such a costly toll in the past experience of the party in this country; and not only in this country.

It is against that error that I am campaigning. I am bent and determined on the training of a proletarian leadership for the proletarian party of the future. In order to do that seriously, that is, properly, we must provide, at a certain stage in the advancement of the most talented workers, for a fairly extended period of full-time study to prepare them for more important political responsibilities. That cannot be contemplated—it is vicious stupidity even to talk about it— unless the party makes practical arrangements to pay their expenses. Again I grant that such a project is not entirely free from dangers. But we must risk them. I am more worried about the other dangers.

Naturally, we must not expect miracles from the National Training School. Rather, we should view it, in all its aspects, as the *beginning* of a new stage in the general development of the party and also in the personal development of new leaders and potential leaders. By putting the accent on the educational qualifications of candidates for party leadership and making generous provisions to aid them to improve their qualifications in this respect, the party will have fairly gained the right to demand more from the leaders.

That will be a new gain, and a fairly important one. At the same time, the militants who have profited by the new educational facilities will, it may be assumed, do their work better and with more assurance, and should feel more closely bound to the party which has valued them so highly and invested so much in them. That will be an important new gain too. (End.)

LETTER 165

SANDSTONE, JANUARY 15, 1945

I am getting badly crowded for time and space, and am working myself to a frazzle trying to finish writing up all my notes before leaving here. As it is, I will have to send the rest of them to you in very abbreviated form and elaborate them later. I will be glad when I get out of here and have some free *time* at my disposal.

＊

We note with interest and satisfaction that inquiries are being made "for clarification." This coincides with our own idea that more clarification is needed and we will try our best to provide it.

"Democracy or Snobocracy." Add a chapter on this theme to the pamphlet "Reflections on the Recent Party Discussion." A critical analysis of the attitude of Morrison, Cassidy and Logan, as manifested in their proposals, arguments, formulas and actions. See Grote on the arrogant assumptions of the ancient oligarchs that they were the "best" and "most honorable" people. The idea of a self-selected elite of independent thinkers, counterposed to a stupid mass of blind followers, hand-raisers and hero-worshipers, is not a democratic but a snobocratic conception. It is founded not at all on an actual division within the party membership but on the petty-bourgeois self-centeredness and conceit of its authors.

One of the best and most progressive demonstrations of the party convention was the mass demand that Bennett, who had apparently abused her high office just a little too much, be reduced back to the status of an ordinary party member. That would have been a most salutary lesson in real party democracy. It will be a great day for the party when such procedure becomes normal, to be taken for granted, like the angry bite of a good natured watch dog if he is provoked too much. Some people must be "learned" that democracy means the *rule* of the people *(demos)*. The convention demonstration in the case of Bennett was a way of saying: "Take warning! *Demos* is the master of this house. If you offend him too grossly he will throw you out on your ear."

*

One of my notes reads: "Write a letter on 'The Rich Year of Party Work and Development.'" Alas, this will have to wait—it would take too many letters.

*

My party method: Not merely to learn, think and do myself, but to *organize* others to learn, think and do. Our strength is in our combination. The "machine" (human) is stronger than any individual can be. Teamwork is better than the prima donna system in any field; in the field of party leadership above all. Those who feel themselves qualified and called to leadership must *learn how to work together* and permit no anarchistic individuals, no matter how talented they may be, to disrupt the "machine."

It is idle to speak about Trotsky and his decisive *personal* role. All laws and rules bend a bit when genius appears on the scene. But geniuses do not grow on trees. We need methods and working rules to govern the functioning of people who fall short of genius. That is the kind of material we have, and most probably that is all we are going to get. In this there is no ground for pessimism, for weeping and wailing, for bawling like lost calves. Men of common clay will suffice to lead the party and the revolution provided only that they know how to organize themselves, to work together.

"Boohoo," say the Babes in the Wood, "it would be so much better if Trotsky were here. Cannon doesn't take the place of Trotsky." I never promised to take Trotsky's place. I promised to take Cannon's place, and I am keeping my promise. Let all the others do their part from the same point of view and quit crying for the impossible. Less moping, please, and more attention to reality! Less whimpering about the defects of others and more emphasis on personal performance!

Trotsky said he was sure of the victory of the Fourth International, although he knew that he could not participate in it personally. Those who are so ready to discount the present leadership, and that in process of development, don't realize that their pessimism manifests their own addiction to the cult of the leader. They trusted Trotsky the man but do not trust the power of his ideas to create other human instruments. But Trotsky's greatness was above all in his ideas.

LETTER 166

SANDSTONE, JANUARY 16, 1945

Dear Walta,

In my French lesson the other day I read the *Déclaration des Droits de l'Homme et du Citoyen* (Declaration of the Rights of Man and Citizen). I felt that I was standing on one of the great mountain peaks of man's history from which one could see even higher ranges rising in the future. Long live the rights of man! They were worth the Great Revolution. They are even worth another revolution which will really secure them.

＊

I also read a Dumas story, *L'évasion de M. de Beaufort.* It is a prison story of the seventeenth century. All my sympathies were with the prisoner. Marvelous is the Dumas insight in describing the actual moment of the escape. Beaufort had seized the dagger, smuggled into the prison in a chicken pie, and pressed it to the breast of the guard, La Ramée. "My friend, I am sorry, but if you make a move, if you utter a cry, you will die!" "Oh! Monseigneur, you would not have the heart to kill me." "Not unless you try to stop my escape." "But, Monseigneur, if I let you escape, I am a ruined man . . .

I have a wife and four children." All prisons are the same, and so are all the people in them.

※

Here is a problem for my philosophy teachers. I am studying Spinoza, but as the time for my "evasion" draws near, I find my thoughts straying from the abstractions of philosophy to the prospect of snacks of cold chicken, a round loaf of Italian bread, sweet butter and black olives and a bottle of chilled white wine. Is that good or bad?

※

Mickey is to have a sled *and* skates. The most painful decision I can remember from my boyhood was the decision I had to make between a sled or a pair of skates on Christmas. This was the first Christmas when I already knew for sure that Santa Claus was only a pseudonym for my parents and that there was no use appealing from them to him. Perhaps the decision was even harder for my mother than for me, but I never thought of it that way then. She explained that we were simply too poor; we couldn't afford more than the one present.

But I had set my heart on both a sled and skates. Sometimes there was no snow and all the kids were on the ice. Again, after a snowfall, they were all on the hill with their sleds. I wanted with all my heart to be equipped for either emergency. But there was no evading the decision; I must choose. It was not easy, but after a long soul struggle I decided in favor of the sled, arriving at the choice by a combination of esthetic sensitiveness and shrewd practical sense. The bright green, red and yellow flower design on the sled at the hardware store had lured me with a mysterious power. I *wanted* that sled. I simply *had* to have it.

I wanted the skates too. But then, I reasoned—there is nothing like being confronted with tough decisions to make a kid learn to use his noodle—that even when there was no snow I could run and slam the sled belly-buster on the ice and take a ride. But skates were absolutely useless in the snow. So I painfully decided for the sled. I got no skates then or ever, until I bought a pair with my own money after I went to work.

I remember all this as vividly as though it had happened yesterday. The lack of skates was a wound that never healed. I feel poignantly sorry for that kid who was hurt so badly by the lack of such a little thing. That is why the determination to see to it that little Mick gets a sled *and* skates is not the least important of the "projects" I have laid out for myself.

*

Prison takes one away from activity and freedom and friends and home, and all that appertains thereto. Otherwise it is not so bad. There are some things about it that I really like. Time for study and contemplation is good to have. The [janitor] work I do is useful and I take pride in doing it right. All the necessary tools and materials for my work are supplied on requisition. No money is required; food, lodging and overalls are automatically provided.

That, plus freedom, etc., is all one really needs—plus, in my special case, medicaments for my stomach—light wines and beers—and a nip or two of good whiskey to fend off rheumatism on frosty days.

So long. Put candles on the Christmas tree.

Love,
Jim

LETTER 167

SANDSTONE, JANUARY 19, 1945

Macdonald *e tutti quanti* construe our assertion of the historic importance of our movement, and thereby of the work of our leading people, as a sign of exaggerated personal conceit. The literary and academic world generally is painfully limited in its judgment of people and their motivations. They seek always for personal interests and concerns, and of these they take the mean and petty as the norm. See Hook's explanation of the motivations of Baldwin; Durant's explanation of Wagner's action in his chapter on Schopenhauer, etc.

Since personal conceit is a very unattractive vice, it may perhaps be worth while to take up this accusation and show that people who judge everything, including themselves, from a historical materialist point of view, can be least inclined of all to attribute a role to themselves not conditioned by their historical milieu. We as individuals are significant insofar as we consciously express, and thereby accelerate, the progressive tendencies inherent in the historical process of which we are a part. An elucidation of this question might help our young militants to see the situation, and their part in it, more clearly and—as a by-product—put the pigmy critics in their places.

We are important because our ideas are going to change the world. Without this conviction we could never build the combat party which is destined to be the instrument of this historic mission. See what Trotsky said on this line about the convictions of the Russian Marxists in the depths of the post-1905 reaction—that they, a persecuted handful, were superior to the ruling powers. See what he wrote on the same theme in *War and the International* when reaction was triumphant everywhere and "the death of Marxism" was being universally celebrated. See what he wrote to the conference of the French youth: "You are more important than all the generals and all the statesmen because you alone represent the future."

See what he told me in 1934 about the role of Molinier and Naville. He commissioned me to go back to Paris, cutting down my long deferred visit with him to a single day, to make one final effort to reconcile them. "They have a great responsibility," I said. He answered: "They have the greatest responsibility in the history of the world, and they quarrel and split over trifles."

It is really a bit painful to have to explain that we are not "bragging" when we say our party is better than the other parties, for they are no good whatsoever.

✳

On democracy and criticism: Free criticism is the essence of democracy, the condition for fruitful collaboration. A leader who "resents" criticism, reacting to it subjectively, is guilty of two glaring faults insupportable in a leader:

1) He unconsciously sets himself against democracy in process, for democracy expresses itself precisely in criticism. If one "resents" criticism, what is the use of talking about democracy, about the theory that many heads are better than one?

2) By setting up "defenses" against criticism and reacting to it resentfully, a leader cuts himself off from one of the best, in some respects *the* best, ways of learning. That means—he is not yet a real leader.

A leader should be measured not by what he knows, but by his capacity to continue learning. When he gets "old," that is to say when he stops learning, he ceases to be useful. I think that is what Lenin meant when he said: "Revolutionists, when they reach the age of fifty, should be shot."

✳

Notes on leadership and the leader cult: The "leader cult" theory, as we have heard it explained lately, is a version of the anti-leader prejudice of the syndicalists which was shared in part by Menshevism. A nihilistic attitude toward leadership ("iconoclasm") is absolutely fatal to the design to organize a combat party; without a *firm, authoritative* and *continuing* central leadership the combat party must remain in the realm of daydreams. See the theory of "leaders *versus* masses" of the German KAPD. See the IWW *constitutional provision* for a complete change of officers every year.

Lenin, who was in dead earnest about organizing a revolution, exalted the concept of leadership higher than anyone had ever done before. Perhaps that was his most distinctive, his most *Leninist* contribution to the theory of organizing the party and the revolution. See the polemics against him by Martov, Luxemburg, Trotsky and others. See Trotsky's later evaluation of this dispute. See *What Is To Be Done,* and *Left Sickness* and the early theses of the Comintern.

In the genuine "leader cult" the "leader" is *arbitrator*— this is the key to an understanding of the problem. It is a *social* formation; there must be *interests* to arbitrate; and there must be the element of *compulsion* in the last resort.

The *leader principle* is not confined to the single individual at the apex of this social formation. That is a purely idealistic conception of this historical phenomenon. The *leader principle* goes all the way to the bottom, down to the basic units of the social organism in question. The ancient Persian satraps under the "Great King," the feudal lords under the absolute monarchs, the Catholic bishops under the Pope, the gauleiters under the fascist fuehrer, the provisional district presidents under Lewis, and the district secretaries under Stalin—they all reign supreme in their own domains and exercise the same arbitrary powers as the Lord over All.

It is necessary to remind careless thinkers that "ideas do not fall from the sky." This includes the idea of the supreme leader which is a solidly based social manifestation which, under given conditions, is *necessary* and *therefore* is invented. And its main instrumentality is not "hero worship" but *compulsion*.

LETTER 168

SANDSTONE, JANUARY, 1945

Notes:

[Laura] Gray and Kovalesky, new types of propagandists who express the orientation on the new post-1940 party, speak to workers. No "sect" can speak in this language. Perhaps the publication of selections of my old writings would help train the new people to speak to the workers. The *old* American movement (pre-communist) had many propaganda devices and techniques which we, as heir of all the past, must learn and appropriate.

❋

File all my letters in loose-leaf folders, number the pages and index and cross-index by subject for easy reference.

❋

Invariable rule: Read at desk with note pad at hand. *Always* make notes of ideas as *they occur.*

LETTER 169

SANDSTONE, JANUARY 12, 1945

Notes on the School:

Get statistics on the extent of the active workers' formal education by states; if possible, by occupations.

Murry should systematize his studies in preparation for a West Coast branch of the training school. Perhaps I can be a visiting "professor."

Journalism must be taught in the school. Every new functionary must learn how to write. Morrison's remarks about Smith [Dobbs] as editor at the fifteenth anniversary plenum. He will get his final answer when Smith becomes the *teacher* of journalism at the training school. He will illustrate in person our central thesis: Workers can learn anything that others can learn if they have time to study and someone to lend them a hand.

A special project: An annual two- or three-week course for field correspondents, open only to actual correspondents of the paper. Give the youth something to aim at all the time: attainable goals, prizes to be won.

Teach foreign languages. Use Linguaphone records and organize special groups with teachers, to practice *speaking* foreign languages.

Refer to the 1941 plenum speech about the provision of study time for party organizers. A check should be made on this. The special requirements of each organizer should be ascertained, directions given for special studies, checks and reports.

We must look ahead to the new crops of candidates. There will be many. We think and plan always in terms of change and growth.

Inspire the young militants to study, and teach them how. This is the most important thing. Those who aspire to leadership must form *habits* of study. See Trotsky (in [the Dewey] Commission testimony, I think): "I never lost my interest in study." Teaching *and* learning are complementary obligations of every leader. Everyone must be a *student* of what he doesn't know and a *teacher* of what he has learned.

Inspire students with the idea that they are to be teachers; teach them how to teach, not only to learn.

Study pedagogy. Our college men on the whole made a very poor showing in this very field where they might have been useful. With very few exceptions, they never taught me anything, although I am and have always been a willing learner. They learned (what they learned) for themselves.

The idea of a priesthood and a priestcraft of learning must be demolished. What *we* learn we must teach to others. The party scholars must take the rebel worker and teach him all they know. My thesis is a polemic in behalf of the ambitious worker who has been deprived of adequate formal schooling. I know that man, and I am on his side.

*

My first and lasting impression of the Russian leaders, whom we first heard of in 1917, was of highly educated men well able to cope with the ideologists of the class enemy. This was a new revelation. Previously the American movement, especially its syndicalist wing, had stressed the cult of action. Even so, this was better than the parliamentary socialist wing, which shrank from militant action and taught a bloodless theory. "Clarity and action," the original slogan of the Communist youth movement, should be adopted as our own.

LETTER 170

SANDSTONE, JANUARY 21, 1945

Notes:
Ask Haldeman-Julius where files of the *Appeal* may be found. Crerar? Wisconsin?
Read Maccabees 1 and 2.
Check at library on "speed writing."
Check issues of *New Masses* devoted to Hook and Calverton.
Get Farrell's obituary articles on L.D. in *Partisan Review* and *Labor Action*.
Explain why organizers must be shifted, not allowed to "settle down" in comfortable grooves. Professional revo-

lutionists must keep footloose. Shake up and shift center people too.

Check *What Next?;* chapter on SAP and United Front.

See Chicago motion on defense work, December 1943.

✷

Study techniques of Durant and other successful popularizers. Bird's-eye view of field as a whole is the best means of preparation for intensive study in detail. See *Loom of Language* on this point. First get a picture of the whole in rough outline. Then examine more clearly each part in detail and relate each part to the generally understood whole. Why can't this be done for Marxism? For labor history, etc.? We should perhaps adopt this method of popularization and also write an article explaining the method so that others can learn to use it in their propaganda work. The question raised by Held's interesting article [*New International*] on Levi, etc., requires further elucidation on the basis of historical facts and Lenin's method. Shows need of history of Comintern. Lit Sec to assemble material for an article or two.

✷

Right and *left:* One's general tendency is shown over a period embracing a number of different conflicts.

Note Trotsky's analysis of Shachtman's tendency, not by a single incident but by a long series over a period of years. Line-ups are a certain indication. Shachtman lined up with Naville, Landau, Nin, etc., in the most critical situations in the formative period of the Left Opposition. He was never convinced but yielded to the joint pressure of L.D. and our own party majority.

His first manifestation of political *independence* took the form of opposition to us, and every *independent* step thereafter. His position was a simulacrum of Bolshevism when he worked under the influence of others. His own instinctive tendency is always opportunist. For example, he never could fully understand why we would hear nothing of unity, or even of united front, with the Lovestoneites. His unification with us (1933) after four years of falsely motivated factional struggle was made unwillingly, under compulsion: the disintegration of the faction and the pressure of L.D.

He fought hand in hand with us against Oehler and Muste. Then he appeared at his best and was taken by many for a real leader. That was a fight *against the left*. When later events brought the struggle *against the right* to the center of the stage, Shachtman found his natural place with a sure instinct.

Many similar illustrations could be shown in the history of the Comintern. The opportunists always sound like Bolsheviks when the fight is directed against the left. It is necessary to observe the attitude of a leader in more than one internal struggle in order to judge his own tendency. Shachtman is not a real *leftist* like Oehler. His radicalism is literary.

The labor party pamphlet: Seen but not read. A revolutionary step forward in propaganda and technique. Designed to attract new people. A professional job. Invite the designer to become a charter member of my new order: "The League of Embattled Saints in the Holy War against Amateurism." We need next an investigation of prices and all details on a *color* job of an illustrated pamphlet in *fifty thousand* lots. Mass distribution is our next goal. A quota of fifty pamphlets per member is not too much for a special campaign on a cheap pamphlet.

Appeal to the young: This is the key to *all* our work. The young relate the word to the deed. They are moved and inspired by *example*. That is why they demand *heroes;* nobody can talk them out of it. The young have better eyes, they see farther. Youth is not petty, timid or calculating. Far goals and grandiose ideals seem attainable to the young, as in fact they are. They see truth beckoning in the distance and run to meet her.

＊

Blanqui: "Tomorrow does not belong to us." The citizens of the communist future will know far better how to manage their affairs than we can possibly imagine. Our preview, therefore, is not a *program*. This distinction between our speculation about the future society and that of the utopians must be explicitly drawn.

But the people love the thought of a better future, even if they personally will not participate in it; nothing appeals more strongly to the imagination, nothing moves and inspires people more powerfully, than the hope for a better future. This must occupy an important place in our propaganda. Marxism entitles us to project the broad outlines of the future society; and as Marxists, we can entertain no doubts that the future man will fill it with an infinitely richer content than we, groping in the gray dawn of precivilization, can hope to visualize. Explain this to the people. Show how we realize our ideal by living a communist life in the struggle for communism.

＊

On "The Wave of the Future": Hitler's "new order" unable to wage political warfare outside adjacent national groupings. Compare with real new orders in history: (1) French Revolution and Napoleonic wars; (2) first phase of Russian Revolution. Show once again that fascism is a resort of *dying* capitalism. Show brevity of its rule: (1) Italy; (2) Germany. Its economic, political and moral exhaustion. Its loss of mass base (petty bourgeoisie destroyed in the war). (See *Reader's Digest* article.)

What perspective does this leave capitalism on a historical scale? Where now are the prophets of "The Wave of the

Future" and *The Managerial Revolution*? The perspectives of communism alone remain undimmed. The blind alley of democratic capitalism. The absolute inability to stabilize society without a social revolution.

Social-Democrats and Stalinists: Note that Social-Democrats and liberals work with Stalinists in Italy. See Montana's letter (*Times*, April 26, 1944). Calls them "Communists." Warns that "Communists" will control, as though it meant a soviet revolution. Pathetic to see their appeal to the bourgeoisie, when it is evident that bourgeois-Stalinist collaboration is the essence of the matter. The crime of Stalinism is propping up capitalism in Europe. [Macdonald's] *Politics* speculates on how bad a Stalinized Europe will be. Essentially defeatist. When the defeatists howl that we don't recognize the danger of Stalinism, they mean that we don't recognize its right to victory in advance.

LETTER 171

SANDSTONE, JANUARY 21, 1945

Notes on Dewey's philosophy:

Dewey's superiority to his scholastic contemporaries, as man and as thinker, is manifest. It was his destiny, however, to become the most authentic philosopher and the first political thinker of American capitalism in its democratic form just at that historic moment when it was passing over the peak of its development and entering into its catastrophic decline. A theory of evolution without the dialectic is helpless in the presence of decay leading up to catastrophic explosions and the emergence of life in new forms. Revolutionary shake-ups rudely interrupt the schemes of orderly progress engineered by "experimental intelligence" and leave the experimentalist gasping with surprise.

"The future cannot be predicted," says Dewey. Indeed it can't, if one rejects the theory that inherent laws at work in the present social order prepare and indicate the line of future development. The foundations of the imposing structure of Dewey's authority were already being undermined while he was still at work shingling the roof. His philosophy became anachronistic during his own lifetime. His influence will be recorded as the most *transient* of all the philosophers who made a serious impression on the thought of the world.

Dewey doesn't refute Marxism, but attempts to dismiss it. Apparently he never took the trouble to study Marxism attentively. This was a most grievous oversight on his part and will prove his undoing. Yankee shrewdness will find its nemesis in Marxism. Dewey's reputation as a philosopher will not stand up under the critical examination of the new generation of Marxist scholars. Dewey's philosophy is the source of all the ideas of the whole pigmy breed of American neo-revisionists and Marx baiters. A critical analysis of the master's theory will dispose of them in passing.

*

An article on the bankruptcy of bourgeois apologists. Dewey and Eastman in the *New Leader*. Morals! Nothing about the "morals" of killing some tens of millions. Nothing about how this slaughter is going to make the world better.

Begin now to make a systematic collection of quotes of those who explained the democratic purposes of the war. Prepare a dossier for future reference.

*

Objectivity and subjectivity in politics. If "subjectivity" is taken to mean passion, enthusiasm, etc., each is necessary. The thing is to keep each in its right place. Mere objective "observers" and urbane commentators are no good. "Nothing great was ever done in the world without passion."

＊

On the press: We should now make an effort to *organize* the work of a large number of *new* contributors, each of whom will be responsible for *one* single little feature, or one special type of item. Examples:

1) "Society notes." Contrasting news items showing extravagance and luxury of the rich and harsh conditions of the poor, quoted verbatim from the press, giving the source and making no comment; let the items speak for themselves.

2) "Facts for Today." A very brief feature relating one or two important facts of interest to workers in each issue. Dig up unusual and not well-known facts.

3) "The Revolutionary Calendar." Printing the significant dates for the week.

＊

The *Party Builder* can perhaps become a medium to draw the membership into the committee-thinking about practical party problems. Perhaps articles on the press and school could be included from this point of view.

The increase in recruiting should lay the ground to increase the number of field organizers. An interesting point to investigate: the proportion of functionaries in the center to the field. We must not become too top-heavy at the center. We must not wait till crying need for new organizers compels us to make experiments. Instead of that, we should force the issue and *make new places* to be filled. All, of course, within the limits of reason and the budget.

Short training courses. An organizer's handbook. (Work over the budget with Moish.) Explain the background of the system of tight normal economy, pinching pennies on nonessentials in order to go all out when money is needed for important projects. St. John's method. The staff comes first. Then equipment (tools and materials for efficient work). No frills, no wasting money on extravagant and unnecessary experiments.

Try out a new type of organizers—"ground-breakers" in new territory. Young couples to lay basis for contacts and new branches by house-to-house work or trial subs. Get full report of Pittsburgh experience. Auto loads of comrades from one city to nearby one for Sunday house-to-house work to build up contact lists of weak branches. Detroit to Flint?

New project. Open extensive personal correspondence with foreign comrades.

Lenin said: "It is very hard to find a conscientious opponent." That was in Russia. In America it is impossible.

Check fifteenth anniversary plenum speech.

The party can work wonders but like the British parliament it can't make a man out of a woman, or vice versa. Neither can it make a silk purse out of a sow's ear. The party can and will make a man out of you—on one condition. You must furnish the raw material.

Pericles' speech: "Here everyone lives as he pleases."

See Grote on the great transformation wrought in the people by the democratic revolution on the island.

LETTER 172

SANDSTONE, JANUARY 21, 1945

Notes:

Get *How to Read Better and Faster*—C. Crowell ($2.50); Thalheimer's *Dialectic Materialism*; everything possible of Mehring's writings; Steffanson in *Treasury of Science* and all other sources on ethics of primitive man; *Revolution Betrayed* on want as the source of "all the old junk"; see Pope's *Iliad* 27, line 929.

*

My pals here are agitating for their own version of Roosevelt's Supreme Court reorganization scheme, to wit: All national secretaries of the party shall automatically retire at the age of fifty-five. They are breathing hot on the neck of the present one (me) for he will reach that age February 11, 1945. I point out that the constitution cannot be amended before the next party convention. But they say that is easily fixed. He should just get out and they will take care of the constitution later. They have learned something, however, from Roosevelt's defeat on the Supreme Court Bill, and state their objects more positively, more euphemistically, than I have outlined them above. Their slogan is: "Put the present secretary on the farm where he can rest and write!"

*

Pioneer: Make a study of *Times Book Review* ads, especially those run in series, and copy some of the features for our advertising campaigns. Get information on cheap process of printing from rotary presses such pamphlet-size magazines as *American Mercury* and *Reader's Digest*. We must look ahead to 50,000 editions of popular pamphlets. I think the new process is applicable in such quantities. Later on we may issue cheap editions of our standard pamphlets and even books in this form. It is well worth investigating.

*

The Press: My pal here who knows newspaper technique very well because he has studied it assiduously in the textbooks of experts, made some sharp criticism of recent makeup innovations in the paper and explained precisely what is wrong about them. I proposed that he write up his criticisms and send them in. He answered: "That would be a waste of my time. I sent in other suggestions and no atten-

tion was paid to them; they were not even acknowledged."
These remarks were the harshest criticism I have heard—one
is almost tempted to say, the harshest criticism one could
hear—of the administration of the paper.

Resentment or insensitivity toward criticism is one of
the most terrible weaknesses a leader can be afflicted with.
I believe one of the characteristic marks of a real leader is
the capacity to listen attentively to criticism. Those who
can't do that shut themselves off from one of the best ways
of learning. One who resents criticism inspired by good
will is simply impossible, too childish for the role of leader.
But even criticism inspired by malice sometimes contains
a kernel or half-kernel of truth which one may profitably
heed and appropriate. I personally learned more than anyone knows precisely this way. Lenin answered the SR's when
they accused the Bolsheviks of appropriating their land program: "Did we ever promise that if you had anything good
we would not take it?"

"This paper does not belong to you." That motto should
be printed on the minds of every member of the staff, if not
on the office walls. The spirit which impels a man to regard
the party office, post or institution in which he works as "his
own," and to resent criticism of his handling of it, is a petty-
bourgeois spirit, a form of the private-property spirit.

Ask in the paper for suggestions from readers for new
small features. Out of the letters we answer—which should
all be printed in the Workers' Forum—select half a dozen
good ones and farm them out to comrades who want to work
for the paper.

The sacrosanct magazine must be knocked apart and put
together again and subordinated to the party. This lady has
been abusing her authority and "thinking" more or less
"independently" since the very beginning. I will take great
pleasure in leading a rough assault on this last bastion of
institutional autonomy and hoisting the party flag on the

rubble. This magazine—this pretentious faker—must change her ways—but fast—and adapt herself to the new regime of efficiency and smooth coordination of all departments under the unquestioned domination of the NC.

As a party *patriot,* judging the magazine in comparison with any other magazine pretending to elucidate theory, I am proud of the *FI.* But as a party *organizer,* believing and insisting on the systematic exploitation of every potentiality, I am ashamed of it, and sick and tired of it, especially of its pretenses.

*

Two Trotsky anniversary articles: (1) A roundup story of the seven secretaries who lost their lives in his service. Here is a theme for one of the greatest, most heroic stories in history. Our youth, who need heroes, should be told this story. (2) A story of the guard at Coyoacan.

The *Party Builder:* An excellent medium, not only for routine circulars and departmental material but also to draw the membership into our thinking and discussion on practical problems. Print the press and school letters from this point of view.

LETTER 173

SANDSTONE, JANUARY 14, 1945

Reflections on the recent party discussion:

The outburst of factional struggle took the party membership by surprise. The appeal against the leadership was not nourished by any sentiment of discontent in the ranks. On the contrary, the opposition made its appearance at the moment when the party morale was perhaps at its highest point, an expression of satisfaction with the visible progress of the party and confidence in the leadership.

The open attempt to discredit the leadership struck the party ranks as a crosscurrent, and resulted only in inflicting the most damaging blows to the prestige and authority of its authors. Seldom has an opposition headed by prominent leaders met such a prompt and crushing repudiation. One simply cannot escape the conclusion that the source of their feverish excitement was in themselves, not in the general situation of the party.

Since the liquidation of the factional struggle with the petty-bourgeois opposition four years ago the internal life of the party has been marked by a spirit of unity and good will based on a great solidarity of views. The relationship between the party ranks and the elected leadership was one of mutual confidence. Harmonious collaboration was the rule in carrying out the party tasks. Our political unity had been effectively demonstrated at the plenum-conferences of 1940 and 1941, and again at the tenth party convention (1942). Incidental disputes of a local character, which arose throughout this period, were resolved to the general satisfaction of the membership.

During these four years many things happened, and the party was dealt heavy blows. The tragic death of Trotsky, the greatest calamity, struck us very soon after the split. The great trade-union struggle in Minneapolis, the arrests and the trial, the entry of the United States into the war, the imprisonment of the eighteen, followed—one shock after another to a small party whose ranks had been decimated by a deep split. But thanks to its political homogeneity and its internal solidarity, the party stood up under these blows, and even made substantial progress.

Party work and activity expanded on all fronts; the professional staff of the party was strengthened in quantity and quality; and recruiting proceeded at a faster pace than ever before in our history. If neither the optimistic fighting morale of the ranks nor the authority of the leadership could be seriously disturbed by the opening of the factional struggle, it was because they were both solidly based on real accomplishments, on real triumphs over difficulties.

The appearance of an unexpected opposition just at the time when the party was making its greatest advances, in the absence of the most prominent leaders, only underscored its untimeliness and made it incumbent upon the leaders of the opposition to give reasons of more than ordinary import and urgency. This they could not do.

The acting leadership conducted the dispute in a manner which leaves little to criticize; and did it, moreover, without permitting the constructive external work of the party to be demoralized or even interrupted. That was a great achievement, a great step forward, in the development of most important and hardest-to-build of all workers' organizations—the democratic combat party.

It was correct, and fully in line with our tradition, to first clear the ground of secondary issues and to make every reasonable concession to redress grievances, real or imaginary, so as to center the attention of the party on the discussion of important questions. Bolsheviks do not waste time and energy fighting over trifles. (More.)

LETTER 174

SANDSTONE, JANUARY 14, 1945

A great deal of nonsense is disseminated about our "aversion" to discussion; the Shachtmanites specialize in this chatter. It is true that we don't believe in conducting aimless discussions around the clock and around the calendar, like a club of bohemian freethinkers. But if anyone wants to bring serious criticisms of the policy and conduct of the leadership, then by all means let them be presented to the membership for full and free discussion.

Despite all the fantastic and hysterical accusations to the contrary, the record shows that this has *always* been our method of dealing with serious disputes. Our party, the most democratic in the world, has never known any other procedure. In the recent discussion the party remained true to its great tradition. It will do the same, it can safely be said, in the subsequent handling of those issues which were implied or adumbrated in the recent discussion but not fully clarified. The most fundamental issues which lay at the basis of the opposition but were not fully developed remain yet to be discussed in full scope and thereby fully clarified.

If many of our critics and opponents in the past have more sincerely believed that we are "against" democracy, it was because they understood democracy in a very one-sided manner—in the sense of unlimited self-expression. We conceive democracy in a broader sense and want to put it to a more definite use. If they want to discuss for the sake of discussion, we want to discuss in order for the party to decide.

Nothing is more barren than aimless discussion, endlessly prolonged, that leads to no conclusion. This is the worst feature of the disputes within isolated groups which lack a proletarian rank and file, a power which can intervene in the disputes and decide them and call the leaders to order. It was precisely this lack of a proletarian deciding force in the dog days of the Left Opposition which permitted the intellectual anarchism and irresponsibility of some of the leaders to assume such monstrous forms and to make them unfit for assimilation into a normally functioning proletarian party.

That is the trouble right now with such demoralized leaders of the emigration as the authors of the "Three Theses." They recognize no restraints and one could argue with them in closed committee circles from now to doomsday

without gaining a single inch. A few hundred revolutionary workers would soon put these anarchists in their places!
Insofar as we conduct a debate with them it must be clearly
understood as an appeal to workers against them. A broad
international discussion is now obviously necessary, but it
must be pointed toward a *decision* by the rank and file and
a stern regulation of all the affairs of the movement on the
basis of this decision.

The artificial debate over "democratic demands" does
not arise over "tempo," as is alleged, but over *perspectives.*
Democratic slogans have an applicability also in periods of
rapid tempo. But the specific slogans to be raised, withdrawn,
modified or emphasized must be determined by an analysis
of the concrete situation regardless of whether the tempo
is rapid or relatively slow. "The blueprint" approach is false
in either case.

A fruitful debate among Leninists can only occur over
the applicability of *specific* democratic slogans in a *concrete*
situation. And such questions, as a rule, can be decided only
on the basis of full information as to the actual state of affairs; that is, on the spot. Why should the American party
assume that we are called upon to give such detailed advice
from afar? It is our duty, rather, to aid European parties in
the struggle for programmatic intransigence.

We don't know of any proposals to reject the use of democratic slogans as a means of mobilizing the masses in a given
situation. We do know of attempts to substitute a so-called
democratic program for the program of proletarian revolution.
That is the significance of the "Three Theses." That danger
is real, not imaginary. We are fighting against that. All the
clamor raised in the artificial struggle against our alleged
opposition to democratic slogans is nothing but a form of
indirect support of the authors of the "Three Theses."

The attempt to witticize on the subject of optimism and
pessimism is not very well placed. It is no laughing matter.

Nobody ever yet made serious preparations to organize a revolution which he didn't believe in. The lack of faith in the ability of the workers is the psychological source of all forms of Menshevism. The "Three Theses" illustrate this once again. They were grounded on the assumption that Hitler's "new order" was firmly established on the continent of Europe. This foundation is crumbling away; it wasn't very solid in the first place.

Now we see the same approach to the danger of Stalinism. There can hardly be a real difference of opinion among us as to the danger of Stalinism or the necessity of struggling against it. (More.)

LETTER 175

SANDSTONE, JANUARY 16, 1945

Continuing: The differences arise over the perspectives of the struggle. Shall we presuppose the victory of Stalinism in Europe or the victory of the Roosevelt-Churchill-Stalin alliance and "prepare for defeats"? Or shall we maintain our conviction that the power of the masses is greater and prepare the struggle with the perspective of victory? If there is any ground for a real conflict between us, that is where it lies. That is the meaning of "optimism" and "pessimism." It is not a question of "tempo" but of perspectives.

There is a somewhat disturbing consistency in the various issues raised or adumbrated by the opposition. In addition to the differences over perspectives, masked as a dispute over democratic demands, we hear the astonishing contention that the Fourth International must be on guard against the left danger. If the perspective is revolutionary, if we are witnessing the beginning of a great revolutionary upsurge, we must rather expect manifestations of the right danger in the sharpest form. That is a historical law.

Leaving aside individual aberrations and judging by main currents, we see this law demonstrated over and over again in every new crisis. "Leftism" is fundamentally a sickness of the labor movement at ebb tide. It is the product of revolutionary impatience, of the impulse to jump over objective difficulties, to substitute revolutionary zeal and forced marches for the supporting movement of the masses. Opportunism, on the other hand, is a disease which strikes the party in the sharpest form at the moment of social crisis. It is the product of the sentiment of capitulation before the moral and material power of the bourgeoisie.

In the light of historical experience it seems incredible that anyone should see "leftism" as the main danger at the beginning of the revolutionary crisis. If history teaches us anything, such a posing of the question must itself be characterized as an opportunist manifestation. The greatest danger to the Fourth International right now, at the moment of the revolutionary upturn, is the sentiment of conciliationism toward Menshevism in any of its forms or manifestations.

The "examples" cited in proof of the "left" danger are arbitrarily and one-sidedly selected, and even then falsely interpreted. The principal difference between us and the official British section arose over the proletarian military policy. Objections to this policy in the spirit of pacifist abstentionism scarcely deserve the designation of "left" deviations. But leaving that aside, and the "Three Theses" along with it, let us turn to another and far more significant page of our recent history.

Simultaneously with the outbreak of the war, the Fourth International was plunged into an internal struggle which threatened its existence. This struggle, as is known, centered in the Socialist Workers Party, but its repercussions were worldwide and its leadership was truly international. Was the petty-bourgeois opposition which was strong enough to muster 40 percent of our membership for a split against Trotsky, against our program and against our tradition, a right or a left danger?

And—to carry the inquiry one necessary step further— is the sentiment of conciliationism toward this Menshevik traitor clique a right or a left danger? These questions are very pertinent to the new controversy arising in our ranks on an international scale. When we begin to discuss them we will begin to get down to the nub of the matter.

LETTER 176

SANDSTONE, JANUARY 16, 1945

In discussing every difference of opinion and every proposal, we should aim to carry our thoughts through to the end and draw the whole party into our thinking. For this it is necessary not only to explain to the party what is proposed, but *why* it is proposed. The characteristic defect of all eclectic thinking is that it is only half-thinking. It is marked by the failure to carry a thought through to the end; the tendency to jump to conclusions and formulate proposals midway in the consideration of a subject.

Take the question of the Shachtmanites, for example. We witness an attempt, direct or implied, to revise our estimate of the petty-bourgeois opposition. But the question is not ended with our *estimate* of the Shachtman party; it is only started. What follows from this estimate, or the proposal to revise it? To what end is it pointed? If we keep thinking without stopping halfway, we must recognize that our estimate inexorably leads us either (1) toward reconciliation and unity, or (2) toward a deepening of the split. The discussion and decision are not completed until that question is decided and reasons given for the decision. (More.)

LETTER 177

SANDSTONE, JANUARY 17, 1945

Continuing: We, on our part, assume that the course toward deepening of the split is necessary and correct; our attitude flows from that. Naturally, if someone has a different proposal, we are ready to discuss it. But if that is the case, let us discuss fully and properly, in logical order, from premise to conclusion. Let us go back to the internal struggle or the split in which it culminated, and put the following questions as a basis for the discussion.

(1) Was the analysis of the petty-bourgeois opposition, which we together with Trotsky made at that time, correct or not? (2) Was the attitude we took toward them properly based on the analysis? (3) Was our action in expelling them when they refused to accept the convention decisions the proper action? (4) What changes have taken place in the meantime? Has the Shachtman party come closer or gone farther away from us? (5) Do these changes provide the logical ground to reassert and strengthen our original decision or to change or modify it?

By all means let us discuss the question of the "Workers Party," if anyone really wants to discuss it. But let us not nibble at the question. Let it be discussed fully—to the end.

*

Trotsky's method apropos the question as to whom we consider ours, and whom we can agree to confer with: Carry every discussion through to the end and make a selection of forces on the basis of the decisions arrived at finally. Cover the ground thoroughly in each situation, but never go back and retrace the ground already covered. See:

1) His letter on Landau in regard to Spain.

2) His letters on who should be invited to the interna-

tional conferences of the ICL and who should be excluded. No admittance to those with whom accounts have already been settled. (Bordigists, Landau, etc.)

3) His letter on what an international conference can and cannot give. It can do no more than put the formal seal on decisions and agreements already arrived at by the sections through democratic discussion. The conference cannot enter into the situation as a *new* factor.

This whole question must be elaborated now, on the basis of our past experiences, in the light of G's [Morrison's] proposal.

＊

At a New York membership meeting someone, it was reported, spoke of a "split atmosphere." Such assertions cannot be passed off. No ambiguity whatever on such a question can be tolerated. It is the duty of all concerned to make explicit statements of their attitude and intentions whenever any suggestion of "split" is heard. (See Trotsky's letter—*In Defense of Marxism*—and the subsequent action taken by the majority.) We do not want to hear any talk about "split" even in jest. Our democracy is free enough, elastic enough, to permit the correction of any error of the leadership by normal means. For that reason the public opinion of the party must condemn anyone who even dares to think of splitting the party.

Fair treatment and comradely discussion with all those loyally working *inside* the party, no matter how great the differences of opinion may be; relentless warfare against all those who step outside the party. This is our policy. As for those who actually resort to split, and thereby try to destroy the party—such people are traitors in our eyes.

＊

Regarding conventions and other national and regional gatherings: powerful instinct of people to come from far and near to commingle with their own kind. Refer to ancient Greek (Panhellenic) festivals. Representatives and delegates came from all the Greek colonies throughout the world— from Marseilles on the western European tip to the Asian colonies and even to the farthest eastern outposts on the shores of the Euxine Sea. Search for the driving impulse of these festivals. Work this into an article projecting encampments, etc. Get material on old-fashioned camp meetings of the Socialist Party in the Southwest (see Ameringer's memoirs) and the Jehovah's Witnesses conventions.

*

Thesis: On the Trotskyist method of doing things, doing them right. Consciousness and plan. Bohemian tradition of the old radical movement. Split with the petty-bourgeois opposition and clearing the decks for a new turn. A complete transformation effected. The specific Trotskyist contribution. The Toledo delegates' report at the convention on their "clean headquarters." A very important report! Lay out a plan to educate the party from top to bottom on these matters. Campaign against the spirit of "getting by." Nothing is done well enough until it is done right. Introduce "the element of consciousness and plan" into all fields and phases of party work—including the not unimportant work of making the headquarters and office neat and attractive and keeping them clean.

LETTER 178

SANDSTONE, JANUARY 14, 1945

Opponents and critics of our party busy themselves in the effort to create the impression that the American Trotskyist movement is split in two, that there are "two wings," etc.

Such publications as the [Socialist Party] *Call* and [Macdonald's] *Politics* overlook no opportunity to confuse people by painting up the Shachtmanite organization as one of these "wings," as some sort of "Trotskyites."

Besides the genuine Trotskyites, they maintain, there are some others who are not so bad and do not demand so much; the cut-rate Trotskyites, so to speak—they can get it for you wholesale. The propaganda of the Shachtman group itself is devoted primarily, almost exclusively, to us. After four and one-half years of self-proclaimed independence they are still unable to conduct themselves otherwise than as a mistreated faction of our party. They run after us like a parasite divorced from its host.

Their politics consists in sniffing at the fringes of our movement in the hope of finding some waifs and strays with whom they may limp in sympathy. But we, on our part, long ago turned our backs on this wretched reminiscence of the past and directed all our attention to the awakening workers who are far more important and potentially far more revolutionary than any or all of these moth-eaten cliques of yesterday.

We demand absolutely nothing from Shachtman & Co. except that they carry through their split to the very end. We insist on that. We gained the upper hand precisely by this policy. We have thrived and grown strong by this policy. It was not adopted in the first place without serious thought and deliberation. It has been vindicated a thousand times in practical experience.

That is why ill-considered suggestions or proposals to change or modify this policy, whether directly made or implied, are bound to be given short shrift by the party membership. Such suggestions or proposals, implicit in the attitude taken by the opposition in the recent discussion, run counter to the orientation of the party. To be carried into effect they would require that the lessons acquired in harsh experience be unlearned, and that positions gained in struggle be given up.

The sentiment of conciliationism looks backward, not forward. There is a time to debate with people who infringe on the principles of Bolshevism and call its organizational methods into question, and there is a time to close the debate and proceed to open struggle. It is important to do the right thing at the right time in each case. The time for debate is when the differences and criticisms are presented by loyal members of a common organization. The time to declare open war is when organizational loyalty is violated, when the critics take the road of split and set up a rival organization, outside the party.

We must not mix up these two prescriptions. It was because we kept them separate, each in its proper place, that we defeated the petty-bourgeois opposition, first in the internal discussion, as faction against faction, and then in the open struggle, as party against party.

No change in our attitude toward the splitters can be entertained except to make it stronger, more precise and definite, more intransigent. Our policy in dealing with the petty-bourgeois opposition, which has been correct from beginning to end, was not invented by us, nor did it fall from the skies. It was derived from the theory and experience of the international movement.

Up to the split and for a few months afterward, we had the direct guidance of Trotsky who embodied this theory and experience. After the death of Trotsky we kept in mind what he had taught us and drew further on historical examples. In this connection read Lenin's letter to the German Communists after the break with Levi. Read Trotsky's letter on the Spanish events after the break with Landau. These two letters, so rich in practical wisdom of great fighting political leaders, both say the same thing, almost in the same words. "Stop the sterile discussion with these deserters, forget that they ever existed, and turn your attention to the workers, recruit new cadres."

This was the gist of the advice of Lenin and Trotsky in dealing with people who rejected the discipline of the party. Lenin and Trotsky were leaders of endless patience. They never tired of explaining things over and over again to loyal people who were willing and able to learn. (More.)

LETTER 179

SANDSTONE, JANUARY 14, 1945

Continuing: But they also knew how to judge when patience ceases to be a virtue and becomes a fault. That happens sometimes sooner but never later than the moment when dissenting factions take the road of split, when the ideologic dispute between factions of a common organization is transformed into a struggle of party against party. We learned that from Lenin and Trotsky, and the party has profited enormously by the knowledge. Nobody can teach us differently at this late date, least of all in the question of our attitude toward the enemy party of Shachtman and Co.

Our resolute decision to have no truck with the Shachtmanites is interpreted by some people to mean that we have an attitude of narrow exclusiveness toward all other political organizations, a fear of permitting our members to come into contact with their members lest they be won over. This idea is implicit, if not directly stated, in M's [Morrison's] comments.

The history of our party cuts the ground from under all such assumptions. Our approach to other political organizations is dialectical, not formal. They are all equal to the same thing—that is, they are all rivals of our party—but they are not equal to each other by a long shot. We study each organization concretely, seek to understand its own peculiar qualities, and on that basis determine whether we should go toward them or stand aloof from them.

Above all we seek to ascertain the *origin* of each organization under investigation, its *composition* and the *general direction* of its development. That is the dialectical method, the best way to study anything in politics, and not only in politics.

Let us take some examples from our history. We were expelled from the Communist Party in 1928. Yet, for *five years* thereafter we maintained the position of a faction of the CP, directing the main weight of our propaganda toward its membership. Why? Because the Communist Party had originated as a revolutionary organization, and while the process of Stalinist degeneration had already set in, it was by no means completed and there was a possibility of reforming the party. We were a mere handful, isolated and shut off from participation in the mass movement, while the Stalinist Party and its peripheral movement embraced virtually all of the militant revolutionary workers. For these reasons we concentrated our attention on the CP, called ourselves a faction of it, ran after its members night and day, and recruited our main cadres right out of its ranks. There was not a trace of exclusiveness in our attitude.

It was only in 1933, after the German events, that we recognized that quantity had been transformed into quality, that the Comintern had degenerated beyond the possibility of reform, and proclaimed our independence of it. But even then—yes, and even now—we could not "ignore" the Communist Party, we could not turn our backs on it. It contained, and still contains, too many militant workers in its ranks to permit such an attitude. We still approach the Stalinist workers whenever we get a chance, or at any rate, we should approach them.

Take the case of the Muste organization, the Conference for Progressive Labor Action, later the AWP [American Workers Party]. It originated in 1929 as a mildly reformist, anti-communist substitute for the communistic left wing which had withdrawn from the old trade unions under the influence of the ultra-left swing of the Comintern—the "Third Period." This was a bad origin, and the composition of the CPLA corresponded to it. We took an attitude of out-right hostility to the new formation.

Later, a change began to take place in the direction, and also in the composition, of the Muste organization. Muste and some of his collaborators had a positive quality: their activity in mass work. Under the impact of the crisis this mass work, especially in the unemployed field, took a radical turn. Militant workers, repelled by the bureaucratic regime of the CP and its sectarian policies at the time, entered the Muste organization, shifted the weight in its composition and changed its general direction. The AWP began to turn to the left and proclaimed the necessity of a new political party.

On that basis we completely changed our attitude toward it. Hostile aversion was changed to friendliness and active fraternization. We engaged, on our initiative, in cooperative actions, opened friendly discussions, and eventually fused with them.

Just as our position as a loyal faction of the CP was changed into a decision to break completely with them and select an independent course, so in the case of the Muste organization our attitude was changed in an opposite sense.

But *our* changes were conditioned by the changes which took place in these organizations. Neither whims nor caprices, nor organizational exclusiveness, nor any kind of subjectively motivated considerations had anything to do with our decisions. (More.)

LETTER 180

SANDSTONE, JANUARY 21, 1945

Continuing: Our *fundamental* attitude was the same all the time, and is the same now. We aimed then and we aim now to build *one* party on the basis of *one* program. All methods must be judged by this end. All methods must serve it.

We changed our attitude toward the SP for similar reasons. But since this party was much larger than ours, and would not listen to any talk of fusion, we took the bull by the horns and unceremoniously dissolved our party, sacrificing our cherished independence, and joined the SP without conditions. In that action, conditioned by the left swing of the SP and our own necessity to establish intimate contact with its left wing, it would be very difficult to find a trace, even a single "germ," of narrow-minded exclusiveness and organizational fetishism.

But it should not be forgotten that our attitude toward the SP changed a second time. After we had completed our work there and were obliged to carry through the split in order to free our hands for revolutionary work, we slammed the door on the wreck of N.T.'s [Norman Thomas'] party and paid no further attention to it. Unlike the Stalinist movement, the SP has no serious body of proletarian supporters. It would be a waste of time to bother with it any longer. And time is one thing that revolutionary militants cannot afford to waste.

During this period under review: from 1929 to 1937, while we were clinging to the Stalinists and then breaking with them, fighting the SP, then joining them, then splitting with them and forgetting about them—during this period of changing political tactics conditioned by changes in the organizations mentioned, we unconditionally refused to have anything to do with the Lovestoneites and we expelled the Oehlerite sectarians from our ranks.

The reasons for this were not in the least subjective either. The Lovestoneites were an opportunist sect *going backward*. The Oehlerites, originally Trotskyists, became ossified in a sectarian mold. We had nothing to gain by interminable debate with them. Debate and revolutionary propaganda in general bear fruit only when directed to groups, parties or masses of workers who are in *motion* and *going forward*.

The objective political method by which we steered our course toward other organizations over a period of many years, through the most complicated situations and changes, guides us today in determining our attitude toward the [Shachtmanite] WP. They are not a growing and progressive workers' organization, but a petty-bourgeois clique declining in membership and going backward ideologically. They became hardened in their prejudices and refused to learn anything in debate, even from Trotsky. They refused to learn from events afterward; they only deepened their errors and transformed them into crimes.

They set up an independent "party" against us but still think and act like a faction of our party. This clique is parasitic through and through. On top of everything else, the numerical relationship of forces between their organization and ours shifts steadily in our favor—convincing evidence of the correctness of our policy.

We know all about their situation. Our refusal to have anything to do with them politically does not mean that we "ignore" them. They are our enemies and we are watching them all the time. The 60-40 relationship at the time of the split has changed to an 80-20 relationship. The new members recruited during the past year alone come very close to equalling the total membership of the WP; and the quality is better.

Stewing in their own juice, the Shachtmanites reminisce

about their "golden age," the good old days of factional struggle without organizational responsibility; pilfer internal documents for publication in their press; and dream of creating a supporting faction in our organization.

Leaving them to their own devices, we keep our program clear and direct all our activity to the awakening workers. They sigh for the past, but the past cannot return. The present situation of the party without them is better than the past with them. And the present is only a preparation for the future which will be better yet—provided we stick to our course.

LETTER 181

SANDSTONE, JANUARY 21, 1945

Macdonald contrasts the "arrogance" of the Trotskyists to their numerical insignificance. He speaks for the majority— all the others. Anyone can be in the majority by joining it on its terms. To fight for a majority on one's own terms is a different matter. He didn't like Vincent's high evaluation of the bound volumes of *The Militant* in comparison with the first issues of the [Socialist Party] *Call*. By the way, who does care about the back numbers of the *Call*? Certainly not those who published it. They are all, or nearly all, in the imperialist war camp, working as flunkeys for Roosevelt or as flunkeys for Roosevelt's labor flunkeys.

The party is not what it used to be. A whole process of rebuilding and reeducating the party has been taking place since 1940 and qualitative changes have been effected. Some people failed to notice what had taken place and addressed their remarks to a party that no longer exists. That is why their remarks sounded like an echo of the past.

Perhaps the most stupid and futile of all judgments is that

which blames a person because others blame him, or still worse, blames him because others praise him. One cannot control the sentiments of others and should not be held responsible for them. Most people prefer praise to blame. It is possible that in this respect I belong to the majority. I once heard it said: "The sweetest incense a man ever smelled is the applause of his fellows."

But one cannot *command* the applause of others unless he has material power over their lives and is base enough— and also stupid enough—to use it for such purposes. Even then the joke is on him, for if he has any sense at all he must know that those who praise him through compulsion in public, laugh at his conceit in private. A politician must also be a philosopher and say: "The abuse of the base is the decoration of merit," but the sincere praise of friends is balm to the soul.

*

Lay out a five-year study plan parallel with a five-year literary plan. Time arrangement: Mornings *invariably* for writing without any interruptions *whatever*; afternoons and evenings for reading, study and contemplation. No work Saturday afternoons and Sunday. Daily stint of writing: 1,000 words.

Increasing the volume of literary production is simply a matter of keeping to a routine and organized collaboration and division of labor. The increasing volume of my published material, two books and six or eight pamphlets, all published within the past three years, can easily give the impression that the last ten percent of my thirty-odd years of work in the movement have been the most effective and the most productive; that I have worked harder, and to better effect.

I believe it is true that these last years have been the most effective, if I judge the influence of the published material correctly. But this increased effectiveness accruing from published writings and speeches has been almost entirely due to the technical assistance and division of labor which previously was lacking. I did no more actual work than before, perhaps less. The assumption that the past three or four years of my activity have been the most fruitful is an argument for a more systematic organization of collaboration and division of labor. Hence the project of the Literary Secretariat.

I think the first indicated task is to collect all the material of my previous work, already prepared in the rough, and put it into finished shape; work up all my "ore" dug up by hard pick-and-shovel work in previous excavations. This material is in the form of lecture notes, letters, committee minutes, and old writings unknown to the new generation. I believe my best service now is to *write down* and publish what I have learned in various ways so that it can become the property of others who are willing to learn from it and make use of it. I don't mean only the "theoretical" and political lore, but *everything,* including practical knacks of doing things, learned the hard way. Others, if they are willing, can learn them the easy way from my explanations. There is a reason for everything: the thing to explain is the reason.

Two examples of old and once corrected mistakes cropped up lately to remind me that the previous experience was lost because no record was made of it for the information of new people:

1) The spinners [sailors] are listed as a unit pledging a quota to a certain party enterprise. This is wrong. It was thrashed out and settled for good reasons long ago. But apparently the lesson was buried and lost in the committee minutes and in the memories of the few people who participated in the closed discussion. How many scores—how many hundreds!—of thought-out ways of doing things to the best advantage lie buried in the old minutes and correspondence files? Much gold can be refined from this ore. (More.)

LETTER 182

SANDSTONE, JANUARY 21, 1945

Continuing: 2) Many typographical errors are creeping back into the press. We waged a campaign against this once *on principle* and finally put a stop to it. Now the weeds are spoiling the garden again. Unfortunately, the fight against typographical errors and its motivations remained known only to a few directly involved at the time. This little affair, and many like it, must be written down for the benefit of all.

✳

If the others mentioned finally agree to go along on the Lit Sec proposition, they should have no illusions as to what they are getting into. My proposition—that each do his own writing but submit it to a triple criticism and editing for *style* as well as content—means precisely what it says.

They will find in me a merciless critic of all gingerbread; of all gargoyles and curlicues stuck onto a piece of writing to please the writer's undisciplined fancy; of everything extraneous, arbitrarily inserted, which breaks the line of communication between writer and reader—the object of our writing—and deflects attention pointlessly to something else. Writing which bears the imprint of the Lit Sec must be good writing, without a drop of water or a bubble of wind in it. My own preference is for Thucydidean leanness. If the others want a plumper style, something with a little more flesh on its bones, they will have to convince me that the extra flesh is muscle, not fat.

We have to set a new style in American political and theoretical writing. The academic curse must never taint a single line. Our task is to elucidate the most profound ideas in language accessible to the ordinary worker, without diluting the ideas or "writing down" to the reader. Our great mission, I take it, is to popularize unadulterated Marxism. For my part, I am confident the Lit Sec can do it.

Of all the literary projects laid out, the one closest to my heart is the book on labor leaders, and of that, the chapter on Parsons. I have long felt a strong compulsion to do justice to the memory of "the dear little man" who stands above all others in my affection. It will also be a work of love to restore the towering figures of Debs, Haywood and "the Saint," and DeLeon. The revolutionary militants of the new generation, like all ardent youth, need heroes who personify their far-reaching ideals. I will show them some real heroes—their own predecessors, the pioneers who blazed the trail for them. The sculptor who made Schiller's statue said: "I will make Schiller life size—that is, colossal." This will be my motto in re-creating the heroic figures of our pioneers.

The Hillquit-Berger chapter will give me a good occasion to say what is on my mind about Social-Democrats in general. In their evaluation of Debs, they unconsciously threw a mercilessly revealing light on their own wretched character. They conventionally praised Debs for his goodness, thinking that was expected of them, like shrewd shopkeepers who "respect" the ideals of honest men, but consider them fools who are out of place in this workaday world. I will answer them by showing what Debs really was and what they really were. See Ameringer's and Hillquit's memoirs. I am going to roast these half-men and the breed they typify on a spit over a slow fire until they are really cooked. I aim to teach the youth to despise people who play and dabble with great ideas and do not go all the way for them.

"Trotsky as Organizer." The models for this pamphlet are *State and Revolution* and the *Criticism of the Draft Program.* In each of these productions the task of the author was to restore and prove the actual teachings and methods of another—Lenin of Marx, and Trotsky of Lenin. Hence

the pattern: extensive quotations strung along a line of explanatory and interpretive comment. I believe this pamphlet will be a revelation to those who have swallowed, wholly or partly, the journalistic myth about Trotsky's indifference to organization.

"Trotsky as Educator": a work on the same pattern. Here is Trotsky at the height of his powers carefully writing down and explaining the reasons for everything he did or proposed. His object was to draw the whole movement into participation in his thinking and to teach them how to think. It will be a great achievement, and a great service to the young generation, if I can enable them to see the living figure of Trotsky, the teacher, explaining things to his disciples, and help them grasp his method.

Trotsky's letters to me. Are they collected? I have in mind to write a special article about them, re-creating the situations with which they dealt, and revealing the Old Man at his best in the dual role of teacher and organizer of the work of others—in this case, myself.

In *Labor Leaders,* fit in somewhere a section on the exploitation of the primitive radical movement by individual adventurers and promoters. Note the privately owned press; Wilshire's "Bishop Creek Gold Mine" stocks, and similar frauds on the comrades. See *International Socialist Review* (about 1913) on "Playing the Comrades for Suckers" [by Phillip Russel].

My grandfather on my mother's side was a "joiner." That was the old name for a skilled carpenter. A joiner was a cunning fellow who shaped and fitted sticks of wood together and transformed a pile of lumber into a house, good to look at and useful to live in. A party organizer is a *joiner* of people.

Faithful to my self-prescribed routine, I am finishing here my writing stint for the day, for the week, and for my term here, on time before noon on Saturday, January 20, 1945. The Sandstone assignment is finished. I am ready to go home.

Notes

(Unless otherwise specified, the year of all dates below is 1944.)

January 1944

LETTER 1

Walta. Rose Karsner's daughter.

Baby. Walta's two-year-old daughter, Lorna; also referred to in these letters by such nicknames as Mickey, Mick, Mickus, Sweetums.

Carl. Cannon's son.

Joe. Joseph Hansen.

LETTER 2

Paper. The Militant.

James T. Farrell. The novelist; he served as chairman of the Civil Rights Defense Committee which provided legal defense for the prisoners and financial assistance to their families, and which publicized the case.

Fifteenth anniversary fund. The Militant, a weekly, was sustained by regular fund drives, contributions to which defrayed its deficits. This fund drive had a goal of $15,000.

Branches. Of the Socialist Workers Party. Though contributions to the fund drives came also from individuals, the main contributions were from branches of the SWP, each of which made a pledge at the opening of the drive and then paid in installments until its "quota" was fulfilled.

Appeal. Though the eighteen Trotskyists were the first people convicted under the Smith Act, the U.S. Supreme Court stubbornly refused to hear an appeal in the case.

Plenum speech. Cannon's speech at the October, 1943, plenum, or plenary meeting, of the Socialist Workers Party National Committee. The NC is the party's highest body between conventions. The October plenum was its last meeting before the eighteen began serving their sentences.

Sylvia. Cannon's secretary, Sylvia Caldwell.

LETTER 3

Father. The author's father, John Cannon.

Agnes. The author's sister.

CRDC. The Civil Rights Defense Committee. (See note on *James T. Farrell*, Letter 2.)

Balabanoff's memoirs. My Life as a Rebel, by Angelica Balabanoff, the Russian-Italian socialist. A leader in the pre–World War I Socialist Party of Italy, she participated in 1915 in the Zimmerwald Conference. She had been a patron of Mussolini and helped him to rise to editorship of *Avanti,* the party organ, in his socialist days. She joined the Bolsheviks on the eve of the revolution and in 1919 was made secretary of the Communist International. Her primary loyalty, however, was to the Serrati wing of the Italian Socialist Party, and when it refused to accept the "21 points" for membership adopted by the CI at its world congress in 1920, she broke with the CI and the Bolsheviks. She remained active in the socialist and anti-fascist movements, but became increasingly bitter in her anti-Bolshevism as the years passed.

Lillian Symes and [Travers] Clement. Prominent figures in the left wing of the Socialist Party in California; co-authors of *Rebel America.*

LETTER 4

Robert Emmet's speech. The famous "speech from the dock" by the Irish patriot, who was hanged by the British in 1803 following the failure of an uprising led by him.

LETTER 5

My bust. Duncan Ferguson, an artist who was a member of the SWP, had recently sculpted a bust of Cannon.

Mona. The widow of Cannon's brother Phil.

My history book. Just prior to entering prison, Cannon had completed his book, *The History of American Trotskyism.*

Usick. The name by which his close friends called John G. Wright, a leader and educator of the SWP, who translated many of Leon Trotsky's works into English. John G. Wright died June 21, 1956.

Six-page Militant. The paper was expanded early in 1944 from four to six pages. (These were full-size pages; it was many years later that *The Militant* was changed to its present tabloid format.)

The magazine. The theoretical organ *Fourth International.*

Trial pamphlet. That part of the court record of the Minneapolis Labor Trial containing Cannon's testimony in direct and cross-examination had been printed as a pamphlet under the title *Socialism on Trial.*

E.R. Frank. One of the prominent younger SWP leaders subject to the draft; a writer and editor of *The Militant* and *Fourth International.*

Thomas. Tom Kerry, who wrote under the pen name C. Thomas.

Frank Graves. An authority on foreign affairs, he became editor of *The Militant.*

LETTER 6

Membership campaign. In reply to government repression, the SWP embarked on a campaign to recruit new members.

Moish. Morris Stein, one of the outstanding party leaders who, as acting national secretary, had taken over Cannon's job in the SWP national office.

LETTER 7

Frank Lovell. An SWP member active in the maritime unions.

Evelyn Novack. Assistant secretary of the Civil Rights Defense Committee.

Pioneer Publishers. A book and pamphlet publishing house established in 1930 to print American editions of the writings of Leon Trotsky and other Marxist and socialist literature.

Lillian Charles. In charge of Pioneer Publishers.

LETTER 8

Hollywood suit. Los Angeles comrades had bought Cannon a new suit.

AWP. American Workers Party, founded and led by A.J. Muste. It merged in December, 1934, with the Communist League of America (Trotskyists) to form the Workers Party.

Salutsky. Also known as J.B.S. Hardman, long-time editor of *Advance*, the official organ of the Amalgamated Clothing Workers. He was briefly in the Communist movement in the 1920s and later was a leader in the American Workers Party.

LETTER 9

Bess Gogol. A family friend and old political associate.

Pardon application. Immediately after their imprisonment, the CRDC launched a nationwide petition campaign calling for the unconditional pardon and immediate release of the eighteen prisoners. This made it necessary for the prisoners to make formal applications for pardon.

February 1944

LETTER 10

Freda. Freda Charles, who was on the office staff of the CRDC.

ACLU. The American Civil Liberties Union.

LETTER 11

Lorna. The granddaughter.

Bam. Lorna's nickname for Cannon.

ILD. International Labor Defense, organized by the Communist Party in 1925 to defend class-struggle prisoners and to assist their families. Cannon was its national secretary from its founding until his expulsion from the Communist Party in 1928 as a Trotskyist. In this period the ILD defended not only Communists but anarchists, such as Sacco and Vanzetti, IWWs and trade unionists of varying or no political affiliations.

International Publishers. The publishing house, founded in 1924, which put out the basic works of Marxism and the books and pamphlets sold by the Communist Party.

Larry. Lawrence P. Trainor (pen name Turner) of Boston, who was then SWP organizer in Seattle and had been hospitalized with a ruptured appendix.

Birthday. His fifty-fourth.

LETTER 12

Dot . . . Grant. Dorothy and Ted Grant. The latter had recently become organizer of the New York City local of the SWP.

LETTER 13

Joe's piece about our departure. Article by Joseph Hansen, entitled "How the Trotskyists Went to Jail," in the February, 1944, issue of the magazine *Fourth International.*

LETTER 14

Ruth. Cannon's daughter.

Labor Defender. The magazine of the International Labor Defense.

Leon Sedov. Trotsky's elder son. A political leader in his own right, he was active in the Trotskyist movement in Western Europe, though surrounded and harassed by Stalin's GPU agents. He died at the age of thirty-two in Paris on February 16, 1938, under mysterious circumstances, in all probability assassinated by Stalin's agents.

The Old Man. A term of affection used in reference to Trotsky.

LETTER 15

Scoreboard. The payments and balance due on the amounts pledged by the SWP branches to the fund drive were printed weekly in a "scoreboard" in *The Militant.*

To Washington for approval. Prisoners were permitted to receive only those books which had been approved beforehand by the Federal Bureau of Prisons.

George's accident. George Clarke had been burned in a shipboard accident.

Frank's little finger. Frank Lovell had undergone surgery on his hand following a shipboard accident. (See note to Letter 7.)

The headquarters. The SWP national office and the New York local office had been in an old, poorly heated building at 116 University Place since the party's founding in 1938. In 1966 the headquarters was moved to 873 Broadway.

Oscar Ameringer. A well-known Socialist Party writer and editor, he published the socialistic *American Guardian* in Oklahoma City into the 1940s. His autobiography is entitled *If You Don't Weaken.*

LETTER 16

Farewell speeches. The send-off for the eighteen, who were due to enter prison on New Year's Eve, was a farewell banquet in New York on December 26, 1943. Six of the defendants made speeches at the banquet.

LETTER 17

Natalia. Trotsky's widow, Natalia Sedova.

Wil and the others. The two Trotskyist groups in Great Britain, the Workers International League and Revolutionary Socialist League, agreed to merge and, in a joint convention in March, 1944, took the name of Revolutionary Communist Party.

Dewey. The American philosopher and educator, John Dewey. He had been chairman of the Commission of Inquiry into the Charges Made Against Leon Trotsky in the Moscow Trials. The Commission went to Mexico and heard testimony from April 10 to 17, 1937.

March 1944

LETTER 18

Struggle book. The Struggle for a Proletarian Party, by James P. Cannon, New York: Pioneer Publishers, 1943.

LETTER 19

Frank's draft status. See note on *E.R. Frank,* Letter 5.

Introduction to my Struggle book. Objection by a group forming around Felix Morrow, editor of the magazine *Fourth International*, to the wording of a section of John G. Wright's introduction to *The Struggle for a Proletarian Party* had resulted in the book being taken off the press while the introduction was amended and reset.

The "march." The defendants assembled in the SWP headquarters in Minneapolis on December 31, 1943, and then marched in a column of two's through downtown Minneapolis to the federal courthouse, where they surrendered themselves to the federal marshals. They were then marched to the county jail.

LETTER 21

Farrell Dobbs. A leader in the Minneapolis Teamsters strikes and later head of the eleven-state over-the-road organizing drive of the International Brotherhood of Teamsters. He later resigned his post with the IBT to become labor secretary of the SWP. He was one of the eighteen prisoners.

Edith and Mike. The Bartells of Los Angeles; they had left the SWP with the Burnham-Shachtman minority in 1940 but later quit the Shachtmanite Workers Party and rejoined the SWP.

Place on Long Island. A cottage at Sea Cliff, New York, rented for the summer.

Wong. John G. Wright's dog.

LETTER 22

National Office. The SWP national headquarters in New York City.

Appeal to Reason. The most popular socialist newspaper of the pre–World War I era; published in Girard, Kansas.

Thermometer. The progress of the fund drive was illustrated in *The Militant* by the drawing of a thermometer with a rising column of mercury.

World-Telegram story about the CP. Early in March, 1944, stories began appearing in the New York newspapers of disputes in the Communist Party leadership occasioned by the line laid down by CP General Secretary Earl Browder of dissolving the Communist Party into a Communist Political Association and continuing the wartime suspension of the class struggle into the postwar period.

William Z. Foster. The most prominent trade-union figure in the CP, but outranked in the leadership in this period by Browder.

ILGWU. The International Ladies' Garment Workers Union.

Jefferson School. Educational institution set up in New York with Communist Party backing.

LETTER 23

International Secretariat. Of the International Left Opposition and later (after 1938) of the Fourth International.

Old Labor Action. A paper edited by Cannon in 1936–37, during the period the Trotskyists were in the Socialist Party. It was the official organ of the Socialist Party of California. The Burnham-Shachtman faction, which split from the SWP in 1940 and formed the Workers Party, revived the name *Labor Action* for its newspaper.

LETTER 24

L.D. Trotsky's initials (for Lev Davidovich). His friends frequently referred to him by these initials.

"The boy." Trotsky's orphan grandson, Seva, who lived with Natalia in Mexico.

Don and Demila. Duncan and Demila Ferguson, who had been assigned by the SWP to live in Mexico and to look out for and assist Natalia and Seva.

Dwight's new magazine. Dwight Macdonald's *Politics.* Macdonald had been a prominent member of the Burnham-Shachtman faction and of the Workers Party. When he split from the WP he started his own magazine.

Charlie's movements. C. Charles, then serving in the army overseas.

Brownie. The baby's dog.

NI. The initials of the magazine *New International.* Originally it was the theoretical organ of the SWP, but at the time of the Burnham-Shachtman split, the magazine happened to be registered in the names of members of that minority faction and they appropriated it for their new Workers Party.

Ciliga. Anton Ciliga, a leader of the Yugoslav Communist Party, imprisoned by Stalin in the 1930s but allowed to leave the USSR because of his foreign citizenship. He revealed much about conditions in Soviet prisons but his anti-Stalinism soon turned into anti-Bolshevism.

LETTER 26

Our "Senator." Grace Carlson, the only woman among the eighteen prisoners. She had been the SWP candidate for Senator from Minnesota in the 1940 campaign. She was imprisoned in the federal penitentiary for women in Alderson, West Virginia.

April 1944

LETTER 27

Aiken's speech. Senator George Aiken of Vermont. See *Militant* article of April 15, 1944, entitled "Seamen's Bonus Cut; Profits Skyrocket."

Hillman and Dubinsky. Two of the leading labor bureaucrats of the period. They headed factions in New York's American Labor Party which eventually split it, with Dubinsky's group forming the rival Liberal Party. In the faction struggle, Sidney Hillman, Roosevelt's chief wartime labor lieutenant and head of the Amalgamated Clothing Workers, was supported by the Stalinists; David Dubinsky, head of the International Ladies' Garment Workers Union, was supported by the social-democrats.

LETTER 28

Cartoonist. Laura Gray, who would contribute cartoons to *The Militant* until her death on January 11, 1958.

Second-class mailing rights. After the Minneapolis Labor Trial, and at the suggestion of U.S. Attorney General Francis Biddle, the Postmaster General began ordering the confiscation and destruction of issues of *The Militant*. At a Post Office departmental hearing the government attorney read into the record numerous excerpts from *Militant* articles exposing State Department policies, Jim Crow practices in the armed forces, wartime profiteering, and anti-labor legislation as evidence of the need to suppress the paper. "We are not concerned here with questions of truth or falsity," he declared. "It does not make any difference if everything *The Militant* says is true." On March 3, 1943, the paper's second-class mailing rights were canceled, thus effectively barring it from the mails. An extensive protest campaign organized by the SWP won considerable backing from civil-liberties supporters. This resulted in the Roosevelt administration backing down and restoring *The Militant's* mailing rights on March 18, 1944.

GPU. The initials of Stalin's secret police organization.

Tito-Brezovich. This referred to a theory that Tito, the leader of the Yugoslav partisans, had been a GPU agent in Spain under the name Brezovich.

Mihailovič. Yugoslav monarchist general who led the right-wing, pro-capitalist Serbian partisans.

LETTER 29

George. George Clarke. (See note on *George's accident*, Letter 15.)

Darcy. S.A. Darcy, a leader in the California and Pennsylvania Communist Party.

DeLorenzo case. Thomas DeLorenzo, president of UAW-CIO Local 365 (Brewster Aeronautical), an opponent of the no-strike pledge, was persecuted by the federal authorities because of the militant policies which had won his local the best wages and conditions and the only union-shop contract in the aircraft-frame industry. Local 365 had been singled out for investigation by the House Naval Affairs Committee. Just before the union elections, the House Committee announced with great fanfare that DeLorenzo would be prosecuted for false statements. Nonetheless he and his slate were reelected. Soon thereafter, in April 1944, he was indicted by the federal government on charges of having made false statements about his previous employment in applying for a civil-service job some years before.

LETTER 31

PC. The Political Committee, a subcommittee of the SWP National Committee. It consisted of NC members resident in the New York area who could meet frequently. In turn it had a smaller subcommittee, called the Secretariat, which could meet on a day-to-day basis when necessary.

LETTER 32

Internal and International Bulletins. Intra-party publications for SWP members. The *Internal Bulletin* was open to contributions from all members. In pre-convention periods it carried articles, pro and con, on all issues before the membership. The *International Bulletin* carried informational as well as discussion articles about the world movement.

George's visit. George Novack, secretary of the CRDC, had received official permission to visit Sandstone to discuss the legal status of their case and the progress of the pardon campaign with the prisoners.

My "Twenty Years." A projected book.

LETTER 33

Italian manifesto. The Militant of April 8 had reprinted a manifesto from Italy issued in the name of a "Provisional National Center for the Building of the Communist Internationalist Party (Fourth International)."

POUM. Partido Obrero de Unificación Marxista (Workers Party of Marxist Unification), a left-centrist socialist organization which participated in the Popular Front government during the Spanish Civil War but was nonetheless persecuted and suppressed by the Stalinists as "Trotskyist." One of its principal leaders, Andrés Nin, a former associate of Trotsky, was assassinated by Stalin's secret police.

German reports via Stockholm. The Militant of April 8 had noted the dispatch in the *New York Times* about the underground activity of a "new crop of German Communists [who] are convinced internationalists."

Norman, Bill D. . . . Marguerite. Norman Tallentire, Bill Dunne, Marguerite Dunne, leading figures in the anti-Browder opposition in the Communist Party.

LETTER 34

Bill Haywood. William D. ("Big Bill") Haywood, American syndicalist leader. He was secretary-treasurer of the Western Federation of Miners; presided at the founding convention of the Industrial Workers of the World in 1905; was most prominent public spokesman of IWW and in 1914 took over post of general secretary-treasurer. He was arrested during World War I witch hunt; convicted at mass trial of IWW leaders and sentenced to 20 years; jumped bail in 1921 while case was on appeal and went to Soviet Union; died there in 1928. His uncompleted autobiography was published posthumously under the title, *Bill Haywood's Book.*

LETTER 35

Max Eastman. Writer, editor, lecturer. He edited the *Masses* and the *Liberator;* opposed World War I and supported the Russian Revolution. Joined the Communist Party in the early 1920s and went to the USSR where he became fluent in Russian and conversant with issues and factions within the Bolshevik Party. He became a supporter of Trotsky and a translator of Trotsky's writings, and was the first to acquaint the American public with the issues of the Trotsky-Stalin struggle. In the mid-1930s he began a retreat from Marxism and at the end of the decade repudiated socialism.

LETTER 36

Debs' Canton speech. Eugene V. Debs' speech in Canton, Ohio, on June 16, 1918. This speech denouncing the imperialist war and supporting the Bolsheviks served as the basis of his trial and ten-year sentence under the Espionage Act. Debs' sentence for leading the American Railway Union strike against the Pullman Company had been served in Woodstock, Illinois, in 1895.

Fred Beal. Communist union organizer in the Gastonia, North Carolina, textile strike of 1929. Framed and sentenced to twenty years' imprisonment, he jumped bail and fled to the Soviet Union. Disillusioned there with Stalinism, he returned secretly in the mid-1930s to the United States, where he lived in hiding and wrote *Proletarian Journey,* an autobiography. Apprehended by federal authorities, he was returned to North Carolina to serve his sentence. After his release, he worked in a garment factory. By this time he had renounced Marxism and was an IWW sympathizer.

May 1944

LETTER 39

Cartoon on Italy. Laura Gray cartoon in the April 22, 1944, *Militant.*

LETTER 40

Farrell and Harry. Farrell Dobbs and Harry DeBoer, two of the eighteen prisoners. Picture in the April 22, 1944, *Militant.*

Evelyn's visit with our "Senator." Evelyn Novack, assistant secretary of the CRDC, had received authorization to visit Grace Carlson in the federal prison for women in Alderson, West Virginia.

LETTER 41

Muste and the Oehlerites. A.J. Muste and the followers of Hugo Oehler.

LETTER 42

"Colonies" column. The April 22, 1944, *Militant* had carried the first of an intermittent series entitled "In the Colonies" by Li Fu-jen.

LETTER 43

McGuckin. An old-time IWW comrade of Cannon who had helped to organize a meeting in San Francisco protesting the imprisonment of the eighteen.

LETTER 44

Comintern. Contraction of words "Communist International," i.e., the Third International.

Karolyn. Karolyn Kerry, head of the New York chapter of the CRDC.

LETTER 49

Minneapolis strike. In 1934 the truck drivers of Minneapolis, led by Trotskyists, won two bitter strikes (one in May, the other in July) which attracted national attention and established the union on a firm basis in what had been one of America's most notorious open-shop cities. Within a few years the truck drivers had made Minneapolis one of the best-unionized cities in the country.

Bundists. On May 15, 1944, the U.S. Supreme Court consented to review the case of twenty-five officials of the German-American Bund, a Nazi organization, convicted of "conspiring to advise evasion and resistance to the Selective Service Act." The high court's willingness to hear the fascists' appeal stood in contrast to its three-time refusal to hear an appeal of the eighteen against the first use of the Smith Act. The AP case was an appeal by the Associated Press of a conviction for violation of the anti-trust laws.

The "dissolution" of the CP. The Communist Party convention on May 20, 1944, voted unanimously to dissolve as a party and reconstitute itself as the Communist Political Association.

LETTER 51

Two speeches . . . Churchill's and Browder's. In a speech to the House of Commons on May 24, 1944, Churchill had approved of Franco of Spain, the Greek monarchy, and the Badoglio regime in Italy. He also had "kindly words" for Stalin. "Profound changes have taken place in Soviet Russia," he declared. "The Trotskyite form of communism has been completely wiped out."

Addressing a Madison Square Garden rally of the new Communist Political Association, Earl Browder had boasted its program contained "nothing whatever of socialism" and "not the slightest suggestion of confiscation of wealth, nor even of wartime proposals for a limitation upon private incomes of the wealthy classes."

Marvel. Marvel Scholl, organizer of Women's Auxiliary during Minneapolis truck drivers' strikes, columnist for *Northwest Organizer*, wife of Farrell Dobbs.

Reba. Reba Hansen, who was then secretary in the SWP national office.

June 1944

LETTER 52

Book reviewed by Harry. An edition of Trotsky's *The New Course,* including an essay by Max Shachtman, entitled "The Struggle for the New Course," which exceeded the Trotsky piece in length. In the May 1944 issue of the *Fourth International,* Harry Frankel had subjected the Shachtman essay to a devastating criticism.

Murry. Murry Weiss, SWP organizer in Los Angeles.

LETTER 54

Stuart's report. J.B. Stuart, who had recently been in England.

LETTER 55

"Militant Army" columns. The column in *The Militant* written by the business manager.

Grandizo. Grandizo Munis, a Spanish Trotskyist in exile in Mexico. He later developed ultraleft and sectarian positions and left the Fourth International.

LETTER 56

Vincent Dunne. V.R. Dunne, one of the eighteen. A founder of the Trotskyist movement in America and a leader of Minneapolis Teamsters Local 544.

LETTER 57

"The Tribe of the Philistines." Letters 56, 57 and 58, save for a few paragraphs, appeared under this title in Cannon's column, "Notebook of an Agitator," in *The Militant* of June 24, 1944.

LETTER 59

German poem. A translation of the section of the poem quoted by Cannon is as follows:

> You're lovely as a flower,
> So pure and fair to see;
> I look at you, and sadness
> Comes stealing over me.

LETTER 60

Cartoon about Stalin and Eric Johnston. Laura Gray cartoon in June 17 *Militant.* Johnston, president of the U.S. Chamber of Commerce, had been given a banquet in Moscow. In his speech he ridiculed U.S. Communists, declaring, "If you take pepper, they sneeze. If you have indigestion, they belch. They annoy our trade unions more than they annoy our employers." Johnston's "wit" was received with great merriment by the high Soviet officials.

Art Preis. He signed some of his articles with the pen name Joseph Keller. Preis joined the staff of *The Militant* in 1940 and was its labor editor until his death in 1964. Author of *Labor's Giant Step: Twenty Years of the CIO,* New York: Pioneer Publishers, 1964.

LETTER 61

Goldman. Albert Goldman, one of the eighteen and the chief defense lawyer at the Minneapolis Labor Trial. Sharp differences with him over the character and perspectives of the party are reflected in numerous letters in this volume. After the prison sentences had been served, he and Felix Morrow organized a faction which led an unsuccessful fight. Goldman then left the SWP and some years later renounced the socialist program.

LETTER 62

ILGWU convention. The convention of the International Ladies' Garment Workers Union, meeting in Boston, had unanimously passed a resolution asking President Roosevelt to pardon the eighteen.

LETTER 64

Gerland. A European Trotskyist who had come to the United States during the war. (See note on *Logan,* Letter 138.)

July 1944

LETTER 66

Henry's condition. Henry Schultz of the Minneapolis–St. Paul SWP had just undergone a serious operation.

LETTER 67

Cartoonist . . . seriously ill. Laura Gray's health was very precarious. She had spent long periods in a tuberculosis sanitarium and one of her lungs had been removed.

LETTER 68

Abern. Martin Abern, one of the founders of the American Trotskyist movement. He split from the SWP along with the Burnham-Shachtman faction.

New Negro columnist. On February 19 Charles Jackson of Detroit had taken over the writing of the weekly column, "The Negro Struggle," in *The Militant.*

Shop Talks on Socialism. A weekly column in *The Militant* by V. Grey. It educated readers in the principles of socialism with examples and arguments drawn from everyday life.

Letter from a Steel Worker to His Son in the Service. Title of an article in the June 17 *Militant* by Theodore Kovalesky. It was written in answer to Steelworkers President Philip Murray's question at the union convention: "If you did withdraw the [no-strike] pledge, what sort of letter would you write to your boys overseas to explain?"

LETTER 69

Harry's book review. See note to Letter 52.

Morrison. Pen name of Albert Goldman.

Hook. Professor of philosophy at New York University. Morrison's article was entitled "Sidney Hook's Attack on Trotskyism" and appeared in the July, 1943, issue of *Fourth International.*

Control Commission. A body elected at each SWP convention to investigate and report on any accusations of dishonesty, violations of discipline, etc., brought against any member.

LETTER 73

Frank Little. An IWW martyr. On August 1, 1917, during a copper miners' strike in Butte, Montana, where he was a member of the IWW General Executive Board, a gang of company-hired thugs and vigilantes kidnapped Little and hanged him from a railroad trestle.

Stalinist accusations. Infuriated by growing trade-union support

for the pardon of the eighteen Trotskyist prisoners, the Stalinist press opened a massive campaign against "Trotskyite fascists." The article referred to by Cannon appeared in the July 1
Militant under the head, "Stalinists Attempt to Extend Slander
Campaign Into Unions." Among other things it reported that the
West Coast Communist daily, the *People's World*, had printed a
dispatch from Mexico (reprinted by *The Pilot*, the official organ
of the National Maritime Union) accusing Trotskyists there of
"inciting" 75 railroad strikes.

AP Navy story. The July 1 *Militant* carried an article headed,
"AP Uses Anonymous Letter As Vile Anti-Labor Smear." This
described the nationwide press campaign by the daily papers
based on an alleged letter from the crew of the U.S.S. *Coos Bay*
containing $412 to "pay the wage increases . . . that money-
hungry strikers are demanding" at the Wright Aeronautical
plant.

LETTER 76

Evie. Wife of Harry DeBoer, one of the eighteen. She had been on
the office staff of Truck Drivers Local 544 in Minneapolis.

"Snow" Larsen. A young SWP member in the merchant marine;
son of Arne Swabeck.

LETTER 78

Martin. James P. Cannon.

Stuart's report on Cuba. J.B. Stuart had recently returned from a
trip to Cuba.

August 1944

LETTER 79

British trial expenses. The SWP had raised a special Solidarity Fund
to assist four leaders of the newly formed Revolutionary Communist Party who had been railroaded to prison by the Churchill
government. Faced with strikes in the coal mines and shipyards,
Churchill ordered Scotland Yard to raid RCP offices throughout
Great Britain as well as the homes of many RCP members. They

were accused of fomenting the strikes. Breaking British prece-
dent, the four defendants were held forty-two days without bail.
At their six-day trial Ernest Bevin, Churchill's Labor Minister,
was one of the prosecution witnesses. They were convicted June
23. A mounting campaign of protest in the unions and even in
the army resulted in a higher court freeing the prisoners at the
end of August.

LETTER 80

Kovalesky. Theodore Kovalesky was the pen name of the young
steelworker in Buffalo who had written the "Letter from a Steel
Worker . . ." described in the note to Letter 68. The letter had
evoked such a favorable response from readers that he was soon
doing a regular column entitled "Diary of a Steel Worker."

R.J. Thomas letter. The Militant of July 29 reports the support for
the eighteen expressed by Thomas, then the president of the
United Auto Workers, in his letter to the president of Ford Local
600. Kay Burch was the head of the Detroit CRDC.

Murray. Philip Murray, president of the CIO.

Stalinists and the Quakers. Beginning in its issue of July 8 and
continuing throughout the month, *The Militant* reported in
detail the Stalinist campaign against the Quakers and its repercussions in the labor movement. In Seattle the Communist Political Association and the Stalinist newspaper, *The New World,*
had demanded in vain that city officials take action against a
scheduled lecture series of the Institute of International Relations sponsored by the American Friends Service Committee
(Quakers). The first two nights of the Institute lectures were interrupted by heckling, shouting, and war-bond selling speeches
by returned Stalinist veterans. The third lecture was broken up
by vigilante action of about a hundred Stalinists. They marched
onto the platform, shoved the pacifists aside, and commandeered
the microphone.

Fellowship of Reconciliation. The principal pacifist organization
in the United States. It was headed by the Reverend A.J. Muste
who had returned to his religious calling after his break with
Marxism.

LETTER 82

"J.M." who writes from Chicago. An extremely long letter to the editor signed "J.M." had been printed in the August 5 *Militant.* The letter and a reply by the editors occupied practically an entire page.
Green. William Green, president of the AFL.

LETTER 83

The Buffalo experience. The reference is to a situation in a UAW-organized plant in Buffalo, New York, where militants, failing to take into account the changed objective situation with the entry of the United States into World War II, were victimized by the company and the union officials.

LETTER 84

Cassidy document. "The First Phase of the Coming European Revolution," by Felix Morrow, appeared first in *Internal Bulletin* Vol. VI, No. 4 (September, 1944), and later in the *Fourth International* of December, 1944.
O'Neal. Pseudonym of novelist James T. Farrell. His letter appeared in *Internal Bulletin* Vol. VI, No. 6 (October, 1944).
Morrison's letter. Letter from M. Morrison in *Internal Bulletin* Vol. VI, No. 2 (September, 1944).

LETTER 86

Warde. Pen name of George Novack.
George. George Clarke. He was Cannon's junior by more than twenty years.

LETTER 88

Robert Ley's "Labor Front." The Nazi regime in Germany smashed the unions and then imposed its own "labor" organization on the workers. After May 1, 1933, all unions were "coordinated" by the regime, their buildings occupied by storm troops and their leaders imprisoned. A committee headed by Dr. Robert Ley, administrative chief of the Nazi Party, took over the assets and property of the defunct unions. On May 10 the new setup was officially constituted as the "German Labor Front." On May 16 the right to strike was abolished.

Hod Carriers. The AFL Hodcarriers and Common Laborers, a classic example of a conservative and undemocratic union.

Stalinist UE. The United Electrical, Radio and Machine Workers of America, the biggest of the Stalinist-dominated unions in the CIO. When the Murray leadership split the CIO in 1949 by ousting those unions which opposed U.S. cold-war policies, the UE itself split, with a minority forming the IUE-CIO.

Editorial on Warsaw. In *The Militant* of August 19.

LETTER 89

Michaels. Mike Michaels, an outstanding member of the Chicago SWP branch.

Kugie. Paul Kujac, an outstanding SWP activist.

Il Proletario. Radical newspaper published in Bari, Italy.

LETTER 90

Lewis. United Mine Workers President John L. Lewis.

LETTER 91

Trotsky's letter . . . Socialist Appeal. When the Trotskyist-led left wing was expelled from the Socialist Party and constituted itself the Socialist Workers Party, it named its newspaper the *Socialist Appeal.* This had been the name of the tendency paper it had published within the Socialist Party until it was banned. The name was later changed back to *The Militant.* On May 27, 1939, Trotsky had written a letter criticizing the *Socialist Appeal* as "a paper for the workers and not a worker's paper." The letter is quoted on page 112 of Trotsky's *In Defense of Marxism,* New York: Merit Publishers, 1965.

Article on Sacco-Vanzetti. A commemorative article by Ruth Johnson, a staff writer, in *The Militant* of August 26.

September 1944

LETTER 93

Simmon's article. "Trotsky on America's Role in Europe," in the August issue of the magazine *Fourth International,* by William

Simmons (a pen name of Arne Swabeck, one of the founders of the American Trotskyist movement).

LETTER 95

Censure of four comrades. A meeting of the New York SWP local voted to censure them when it was revealed that they had been conducting political discussions with members of the Shachtmanite Workers Party without informing the SWP.

Article by Morrison. "Reply [to Political Committee] from Comrade Morrison" in *Internal Bulletin* Vol. VI, No. 2 (September, 1944).

LETTER 96

Relief for Don and De. Relieving Duncan and Demila Ferguson of their assignment to reside in Mexico and assist Trotsky's widow and grandson.

Henry and Dorothy. Henry and Dorothy Schultz of the Minneapolis–St. Paul SWP.

Bordigists. A dissident Communist group in Italy, so called after Amadeo Bordiga. He led the Communist opposition while it was still in the Italian Socialist Party and became head of the CP after its founding; leader of the "left majority" which held a sectarian position. For opposing Stalin in the Communist International he was deprived of his power in the Italian CP in 1926 and expelled on charges of "Trotskyism" in 1930. Jailed by Mussolini. Trotsky and the International Left Opposition tried to work with the Bordigists but failed because of that group's inveterate sectarianism; they opposed the tactic of the united front, for example, "on principle."

LETTER 99

Solly. Sol Dollinger of the Flint, Michigan, SWP branch.

LETTER 101

Tobin. President Daniel J. Tobin of the AFL Teamsters union; also chairman of the Democratic Party's National Labor Committee.

Biddle. U.S. Attorney General Francis Biddle.

Anderson. Victor E. Anderson, U.S. Attorney for the District of Minnesota, one of the federal prosecutors at the Minneapolis Labor Trial.

LETTER 102

Account of auto convention. The Militant of September 23 carried extensive reports on the Grand Rapids convention of the United Auto Workers union.

Stein's article. "What Are the Real Issues—An Answer to Comrade Morrison" by M. Stein in *Internal Bulletin* Vol. VI, No. 2 (September, 1944).

LETTER 103

Bruno R. Bruno Rizzi, an Italian ex-Trotskyist, who in the late 1930s advanced the theory that the bureaucracy in the Soviet Union constituted a new class with its counterparts in the fascist and Nazi regimes in Italy and Germany and in the Rooseveltian New Deal in the United States. Rizzi gave a full exposition of his ideas in *La Bureaucratisation du monde* (The Bureaucratization of the World), published in Paris in 1939. Trotsky devoted considerable attention to refuting Rizzi's thesis and the subject was thoroughly discussed in the Trotskyist movement internationally before the war. Rizzi's theory later appeared in cruder versions in the "managerial revolution," "bureaucratic collectivism," and "new class" of Burnham, Shachtman, and Milovan Djilas, respectively.

October 1944

LETTER 106

"In Defense of Daniel J. Tobin." This appeared in the October 21 *Militant.*

LETTER 109

Definite relationships (More.) Regulations restricted a prisoner's letter-writing to one sheet of paper. Cannon filled the sheet in the middle of a citation and had to break off there. The sentence is resumed in the next letter.

LETTER 110

Whither England? By Leon Trotsky, 1925.

Martov. Menshevik leader and theoretician. On board of *Iskra* with Lenin. A leader of Menshevik walkout at 1903 congress of Russian Social Democratic Labor Party. Led left-centrist Menshevik-Internationalists in 1917. Went into exile in 1920.

LETTER 112

International Left Opposition. Trotsky had led the Left Opposition in the Soviet Union. After he was exiled he brought together groups expelled from Communist Parties in other countries, which were in agreement with the program of the Left Opposition, into the International Left Opposition. At a congress in 1938 these groups formed the Fourth International.

LETTER 114

Single Taxers. Advocates of Henry George's panacea by which a single tax of the entire economic rent of land would provide society with enough funds for a regime of justice and plenty.

De Leon. Daniel De Leon, Marxist theoretician (1852–1914). Joined Socialist Labor Party in 1890 and was its leader until his death.

Luxemburg and Liebknecht. Leaders of the Spartakus Bund (German Communist Party) murdered by the police during the unsuccessful German Revolution of 1919. Karl Liebknecht was a Social-Democratic member of the Reichstag. He broke with the party by opposing its support of World War I, and was jailed. Rosa Luxemburg, a Polish Socialist leader and theoretician, was also active in the German Social-Democratic movement. She, too, was jailed for her revolutionary opposition to the war.

Noske and Scheidemann. Gustav Noske and Philip Scheidemann were right-wing Social Democrats and the principal governmental figures in the suppression of the German Revolution of 1919 and the murders of Luxemburg and Liebknecht.

LETTER 116

Three dear comrades. Harry DeBoer, Clarence Hamel and Ed Palmquist were released from Sandstone. (Simultaneously, Carl

Kuehn, Oscar Shoenfeld and Alfred Russell were released from the prison in Danbury, Connecticut, where they had chosen to go for the convenience of their families in visiting them.) All had received sentences of a year and a day. With time off for good behavior, they served almost ten months.

Article on Bulgaria. The October 14 *Militant* article was entitled "Stalinist Leaders Curb Uprising of Bulgarian Masses."

The Count. Delaney. An old-time Wobbly.

The Germans. A group of emigrés, former members of the IKD, the German Trotskyist group, who had joined the SWP but succumbed to pessimistic views about the fate of European civilization and the attainability of socialism.

LETTER 119

Morrison-Cassidy tendency. The Goldman-Morrow tendency which later became a faction and split away from the SWP.

LETTER 120

"The Dog Days of the Left Opposition." The title of Lecture V in Cannon's *History of American Trotskyism.*

November 1944

LETTER 124

French POI. Parti Ouvrier Internationaliste (Internationalist Workers Party). This had been the official French section of the Fourth International when that body was organized in 1938. But in the conditions of illegality during the German occupation, the POI merged with other Trotskyist elements to form the Parti Communiste Internationaliste (Internationalist Communist Party). The founding of the PCI took place in October, 1943, largely due to the work of Marcel Hic, a POI leader, who was caught soon after by the Gestapo and was executed in the extermination camp at Dora.

Molinierist group. Split-off from French Trotskyist movement led by Raymond Molinier. (See note to Letter 167.)

La Vérité (Truth). Became the official organ of the new unified party; the official paper of the POI had been *La Lutte Ouvrière* (Workers' Struggle).

LETTER 127

Charles Rumford Walker. Author of books and novels about labor. In 1937 he published *American City*, a study centering around the Minneapolis strikes of 1934.

LETTER 128

Underground convention. Of the Communist Party in August, 1922, at a rural summer resort near Bridgman, Michigan. It was broken up by a raid of U.S. Department of Justice agents. Arrests and trials followed.
Fourth Congress. Of the Communist International.

LETTER 129

Grant, Burch, Murry and Bill. Ted Grant, Arthur Burch, Murry Weiss and William Kitt. The SWP branch organizers respectively in New York City, Detroit, Los Angeles and Buffalo.
Jack. Jack Weber, a well-known figure in the American Trotskyist movement.
Oscar and Al. Oscar Shoenfeld and Al Russell, two of the eighteen prisoners. They had been released from the federal prison in Danbury, Connecticut, three weeks earlier.
Critical support to the SP. In the presidential elections which had just taken place.

LETTER 130

George. George Novack. See note to Letter 32.
Crerar Library. A branch of the Chicago public library which has a special collection of labor and radical literature.

LETTER 131

Haymarket drawing. The November 11 *Militant* carried a commemorative article on the execution of the Haymarket martyrs and illustrated it with a reproduction of the famous contemporaneous drawing of the Haymarket "riot" from *Harper's Weekly*.

LETTER 133

Skogie's bond. Carl Skoglund, one of the eighteen, president of Minneapolis Teamster Local 544. He came to the United States from Sweden in 1911, but never became a citizen. Prior to the Minneapolis Labor Trial federal officials had unsuccessfully tried to make him turn state's evidence by threatening to deport him immediately after he finished serving his sentence. Cannon's concern was that Skoglund not be jailed by the U.S. Immigration Service upon his release from Sandstone, but be free on bail. Immigration authorities did try to deport Skoglund and in 1959 incarcerated him on Ellis Island for six months. At one point they even put him on a ship. But continued legal action saved him from deportation; he was still out on bond at the time of his death in 1961.

Roger Baldwin. Head of the American Civil Liberties Union.

German poem. It is from Goethe's *Erinnerung.* A literal translation is as follows:

> Wilt thou always wander farther?
> Behold, the good lies so near.
> Simply learn to grasp happiness,
> For happiness is always there.

LETTER 135

McNamaras. John J. and James B. McNamara. The former was secretary-treasurer of the AFL International Association of Bridge and Structural Iron Workers. Labor prisoners, they had been sentenced for the Los Angeles *Times* bombing of 1910, James B. for life and his brother for fifteen years.

Schmidt and Kaplan. Trade-unionists indicted along with the McNamaras, but not caught until three years after the trial. Matthew Schmidt was given a life sentence; David Kaplan received a lesser sentence.

Tom Mooney. Prisoner in the most famous labor frame-up in U.S. history. Mooney, leader of the left-wing bloc in the California AFL, and Warren K. Billings, a young left-wing unionist, were railroaded on charges of having bombed the 1916 "Preparedness Day" parade in San Francisco. Originally sentenced to be hanged,

Mooney was saved by Bolshevik demonstrations in Russia on his behalf. Unceasing agitation by the radical and labor movements brought about Mooney's pardon in 1939; Billings was released some months later.

LETTER 138

Logan. A pen name of Gerland. His position was elaborated in an article, entitled "On the European Situation and Our Tasks— Contribution to a Criticism of the Draft Resolution of the National Committee of the SWP," which appeared first in *Internal Bulletin* Vol. VI, No. 8 (October, 1944) and later in *Fourth International* issues of January and February, 1945.

LETTER 139

Flint branch . . . scoreboard. The scoreboard registered progress in a campaign to sell 10,000 sets of four pamphlets about the Minneapolis Labor Trial. The various SWP branches had taken quotas, and standing on the scoreboard was according to percentage of the quota sold. Since the Flint branch had taken a quota of ten (the lowest) and sold 32 sets, it headed the scoreboard, outranking, for example, Toledo, which had taken a quota of 160 and sold 488.

December 1944

LETTER 140

Mike. Mike Bartell, who was going to Chicago as the new branch organizer.

LETTER 143

London Bureau. A loose association of centrist parties not affiliated to either the Second or Third Internationals, but opposed to the formation of a Fourth International. Among its members were the Independent Labor Party of Great Britain, the POUM of Spain, the SAP of Germany, and the PSOP of France.

LETTER 149

George. George Novack. (See note to Letter 32.)

LETTER 152

Wolfe. The novelist Thomas Wolfe.

LETTER 154

Wayland and Warren. Publisher and editor of the *Appeal to Reason* (see note to Letter 22). Julius A. Wayland founded the paper in 1895; Fred Warren took over the editorship in 1904.

LETTER 155

Labor Action. The newspaper of the Shachtmanite Workers Party at that time.

January 1945

LETTER 159

Neue Zeit. Theoretical organ of the German Social-Democrats, founded 1883; edited by Karl Kautsky.

Bernstein. Eduard Bernstein, German Social-Democratic theoretician. His series of articles in *Neue Zeit* in 1897 revising Marxism and foreseeing evolution, rather than revolution, as the vehicle of socialism touched off the great theoretical battle in the international socialist movement. Kautsky was the principal polemicist against him. Bernstein's revisionism was rejected.

Makhaisky. (Also spelled Makhaysky.) Pre-World War I Polish revolutionary, Waclaw Machajski (pen name A. Wolski), exiled to Siberia. His articles around turn of century excited considerable attention in Russian revolutionary circles.

Berkman and Goldman. The famous American anarchist leaders, Alexander Berkman and Emma Goldman.

Dewey-Hutchins controversy. A debate over educational methods between philosopher John Dewey, the father of progressive education, and Robert M. Hutchins, president of the University of Chicago and advocate of traditional, classical educational views.

Sumner Welles. Under Secretary of State in the Roosevelt administration.

LETTER 161

SAP. Sozialistische Arbeiter Partei (Socialist Workers Party). The name taken by a left wing in the German Social Democratic Party led by Seydewitz and Rosenfeld after its expulsion in July, 1931, for opposition to the social-democratic policy of supporting the "lesser evil." The new party was soon reinforced by the adherence of a split-off from the Brandler-Thalheimer KPO (see note to Letter 162) led by Walcher and Froelich, both old Spartacists. A centrist formation, the SAP briefly swung left in 1934 and joined with the Trotskyists in a call for the building of a Fourth International. Under conditions of emigration, however, opportunist tendencies soon became predominant and it adopted a pro–Popular Front line and, after Hitler's defeat, solidarized itself with the Stalinists. Many of its leaders were given minor party and government posts in East Germany; on the other hand, its youth leader, Willi Brandt, became social-democratic mayor of West Berlin.

Blum. Léon Blum, French Socialist Party leader; Premier at head of coalition government with bourgeois Radicals (Popular Front government). Announced, upon taking office, the need for staying within limits of capitalist order.

Hook and Hacker. Sidney Hook (see note to Letter 69) and historian Louis M. Hacker.

The Iron Heel. Novel by Jack London, published in 1907, prophesying a regime comparable to fascism in the United States.

LETTER 162

Brandler-Lovestone. A member of the Spartakus Bund, Brandler became head of the German Communist Party; was made the scapegoat for failure of 1923 Revolution and removed from leadership; lived for several years thereafter in Moscow; was expelled from German CP in 1929; along with August Thalheimer, another expelled Communist, he founded the KPO, or German Right Opposition, whose connections were with Nicolai Bukharin, leader of the Right Opposition in the Soviet Union.

Jay Lovestone was the head of the Communist Party of the United States who was expelled in 1929. The expelled faction he headed first called itself the Communist Party (Opposition), but later took the name Independent Labor League. Its orientation and connections were similar to those of the Brandler-Thalheimer group. It disbanded in 1940.

Stevie. Stephen Geller, teen-age son of Jules and Henrietta Geller, who were prominent in trade-union activity in the Midwest.

LETTER 163

Convention report. "The Eleventh Convention of the American Trotskyist Movement" in the magazine *Fourth International* of December, 1944.

LETTER 164

Elaine. Elaine Roseland, office secretary of Minneapolis SWP.

LETTER 167

Molinier and Naville. Rival leaders in French Trotskyist movement in the 1930s. Raymond Molinier was a leader in the Communist youth who became a Trotskyist and was cofounder of *La Vérité* (Truth) in 1929. Much of the history of Trotskyism in France revolves around the efforts to integrate him and his faction into a disciplined, united movement. Despite Trotsky's interventions these efforts were unsuccessful. After leading a rival party to the official French section of the Fourth International, he dropped out of socialist politics in 1939.

Pierre Naville was expelled from the CP in 1928; a co-founder of *La Vérité;* a member of secretariat of the International Communist League, the forerunner of the Fourth International; opposed "French turn," i.e., entry of Trotskyists into Socialist Party in 1934, but later entered; opposed entry into PSOP and was expelled; mobilized during World War II, he was a prisoner of war; upon return to France he did not rejoin Trotskyists but was prominent among left socialists; best known today for his numerous sociological writings. (See notes to Letter 124.)

KAPD. Kommunistische Arbeiter Partei Deutschlands (Communist Workers Party of Germany). A large split-off from the German CP. The split took place at an underground convention in Heidelberg in the fall of 1919, the year which had already witnessed the defeat of the Spartacist uprising and the smashing of the Hungarian Revolution.

LETTER 170

Haldeman-Julius. Publisher of the famous pamphlets known as the "Little Blue Books." His publishing company was in Girard, Kansas, and was a continuation of what had been the *Appeal to Reason* publishing establishment.

Held. Walter Held was the pen name of Heinz Epe, a German Trotsky- ist who fled to Norway after Hitler came to power in Germany. When Trotsky was granted asylum in Norway, Epe served as one of his secretaries. Shortly before the Nazis invaded Norway, Epe went to Sweden and secured papers to enter the United States. In the spring of 1941 he undertook to travel there via the USSR and Turkey, for both of which countries he had been granted the necessary transit papers. He was taken off the train by Soviet secret police and executed in Saratov. The article referred to was entitled "Why the German Revolution Failed" and appeared in two installments in the December, 1942, and January, 1943, is- sues of the magazine *Fourth International.*

Levi. Paul Levi, well-known lawyer and a leader of the Spartakus Bund, friend of Rosa Luxemburg. He split from the German CP in 1922; later reentered the Social-Democratic Party.

Naville, Landau, Nin. Members of the International Left Opposi- tion who split from it in the 1930s.

Pierre Naville (see note to Letter 167).

Kurt Landau, an Austrian, former secretary of the International Left Opposition; split from Trotskyist movement and headed his own group; went to Spain during Civil War, supported POUM; was kidnapped and killed by Stalin's secret agents.

Andrés Nin, a founder of Spanish Communist Party; went to Soviet Union and served as secretary of the Red International of Trade Unions; supported Left Opposition; expelled from CP in 1927; expelled from Soviet Union in 1930; participated in for- mation of International Left Opposition; broke with Trotsky to participate in formation of POUM, of which he became principal leader during Civil War; kidnapped and murdered by Stalin's secret agents. (See note to Letter 33.)

Blanqui. Louis Auguste Blanqui (1805–1881), French revolutionary socialist whose name has become associated with theory of armed insurrection by small groups of selected and trained men as opposed to the Marxist concept of mass insurrection. Participated in French Revolution of 1830. Organized an unsuccessful insurrection in 1839. Freed by Revolution of 1848, he was jailed during its defeat. Jailed on eve of Paris Commune. Broken in health by thirty-five years of prison life, he was pardoned in 1879 and elected the same year by the workers of Bordeaux to the Chamber of Deputies, but was declared ineligible to sit by the government.

The Managerial Revolution. Title of a book by James Burnham published in 1940.

Montana's letter. A letter to the editor by Vanni B. Montana, secretary of the Italian Socialist Federation and an official of the ILGWU.

LETTER 171

The Party Builder. Like the *Internal Bulletin,* a publication for SWP members. This, however, contained not political discussion articles but articles on organizational matters and methods of work. The comments on the press (in Letters 151–157) and on the party training school (Letters 163–164) appeared as articles by Martin in the *Party Builder,* Vol. I, No. 4 (February, 1945) and Vol. II, No. 1 (March, 1945) respectively.

LETTER 172

Seven secretaries who lost their lives. Four in the Soviet Union were: Glazman, driven to suicide in 1924 by Stalinist persecution; G.V. Butov, arrested and tortured to give false evidence, went on hunger strike and died of its effects; Sermuks and Poznansky, Trotsky's secretaries at the time of his exile to Alma Ata in 1928, attempted on their own to follow him there, were arrested by the GPU, and disappeared in Soviet prison camps. Others were: Rudolph Klement, a Czech Trotskyist, secretary of the Fourth International, murdered by Soviet secret agents in Paris in 1938;

Erwin Wolf, Czech Trotskyist, Trotsky's secretary in Norway, expelled from that country during Moscow Trials when Trygve Lie put Trotsky under house arrest, kidnapped and killed by GPU in Spain; Walter Held (see note to Letter 170).

The guard at Coyoacán. An armed defense guard was maintained and expanded after the first attack on the Trotsky household in Mexico. Most of the guard were young SWP members. One guard, Robert Sheldon Harte, was kidnapped and killed in the May 22, 1940, attack.

LETTER 174

"Three Theses." A document submitted by German Trotskyist exiles which asserted that, in view of the crushing of labor and revolutionary forces by fascism, the struggle for restoration of democracy would take precedence over any program or struggle for socialist objectives for an entire epoch.

LETTER 177

ICL. The International Communist League. The international organization of the Trotskyists which preceded the Fourth International.

LETTER 181

Vincent. Vincent R. Dunne. (See note to Letter 56.)

LETTER 182

Parsons. The Haymarket martyr, Albert R. Parsons.

"The Saint." Vincent St. John, General Secretary-Treasurer of the IWW until 1914.

Hillquit-Berger. Leaders of right wing in pre-World War I Socialist Party. Morris Hillquit, a New York lawyer, and Victor Berger, publisher of the German-language *Vorwärts* in Milwaukee.

Wilshire. Gaylord Wilshire, publisher and editor of *Wilshire's Magazine.* In his checkered career, Wilshire went to Harvard, quit before graduating and mined gold in California, published several socialistic magazines before *Wilshire's,* engaged in banking in New York, and ran for office as a socialist in California, New York, England and Canada.

Index

Building a PROLETARIAN PARTY

The Changing Face of U.S. Politics
Working-Class Politics and the Trade Unions
JACK BARNES

Building the kind of party working people need to prepare for coming class battles through which they will revolutionize themselves, their unions, and all society. A handbook for those seeking the road toward effective action to overturn the exploitative system of capitalism and join in reconstructing the world on new, socialist foundations. $24. Also in Spanish, French, and Swedish.

Revolutionary Continuity
Marxist Leadership in the U.S.
FARRELL DOBBS

How successive generations took part in struggles of the U.S. labor movement, seeking to build a leadership that could advance the class interests of workers and small farmers and link up with fellow toilers around the world. Two volumes:

The Early Years, 1848–1917, $20; *Birth of the Communist Movement 1918–1922*, $19.

The History of American Trotskyism, 1928–38
Report of a Participant
JAMES P. CANNON

"Trotskyism is not a new movement, a new doctrine," Cannon says, "but the restoration, the revival of genuine Marxism as it was expounded and practiced in the Russian revolution and in the early days of the Communist International." In twelve talks given in 1942, Cannon recounts a decisive period in efforts to build a proletarian party in the United States. $22. Also in Spanish and French.

What Is To Be Done?

V.I. LENIN

The stakes in creating a disciplined organization of working-class revolutionaries capable of acting as a "tribune of the people, able to react to every manifestation of tyranny and oppression, no matter where it appears, to clarify for all and everyone the world-historic significance of the struggle for the emancipation of the proletariat." Written in 1902. In *Essential Works of Lenin*, $12.95

In Defense of Marxism

The Social and Political Contradictions of the Soviet Union on the Eve of World War II

LEON TROTSKY

Writing in 1939–40, Leon Trotsky replies to those in the revolutionary workers movement beating a retreat from defense of the Soviet Union in face of the looming imperialist assault. Why only a party that fights to bring growing numbers of workers into its ranks and leadership can steer a steady revolutionary course. $25. Also in Spanish.

The Struggle for a Proletarian Party

JAMES P. CANNON

"The workers of America have power enough to topple the structure of capitalism at home and to lift the whole world with them when they rise," Cannon asserts. On the eve of World War II, a founder of the communist movement in the U.S. and leader of the Communist International in Lenin's time defends the program and party-building norms of Bolshevism. $22

Background to 'The Struggle for a Proletarian Party'

JAMES P. CANNON, GEORGE CLARKE, LEON TROTSKY

The challenges faced by the Socialist Workers Party in deepening its involvement in the organizations and struggles of the industrial working class in the years prior to U.S. imperialism's entry into World War II. The SWP must "orient in practice the whole organization toward the factories, the strikes, the unions," writes Leon Trotsky in a 1937 letter to party leader James P. Cannon. $6

BY JAMES P. CANNON

*Writings and Speeches of James P. Cannon on the fight
to build a proletarian party in the United States*

The First Ten Years of American Communism

REPORT OF A PARTICIPANT

"Stalinism has worked mightily to obliterate the honorable record of American communism in its pioneer days. Yet the Communist Party wrote such a chapter too, and the young militants of the new generation ought to know about it and claim it for their own. It belongs to them."—James P. Cannon, 1962. $22

The Founding of the Socialist Workers Party

MINUTES AND RESOLUTIONS, 1938–39

At two conventions and surrounding leadership meetings in 1938–39, revolutionists in the United States codified some 20 years of experience in building a communist party. Taking the name Socialist Workers Party, they reaffirmed the Marxist approach in the fight against the coming imperialist war, the spread of fascism across Europe, and attacks by the bosses at home. $24.95

Speeches to the Party

THE REVOLUTIONARY PERSPECTIVE AND THE REVOLUTIONARY PARTY

Writing in the early 1950s, Cannon discusses how class-conscious workers, in face of the conservatizing pressures of the emerging capitalist expansion and anticommunist witch-hunt, carried out effective union work and political activity to build a communist workers party. He discusses Washington's failure to achieve its goals in the Korean War and why the rulers reined in McCarthyism. $24

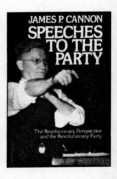

www.pathfinderpress.com

THE TEAMSTER SERIES

FARRELL DOBBS, *a young worker who became part of the class-struggle leadership of the Minneapolis Teamsters in the 1930s tells the story of how the strikes and organizing drives by men and women in the Twin Cities and throughout the Midwest paved the way for the rise of the industrial union movement. They showed in life what workers and their allied producers on the land can achieve when they have the leadership they deserve.*

Teamster Rebellion

How members of Teamsters Local 574 in Minnesota during two 1934 strikes defeated not only the trucking bosses in Minneapolis but strike-breaking efforts of the big-business Citizens Alliance and city, state, and federal governments. $19. Also in Spanish and Swedish.

Teamster Power

How the class-struggle Teamsters leadership used the power workers had won during the 1934 strikes to make Minneapolis a union town and launch an 11-state campaign that brought tens of thousands of over-the-road truckers into the union. $19. Also in Spanish.

Teamster Politics

How the Minneapolis Teamsters combated FBI frame-ups, helped the jobless organize, deployed a Union Defense Guard to turn back fascist thugs, fought to advance independent labor political action, and mobilized opposition to U.S. imperialism's entry into World War II. $19

Teamster Bureaucracy

How the employing class, backed by union bureaucrats, stepped up government efforts to gag class-conscious militants; how workers mounted a world campaign to free eighteen union and socialist leaders framed up and imprisoned in the infamous 1941 federal sedition trial. $19

www.pathfinderpress.com

THE CLASS STRUGGLE IN

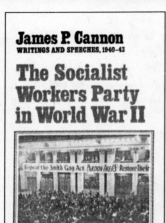

The Socialist Workers Party in World War II
James P. Cannon
Preparing the communist movement in the U.S. to stand against the patriotic wave inside the working class and unions supporting the imperialist slaughter and to join with other working people in campaigning against wartime censorship, repression, and antiunion assaults. $24.95

Fighting Racism in World War II
C.L.R. James, George Breitman, Edgar Keemer, and others

A week-by-week account from 1939 to 1945 of efforts to advance the Black rights struggle in face of patriotic appeals to postpone resistance to lynch-mob terror and racist discrimination until after U.S. "victory" in World War II. These struggles—of a piece with rising anti-imperialist battles in Africa, Asia, and the Americas—helped lay the basis for the mass civil rights movement in the postwar decades. $22

Labor's Giant Step
THE FIRST TWENTY YEARS OF THE CIO: 1936–55
Art Preis
Until union coal miners went on strike in 1943—defying intense pressure to "sacrifice" for the imperialist war effort—"The ruling class looked on the war as their supreme opportunity to destroy union contractual conditions and even unionism itself," writes Preis. "Instead, the miners' victory opened a whole new wave of labor struggle." One of many battles described in this account of labor and political struggles in the 1930s and '40s that built the industrial unions. $30

WORLD WAR II

Teamster Bureaucracy
Farrell Dobbs

How the class-struggle Teamsters leadership in the Upper Midwest organized to fight union busting, racism, and colonial oppression, as they opposed the mobilization of labor behind U.S. imperialist war aims in World War II. How Washington—backed by top AFL, CIO, and Teamsters officials—acted to gag class-conscious workers. $19

Washington's 50-year Domestic Contra Operation
Larry Seigle

As the U.S. rulers prepared to smash working-class resistance and advance their interests through the interimperialist slaughter of World War II, Washington's political police apparatus as it exists today was born. This article explains the political battles within the workers movement over how to combat government and employer attacks against the working class and unions, the Black rights movement, Puerto Rican independence fighters, opponents of U.S. wars, and others. In *New International* no. 6. $16. Also in Spanish

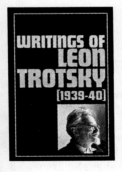

Writings of Leon Trotsky (1939–40)

"The life of Europe and all mankind will be determined for a long time by the course of the imperialist war and its economic and political consequences," wrote communist leader Leon Trotsky in May 1940. In face of this, he said, communist workers continue to "fulfill our basic task: to carry on constant, tireless preparation for the revolution—in the factories, mills, villages, barracks, at the front, and in the fleet." $35

www.pathfinderpress.com

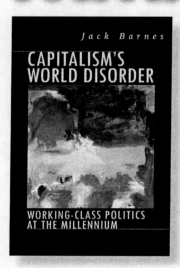

Capitalism's World Disorder
Working-Class Politics at the Millennium
JACK BARNES
The social devastation and financial panic, the coarsening of politics, the cop brutality and acts of imperialist aggression accelerating around us—all are the product not of something gone wrong with capitalism but of its lawful workings. Yet the future can be changed by the united struggle and selfless action of workers and farmers conscious of their power to transform the world. $25. Also in Spanish and French.

Is Socialist Revolution in the U.S. Possible?
A Necessary Debate
MARY-ALICE WATERS
In two talks, presented as part of a wide-ranging debate at the Venezuela International Book Fairs in 2007 and 2008, Waters explains why a socialist revolution in the United States is possible. Why revolutionary struggles by working people are inevitable, forced upon us by the crisis-driven assaults of the propertied classes. As solidarity grows among a fighting vanguard of working people, the outlines of coming class battles can already be seen. $7. Also in Spanish and French.

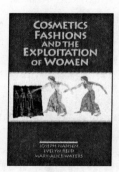

Cosmetics, Fashions, and the Exploitation of Women
JOSEPH HANSEN, EVELYN REED, MARY-ALICE WATERS
How big business plays on women's second-class status and social insecurities to market cosmetics and rake in profits. The introduction by Waters explains how the entry of millions of women into the workforce during and after World War II irreversibly changed U.S. society and laid the basis for a renewed rise of struggles for women's emancipation. $15

www.pathfinderpress.com

The Communist Manifesto
KARL MARX AND FREDERICK ENGELS

Founding document of the modern working-class movement, published in 1848. Explains why communism is not a set of preconceived principles but the line of march of the working class toward power, "springing from an existing class struggle, a historical movement going on under our very eyes." $5. Also in Spanish.

Our History Is Still Being Written
The Story of Three Chinese-Cuban Generals in the Cuban Revolution

Armando Choy, Gustavo Chui, and Moisés Sío Wong talk about the historic place of Chinese immigration to Cuba, as well as more than five decades of revolutionary action and internationalism, from Cuba to Angola and Venezuela today. Through their stories we see the social and political forces that gave birth to the Cuban nation and opened the door to the socialist revolution in the Americas. $20. Also in Spanish and Chinese.

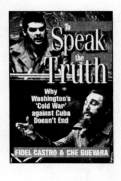

To Speak the Truth
Why Washington's 'Cold War' against Cuba Doesn't End
FIDEL CASTRO, ERNESTO CHE GUEVARA

In historic speeches before the United Nations and UN bodies, Guevara and Castro address the peoples of the world, explaining why the U.S. government so fears the example set by the socialist revolution in Cuba and why Washington's effort to destroy it will fail. $17

Capitalism and the Transformation of Africa
Reports from Equatorial Guinea
MARY-ALICE WATERS, MARTÍN KOPPEL

An account of the transformation of production and class relations in this central African country, as it is drawn deeper into the world market and both a capitalist class and modern proletariat are born. Here also the example of Cuba's socialist revolution comes alive in the collaboration of Cuban volunteer medical brigades helping to transform social conditions. Woven together, the outlines of a future to be fought for today can be seen—a future in which the toilers of Africa have more weight in world politics than ever before. $10. Also in Spanish.

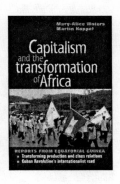

EXPAND *Your Revolutionary Library*

Malcolm X Talks to Young People

Four talks and an interview given to young people in Ghana, the United Kingdom, and the United States in the last months of Malcolm's life. This new edition contains the entire December 1964 presentation by Malcolm X at the Oxford University in the United Kingdom, in print for the first time anywhere. The collection concludes with two memorial tributes by a young socialist leader to this great revolutionary. $15. Also in Spanish.

Thomas Sankara Speaks
The Burkina Faso Revolution, 1983–87

Colonialism and imperialist domination have left a legacy of hunger, illiteracy, and economic backwardness in Africa. In 1983 the peasants and workers of Burkina Faso established a popular revolutionary government and began to combat the causes of such devastation. Thomas Sankara, who led that struggle, explains the example set for Africa and the world. $24. Also in French.

What Is Surrealism?

ANDRÉ BRETON

Writings of the best-known leader of the Surrealist movement. Includes a facsimile reproduction of the 1942 Surrealist Album by André Breton. $40

Puerto Rico: Independence Is a Necessity

RAFAEL CANCEL MIRANDA

Rafael Cancel Miranda is one of five Puerto Rican Nationalists imprisoned by Washington for more than 25 years until 1979. In two interviews, he speaks out on the brutal reality of U.S. colonial domination, the campaign to free Puerto Rican political prisoners, the example of Cuba's socialist revolution, and the resurgence of the independence movement today. $6. Also in Spanish.

www.pathfinderpress.com

Che Guevara Talks to Young People

In eight talks from 1959 to 1964, the Argentine-born revolutionary challenges youth of Cuba and the world to study, to work, to become disciplined. To join the front lines of struggles, small and large. To politicize their organizations and themselves. To become a different kind of human being as they strive together with working people of all lands to transform the world. $15. Also in Spanish.

Women's Liberation and the African Freedom Struggle

THOMAS SANKARA

"There is no true social revolution without the liberation of women," explains the leader of the 1983–87 revolution in Burkina Faso. Workers and peasants in that West African country established a popular revolutionary government and began to combat the hunger, illiteracy, and economic backwardness imposed by imperialist domination. $8. Also in Spanish and French.

Socialism on Trial

JAMES P. CANNON

The basic ideas of socialism, explained in testimony during the trial of 18 leaders of the Minneapolis Teamsters union and the Socialist Workers Party framed up and imprisoned under the notorious Smith "Gag" Act at the beginning of World War II. $16. Also in Spanish.

Pathfinder Was Born with the October Revolution

MARY-ALICE WATERS

From the writings of Marx, Engels, Lenin, and Trotsky, to the speeches of Malcolm X, Fidel Castro, and Che Guevara, to the words of James P. Cannon, Farrell Dobbs, and leaders of the communist movement in the U.S. today, Pathfinder books aim to "advance the understanding, confidence, and combativity of working people." $3. Also in Spanish and French.

www.pathfinderpress.com

New International

A MAGAZINE OF MARXIST POLITICS AND THEORY

NEW INTERNATIONAL NO. 14

REVOLUTION, INTERNATIONALISM, AND SOCIALISM: THE LAST YEAR OF MALCOLM X

Jack Barnes

"To understand Malcolm's last year is to see how, in the imperialist epoch, revolutionary leadership of the highest political capacity, courage, and integrity converges with communism. That truth has even greater weight today as billions around the world, in city and countryside, from China to Brazil, are being hurled into the modern class struggle by the violent expansion of world capitalism."—Jack Barnes

Issue #14 also includes "The Clintons' Antilabor Legacy: Roots of the 2008 World Financial Crisis"; "The Stewardship of Nature Also Falls to the Working Class: In Defense of Land and Labor" and "Setting the Record Straight on Fascism and World War II." $14

NEW INTERNATIONAL NO. 12

CAPITALISM'S LONG HOT WINTER HAS BEGUN

Jack Barnes

and "Their Transformation and Ours,"
Resolution of the Socialist Workers Party

Today's sharpening interimperialist conflicts are fueled both by the opening stages of what will be decades of economic, financial, and social convulsions and class battles, and by the most far-reaching shift in Washington's military policy and organization since the U.S. buildup toward World War II. Class-struggle-minded working people must face this historic turning point for imperialism, and draw satisfaction from being "in their face" as we chart a revolutionary course to confront it. $16

ALL THESE ISSUES ARE ALSO AVAILABLE IN SPANISH AND MOST IN FRENCH AT
WWW.PATHFINDERPRESS.COM

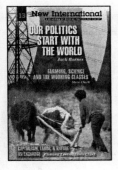

NEW INTERNATIONAL NO. 13
OUR POLITICS START WITH THE WORLD
Jack Barnes

The huge economic and cultural inequalities between imperialist and semicolonial countries, and among classes within almost every country, are produced, reproduced, and accentuated by the workings of capitalism. For vanguard workers to build parties able to lead a successful revolutionary struggle for power in our own countries, says Jack Barnes in the lead article, our activity must be guided by a strategy to close this gap.

Also includes: "Farming, Science, and the Working Classes" *by Steve Clark* and "Capitalism, Labor, and Nature: An Exchange" *by Richard Levins, Steve Clark.* $14

NEW INTERNATIONAL NO. 11
U.S. IMPERIALISM HAS LOST THE COLD WAR
Jack Barnes

Contrary to imperialist expectations at the opening of the 1990s in the wake of the collapse of regimes across Eastern Europe and the USSR claiming to be communist, the workers and farmers there have not been crushed. Nor have capitalist social relations been stabilized. The toilers remain an intractable obstacle to imperialism's advance, one the exploiters will have to confront in class battles and war. $16

NEW INTERNATIONAL NO. 8
CHE GUEVARA, CUBA, AND THE ROAD TO SOCIALISM
Articles by Ernesto Che Guevara, Carlos Rafael Rodríguez, Carlos Tablada, Mary-Alice Waters, Steve Clark, Jack Barnes

Exchanges from the opening years of the Cuban Revolution and today on the political perspectives defended by Guevara as he helped lead working people to advance the transformation of economic and social relations in Cuba. $10

NEW INTERNATIONAL NO. 7
OPENING GUNS OF WORLD WAR III: WASHINGTON'S ASSAULT ON IRAQ
Jack Barnes

The murderous assault on Iraq in 1990–91 heralded increasingly sharp conflicts among imperialist powers, growing instability of international capitalism, and more wars. *Also includes:* "1945: When U.S. Troops said 'No!'" *by Mary-Alice Waters* and "Lessons from the Iran-Iraq War" *by Samad Sharif.* $14

PATHFINDER AROUND THE WORLD

Visit our website for a complete list of titles and to place orders

www.pathfinderpress.com

PATHFINDER DISTRIBUTORS

UNITED STATES
(and Caribbean, Latin America, and East Asia)

Pathfinder Books, 306 W. 37th St., 10th Floor,
New York, NY 10018

CANADA

Pathfinder Books, 7105 St. Hubert, Suite 106F,
Montreal, QC H2S 2N1

UNITED KINGDOM
(and Europe, Africa, Middle East, and South Asia)

Pathfinder Books, First Floor, 120 Bethnal Green Road
(entrance in Brick Lane), London E2 6DG

SWEDEN

Pathfinder böcker, Bildhuggarvägen 17, S-121 44 Johanneshov

AUSTRALIA
(and Southeast Asia and the Pacific)

Pathfinder, Level 1, 3/281-287 Beamish St., Campsie, NSW 2194
Postal address: P.O. Box 164, Campsie, NSW 2194

NEW ZEALAND

Pathfinder, 7 Mason Ave. (upstairs), Otahuhu, Auckland
Postal address: P.O. Box 3025, Auckland 1140